P9-CFH-194

Tribal Warfare

Critical Studies in Television

Series Editor
Mark Andrejevic, University of Iowa

Advisory Board
Lynn Schofield Clark, University of Colorado, Boulder
James Hay, University of Illinois Urbana Champaign
Fredrick Turner, Stanford University

This new series critically examines television, emphasizing in-depth monographic studies on a particular television series. By looking at television through a critical lens, the books in this series will bring insight into the cultural significance of television, and also explore how the lessons apply to larger critical and social issues. The texts in the series will appeal to communication, media, and cultural theory scholars.

Titles in Series:

Tribal Warfare: Survivor *and the Political Unconscious of Reality Television* by Christopher J. Wright

Forthcoming:

The Other Sunnydale: Representations of Blackness in Buffy the Vampire Slayer by Lynne Y. Edwards

Tribal Warfare

Survivor and the Political Unconscious of Reality Television

Christopher J. Wright

LEXINGTON BOOKS

A division of
ROWMAN & LITTLEFIELD PUBLISHERS, INC.
Lanham • Boulder • New York • Toronto • Oxford

LEXINGTON BOOKS

A division of Rowman & Littlefield Publishers, Inc.
A wholly owned subsidary of The Rowman & Littlefield Publishing Group, Inc.
4501 Forbes Boulevard, Suite 200
Lanham, MD 20706

PO Box 317
Oxford
OX2 9RU, UK

Copyright © 2006 by Lexington Books

All rights reserved. No part of this publication may be reproduced,
stored in a retrieval system, or transmitted in any form or by any
means, electronic, mechanical, photocopying, recording, or otherwise,
without the prior permission of the publisher.

British Library Cataloguing in Publication Information Available

Library of Congress Cataloging-in-Publication Data

Wright, Christopher J., 1976-
  Tribal warfare : survivor and the political unconscious of reality television / Christopher
J. Wright.
     p. cm. -- (Critical studies in television)
  Includes bibliographical references and index.
  ISBN-13: 978-0-7391-1165-9 (cloth : alk. paper)
  ISBN-10: 0-7391-1165-5 (cloth : alk. paper)
  ISBN-13: 978-0-7391-1166-6 (pbk. : alk. paper)
  ISBN-10: 0-7391-1166-3 (pbk. : alk. paper)
  1. Survivor (Television program) I. Title. II. Series.
PN1992.77.S865W75 2006
791.45'72--dc22   2006009149

Printed in the United States of America

∞™ The paper used in this publication meets the minimum requirements of American
National Standard for Information Sciences—Permanence of Paper for Printed Library
Materials, ANSI/NISO Z39.48–1992.

For my parents

Contents

List of Figures   ix

List of Tables   xiii

Preface: A Note on Television, Marx, Freud, and Semiotics   xvii

Acknowledgments   xxi

Introduction: "Interrogating the Obvious": *Survivor* as
Cultural Touchstone   1

1   "You Cannot Talk to the Guys in the Boat": *Survivor* as the
False Real   7

2   "Apparently Reprehensible Material": The Political Unconscious
and Popular Culture   15

3   "If It Happens Again . . .": Repression and the Tagi Alliance   27

4   "They're All Lying to Me": Repression Among Contestants   45

5   "A Really Passionate Affair": Repression Through Editing   63

6   "These Three Girls Have All Been Riding Coattails":
Survivor's Gender Wars   73

7   "Thrashing Around Like I'm Thirty-Five": Paradoxes
of Aging on *Survivor*   95

8   "This Thing Runs Deeper Than a Game": *Survivor's*
Troubles With Race   109

Conclusion: "Always Historicize!": Symbolic Resolutions
    and Contemporary Politics   135

Appendix A: Synopses of First Eleven *Survivor* Seasons   145

Appendix B: Contestant Profiles and Ratings   149

Appendix C: Methodology   169

Bibliography   181

Index   189

About the Author   197

List of Figures

Figure 3.1: Final ten contestants on *Survivor: Borneo*, members
of the Rattana Tribe   28

Figure 3.2: Recollected desires of survey respondents as to fate
of *Borneo's* Tagi alliance   31

Figure 3.3: Reaction of survey respondents to *Borneo* outcome   37

Figure 3.4: Percentage of respondents wanting Tagi alliance
to prevail, grouped by social class   38

Figure 3.5: Percentage of respondents pleased by Tagi alliance
prevailing, grouped by social class   39

Figure 3.6: Percentage of respondents pleased by Rich winning
Borneo, grouped by social class   40

Figure 3.7: Percentage of respondents pleased by Tagi alliance
prevailing, grouped by political party   41

Figure 3.8: Percentage of respondents wanting Tagi alliance
to prevail, grouped by annual household income   42

Figure 4.1: Final ten contestants in *Survivor: Marquesas*,
members of the Soliantu tribe   46

Figure 4.2: Desires of survey respondents as to fate
of *Marquesas'* Rotu alliance   50

Figure 4.3: Reaction of survey respondents to *Marquesas'*
Rotu alliance failing   51

Figure 4.4:   Reaction of survey respondents to Vecepia
              winning *Marquesas*   52

Figure 4.5:   Percentage of respondents pleased by Vecepia
              winning, grouped by housing status   53

Figure 4.6:   Percentage of respondents pleased by Vecepia
              winning, grouped by annual household income   54

Figure 4.7:   Final ten contestants in *Survivor: The Amazon*,
              members of Jacaré Tribe   56

Figure 4.8:   Tribal Council results, *Survivor: The Amazon*,
              Episodes 7-13   57

Figure 4.9:   Percentage of respondents seeing *Amazon's* Rob
              as "good," grouped by social class   58

Figure 4.10: Percentage of respondents seeing *Amazon's* Rob
              as "good," grouped by education level   59

Figure 5.1:   Final ten contestants in *Survivor: Africa*,
              members of Moto Maji tribe   67

Figure 5.2:   Percentage of respondents expecting Roger to leave
              Amazon in Episode 7, grouped by political party   70

Figure 5.3:   Percentage of respondents expecting Roger to leave
              in Episode 7, grouped by education level   71

Figure 6.1:   Coded valence of tribes' depictions in *Amazon*
              Episode 1, divided by depiction type   82

Figure 6.2:   Codings of tribes' gendered depictions in Episode 1,
              according to adjectives selected   83

Figure 6.3:   Percent of respondents pleased by Jabaru winning
              first *Amazon* challenge, grouped by gender   85

Figure 6.4:   Percent of respondents pleased by Burton's second
              Pearl Islands ouster, grouped by gender   89

Figure 6.5: Percent of respondents pleased by Jabaru winning
first *Amazon* challenge, grouped by political party 92

Figure 7.1: Game longevity of *Survivor* contestant age groups,
seasons 1-7, 9-10 102

Figure 7.2: Percent of contestants included in game-winning
alliances, grouped by age, seasons 1-7, 9-10 103

Figure 7.3: Percentage of respondents perceiving Tagi and Rotu
alliances as "good," grouped by age 105

Figure 8.1: Mean adjusted audience attitude index for selected
racial groups on *Survivor* 121

Figure 8.2: Percent of respondents pleased by Sean being voted
out of *Marquesas,* grouped by race 127

Figure 8.3: Percent of respondents pleased by Vecepia winning
Marquesas, grouped by race 128

Figure 8.4: Percent of respondents pleased by Sean's ouster
from *Marquesas,* grouped by political party 131

Figure 9.1: Percentage of respondents saying Brian's video
made them want him to win *Thailand* less, as opposed
to it having no effect, grouped by social class 136

Figure 9.2: Percentage of respondents saying Brian's video
made them want him to win less, as opposed to it
having no effect, grouped by political party 137

Figure 9.3: Percentage of respondents saying Brian's video
made them want him to win less, as opposed to it
having no effect, grouped by income 138

List of Tables

Table 6.1:   Key contestants in Episode 1 of *Survivor: The Amazon*   77

Table 6.2:   Final five players in *Survivor: Pearl Islands*   87

Table 7.1:   Stereotypes of older persons, with corresponding
             Survivor contestants age 50 and up   96

Table 7.2:   Age distribution of 150 contestants appearing
             on *Survivor* seasons 1-7, 9-10   97

Table 7.3:   Age of contestants appearing on *Survivor* seasons
             1-7, 9-10, vs. TV characters in 1975 and 1990
             and subset of U.S. population   97

Table 7.4:   Common descriptions of *Borneo* contestants
             over age 50, as cited by respondents   100

Table 8.1:   Selected African-American stereotypes in entertainment
             media as described by Bogle (1989) and Jewell (1993)   111

Table 8.2:   Summary of depictions for sixteen African-Americans
             featured on first ten seasons of *Survivor*   116

Table 8.3:   Final five players on *Survivor: Marquesas*   124

Table 9.1:   Best-fitting overall structure of first eleven
             Survivor seasons   141

Table B.1:   AAAI rankings of contestants from first ten
             Survivor seasons   151

Table B.2:   Contestants on *Survivor: Borneo*   152

Table B.3:   Contestants on *Survivor: The Australian Outback*   153

Table B.4:   Contestants on *Survivor: Africa*   154

Table B.5:   Contestants on *Survivor: Marquesas*   155

Table B.6:   Contestants on *Survivor: Thailand*   156

Table B.7:   Contestants on *Survivor: The Amazon*   157

Table B.8:   Contestants on *Survivor: Pearl Islands*   158

Table B.9:   Contestants on *Survivor: All-Stars*   159

Table B.10: Contestants on *Survivor: Vanuatu*   160

Table B.11: Contestants on *Survivor: Palau*   161

Table B.12: Contestants on *Survivor: Guatemala*   162

Table B.13: *Survivor* contestants perceived significantly
           differently by male vs. female respondents   163

Table B.14: *Survivor* contestants perceived significantly differently
           by respondents age 50 and older vs. 30 and younger   164

Table B.15: *Survivor* contestants perceived significantly differently
           by white respondents vs. nonwhite respondents   164

Table B.16: *Survivor* contestants perceived significantly differently
           by politically independent respondents vs.
           non-independent respondents   164

Table B.17: *Survivor* contestants perceived significantly differently
           by Republican respondents vs. non-Republican
           respondents   165

Table B.18: *Survivor* contestants perceived significantly differently
           by Democratic respondents vs. non-Democratic
           respondents   165

Table B.19: *Survivor* contestants perceived significantly differently by respondents with household incomes of $100,000 or more vs. respondents with household incomes of $35,000 or less   165

Table B.20: Frequency of use of adjectives chosen by respondents to describe *Survivor* contestants, grouped by gender   166

Table B.21: Frequency of use of adjectives chosen to describe *Survivor* contestants 50 and older, overall and by gender   167

Table B.22: Frequency of use of adjectives chosen to describe select *Survivor* contestants, by race and gender   168

Table C.1:   First 1,000 vs. last 508 cases in 2004 survey   172

Table C.2:   Change in frequencies, first 1,000 vs. last 508 cases   173

Table C.3:   Adjectives used in 2005 survey, question No. 2   176

Preface

A Note on Television, Marx, Freud, and Semiotics

MUCH ANALYSIS OF CULTURAL OBJECTS focuses on "high culture"—sculpture, classical music, plays, and the like. Universities offer countless courses in poetry, the novel, and art history, focusing on works filled with meaning and able to support deep, sustained analysis. Thousands of students graduate every year having studied the "classics." Some continue to do so in their professional lives, while others never view a Picasso again.

Indeed, as these are forms of high culture, the meaning inherent in them will primarily be absorbed by the sociocultural elite, who have the money, education, and social background to view and "appreciate" them. Generally, the middle and lower classes will not enjoy the same long-term exposure to this "more meaningful" cultural output. Along with the elites, however, they will enjoy potentially unlimited exposure to popular cultural productions such as film, television, rock music, and video games.

These media sometimes are dismissed as objects of serious study. "There's a fallacy here, in assuming that the common run of literature is comparable to Melville," New York University's Mark Crispin Miller said in *The New York Times* upon the opening of Syracuse University's Center for the Study of Popular Television (Mifflin 1997). "Most TV drama is aesthetically appalling, and most TV comedy is too."

The Center's director, Robert Thompson, countered that "[i]t is tragic and in many ways dangerous that we are so ignorant as intellectuals about a medium [television] that has such a profound effect on us" (Mifflin 1997). Indeed, academics who scoff at studying TV may be overlooking that the point is not necessarily to equate *A Doll's House* to *Full House*. Rather, the focus is that, because "television is one of the primary socializing agents of contemporary society, it is necessary to determine which programs have the largest viewership and investigate what we are learning from them" (Roth 2003, 35). Although there is little evidence of a systematic cause-and-effect link between media content and behavior, "contemporary studies are finding that media messages influence viewers' perceptions of reality in a systemic manner. This evidence suggests that media representations are incorporated into the knowledge base of audience members" (Eschholz et al. 2002, 301).

In recent years, certain popular media artifacts have come to be studied through programs in cultural studies, but the so-called reality television genre has until recently been ignored. At first glance, this seems reasonable: What meaning can there possibly be in sixteen people stuck on an island, or in forcing swimsuit models to eat live crickets? But such programs must not be so easily dismissed. Television is beamed to millions of people at once, with the ability to impact our lives in ways that high culture today simply cannot. For this reason alone, it is worthy of study. *Tribal Warfare* will pursue this avenue, using as its backbone a concept—the political unconscious—that is based on the ideas of philosopher Karl Marx and psychologist Sigmund Freud.

Marx and Freud

Briefly, Marx argued that relations among people were determined by their economic relationships, especially in capitalistic societies. The few in power—the state, the "haves," the bourgeoisie—exerted control over everyone else, the "have-nots" or proletariat. As Louis Althusser wrote, the state can exert this control through actual or symbolic violence (such as police and courts) or through ideology, which for these purposes is defined as the dominant beliefs and representations that legitimate and perpetuate power relationships. That is, ideology promotes and upholds the dominant group's interests. It is disseminated through the family, schools, church, and perhaps most of all, the media—or generally, through socialization.

Clearly, the application of so-called Marxist idealism, in the guise of communism, has proved to be an unmitigated disaster worldwide. However, "Marxism is something very different from the reductive political programs that have been derived from his writings; as [Marx] himself said later in life... 'All I know is I am not a Marxist'" (Roberts 2000, 17). It is critical, therefore, to separate Marx's analysis of the structure of capitalism (haves vs. have-nots, etc.) from how totalitarian regimes have tried to put his ideas into practice.

Freud, meanwhile, focused his analysis on the individual level, as opposed to Marx's examination of society at large. He suggested that one's consciousness is made up of three parts. First is the ego, the part of someone who thinks "I am me." It is "the conscious, self-aware aspect of consciousness"; then there is the super-ego, the "inner policeman...that manifests itself in feelings of conscience, shame and guilt and acts as a break on desires and urges"; finally, the unconscious or subconscious id houses our primitive desires, urges, and fears. "It just wants, and it doesn't care how or why" (Roberts 2000, 56). This id is inaccessible to conscious thought, yet still affects all our actions; for example, it is blamed for "Freudian slips," and much psychotherapy involves extracting the id's contents.

Indeed, the id houses repressed thoughts as a psychological defense mechanism. "Thoughts, responses or impulses that are unacceptable or too painful for the conscious mind to cope with are buried in the subconscious. This is a form of denial, a squashing down of whatever it is that makes the individual feel anxious in an attempt to get rid of it" (Roberts 2000, 60). But these thoughts do not disappear. They may remain "latent," or below the surface, yet may manifest themselves from time to time in other forms— such as an irrational fear of spiders being a symbol for a deeper, latent fear. This idea of symbols is related to semiotics, another concept that will come into play in this book.

Semiotics

Semiotics, or the "science of signs," derives from the lectures of Swiss linguist Ferdinand de Saussure. A sign consists of a signifier (an image, sound, or series of letters) and the signified it conjures (the concept). To cite a famous example, the signifier "t-r-e-e" evokes the signified, an image of the living thing that those who speak English call a tree (Chandler 2002). For those who speak Spanish, the signifier "a-r-b-o-l" evokes that same signified. The signifier and signified "form an indissociable unity, like two sides of the same piece of paper" (McNeill 1996). This is the sign (the word "tree"). This sort of sign is arbitrary, random—that is, "t-r-e-e" could just as easily have signified a llama rather than a tall plant if that was how English had evolved.

Linguist Roland Barthes later distinguished between two types of signifieds, denotative and connotative. Saussure's work focused on denotation— that is, the literal, definitional, obvious meaning of a sign, such as "t-r-e-e" conjuring the image of a tree. Connotation, however, refers to "sociocultural and personal associations (ideological, emotional, etc.) of the sign. These are typically related to the interpreter's class, age, gender, ethnicity, and so on" (Chandler 2002). Connotations, then, are more open to interpretation. For instance, the sign of tree could mean environmentalism to one person, Christmas to another, even Stanford University (whose mascot is a tree)—or all of these. However, the Stanford connotation would have limited legitimacy, as responses not shared by many members of a given culture will have little impact (McNeill 1996).

To Barthes, the sign formed by the denotative signifier and signified becomes the new signifier, from which the new connotative signified extends (Barthes 1988, 115). As this often has cultural meaning (and indeed the denotative signified can, too, in a subliminal way), "objects and events always signify more than themselves; they are always caught up in systems of representation which add meaning to them." This is the domain of myth, a "second-order semiological system" (Barthes 1988, 114). Barthes used this to delve into seemingly innocuous objects of culture, those that he felt masked subjective ideas as objective fact—in his words, transforming "history into nature." Barthes is critical to the study of culture "because he was amongst the first to take seriously 'mass culture' and to apply to it methods of analysis formerly the preserve of 'high culture'" (McNeill 1996).

One scholar, Nick Couldry, has even said that every game-style reality program "has a specific myth about how it represents the social world" (2004, 63). Indeed, as will be shown, Barthes' ideas about myth—especially when used in tandem with those of Freud and particularly Marx—play a pivotal role in analyzing *Survivor*.

Acknowledgments

THIS BOOK WOULD NOT HAVE BEEN POSSIBLE without contributions from a number of individuals. *Tribal Warfare* originated as a thesis project at Georgetown University's program in Communication, Culture, and Technology; my primary and secondary advisers, Dr. Matthew Tinkcom and Dr. Diana Owen, lent their enormous expertise to me on numerous occasions. Dr. Tinkcom was endlessly helpful in dealing with the theory end of things, and it helped that he too is a *Survivor* viewer. Dr. Owen, meanwhile, answered my never-ending statistics questions, and helped enormously with my survey research, both of which continued well after I had graduated.

A number of others must also be thanked: series editor Dr. Mark Andrejevic; Erin Hill-Parks, my former editor at Lexington, who was particularly instrumental in the book's development; her successor, Joseph Parry; production editor Molly Ahearn; viewers M. Catts, Chris Huffine, B.C.N., and Dr. Carol Wharton of the University of Richmond, who read drafts of all or some of the work; Christine Cupaiuolo, who gave me my first outlet to write about *Survivor* in 2001 on *PopPolitics.com*; the anonymous reviewers who provided invaluable advice; Helen Glover, who gave me a contestant's insight; my parents, for their continued support; and Oliver and Sierra, for being by my side.

Thanks also to the tens of thousands of members of the online *Survivor* community, particularly those at SurvivorSucks and its "splinterverse," who collectively helped inspire my academic interest in the program. More than 1,000 of them also took time to complete my surveys (and message board moderators were kind enough to let me prominently post them there), with several also providing helpful insights and the occasional tape of an episode I had lost; leaders of the team behind "edgic," a content analysis of sorts, were kind enough to work with me to include those ratings in an appendix.

Finally, we *Survivor* viewers would have nothing to obsess over were it not for the game's many players and its brilliant man behind the curtain, executive producer Mark Burnett (who, for the record, was in no way involved in this book's production, nor was CBS television).

"A baby raised in isolation, we understand, would not be a human being, and an adult going to a desert island takes his society with him."
— William Dowling, on the political unconscious (1984, 115)

"If Tagi were the island's 'haves,' Pagong were definitely the 'have-nots.'"
— executive producer Mark Burnett (2000, 89) on *Survivor: Borneo*

Introduction

"Interrogating the Obvious"
Survivor *as Cultural Touchstone*

REALITY TELEVISION FAILS to live up to what its name implies. The word "reality" connotes truth, that we are shown events as they happened, along with objective portraits of contestants. Yet existing literature demonstrates the genre is contrived, less *The Real World* than the unreal world—a manufactured reality designed to make us forget cameras and time compression. Therein lies the danger: If reality TV is not "real," but presented as such, the ideologies therein may more greatly impact viewers than obviously fictitious work.

Before the summer of 2000, reality television—a genre based on the recording of events in people's lives, be they "normal" daily activities or those resulting from a contrived game-show style setting, and the editing of this material into a packaged television program[1]—was little thought-of. It was seen primarily in programs such as *Cops, America's Funniest Home Videos*, to some degree *Unsolved Mysteries*, and of course MTV's *The Real World*. The latter program, in fact—with its serialized nature and young, conflicted roommates in a swanky house full of cameras and microphones, including a room for "private" "confessionals"—birthed "many of the textual characteristics that would come to define the genre's current form" and arguably "trained a generation of young viewers in the language of reality TV" (Ouellette and Murray 2004, 3). The reality genre is rooted, however, further in the televisual past: "Reality television may not be such a recent phenomenon as many researchers and practicioners assert. Shows from previous decades, such as *Candid Camera* and *Real People,* are often cited as the instigators of this genre" (Baker 2003, 57).

In the late 1990s, reality television seemed so irrelevant[2] that CBS rejected executive producer Mark Burnett's concept for *Survivor* at least twice before finally giving him the green light (Farhi and de Moraes, 2000). Despite its low production costs and similar programs' success overseas, *Survivor* was seen as too different, something that American audiences—

programmed to care only about whether that week's *ER* patients would survive and whether *Friends'* Ross and Rachel would get back together—would never accept.

Even when Les Moonves and company finally approved the show, they banished it to summer air, when fewer people watch TV. Debuting in May 2000, the original *Survivor,* along with its sequels, features sixteen to twenty people[3] dropped off in a remote jungle or other locale, where they form "tribes" and create mini-societies. Cameramen follow the contestants, filming their every move as the "castaways" interact with their environment and one another. Producers also interview the contestants for "confessional" soliloquies. The contestants receive basic supplies but generally must find their own food, water, and shelter. They also compete in "challenges" run by the show's host, Jeff Probst. The challenges may consist of an obstacle course, a giant jigsaw puzzle, a quiz, an archery contest, or any of other countless inventive activities. The winning tribe collects either a reward (such as food or fishing gear) or "immunity." Every three days, the tribe without immunity must trek to Tribal Council, a location that takes on a religious aura, where one member is voted out of the game in dramatic fashion, often determined by membership in various player "alliances."

Midway through the game, remaining members of the tribes merge into one, at which point reward and immunity contests become individual. All players go to each Tribal Council, with only the immune contestant(s) safe from the vote.[4] By the thirty-ninth day only two players remain, and the last seven previously dispatched contestants return to select the winner, who receives $1 million.

Initial reviews were mixed. "*Survivor* is drama distilled—and addictive," wrote the *New York Daily News'* David Bianculli, calling it "the rare sort of TV show...that will increase in appeal each week as the stakes get higher, and the word of mouth gets even louder.... Even more will be watching it next week" (2000, 100). On the other hand, the *Washington Post's* Tom Shales wrote that "the show is a revolting and ridiculous bore.... We're voting ourselves off that rat-ridden island right this minute" (2000, C01).

Bianculli was proven prescient—and Shales quite the opposite—as *Survivor* quickly became a cultural phenomenon, with water cooler chatter centering around it and multiple Internet sites springing up and following the program's actions. For the premiere episode, a healthy 15.5 million viewers tuned in (*Post-Gazette* 2000), and ratings rose on almost a weekly basis, with 51 million viewers—a summer non-sports viewing record—watching the August season finale to see contestant Richard prevail (Magder 2004, 137). The second edition, *Survivor: The Australian Outback*, aired in spring 2001 and was the 2000-01 TV season's highest-rated show (de Moraes 2001, C05). The viewing audience has hovered at approximately 20 million per week since, with two editions of *Survivor* being churned out per television season, and the show has remained a Top-Ten fixture among total viewers in the Nielsen ratings.[5]

The Unreal World

Haralovich and Trosset, quoting *Variety*, note that *Survivor* is not your run-of-the-mill reality production: "Burnett knew American viewers expect top-notch production values in primetime programs, so he eschewed the cheap-is-better convention of most reality shows and gave *Survivor* a virtually cinematic look that made the show look as good as (if not better than) the typical network drama" (2004, 77). The fact that the program is filmed entirely in advance also gives producers a leg up, enabling them to edit in overarching storylines, symbolism, and imagery.

This timing also, however, enables them to manipulate the show's construction at will, while maintaining an aura of realness:

> By emphasizing the "reality" of reality TV, producers and networks privilege the "ordinariness" of the competitors, erasing the "TV" part of the phrase—the manipulation of the situation and the mediation of the footage. In the words of Jean Baudrillard, "it is rather a question of substituting signs of the real for the real itself." (Delisle 2003, 44)

The danger is that, because what we are seeing is billed as "reality," any ideological messages presented will seem more natural on *Survivor* than they ever would on *Lost* or *Desperate Housewives*, where at least viewers know they are watching fiction. Reality television, therefore, must be probed for its meaning and messages. As Roland Barthes—as noted in the preface, one of the first scholars to take seriously "mass" culture and apply to it methods of analysis normally exclusive to "high" culture (McNeill 1996)—believed, we must unearth the meaning of the seemingly banal. We must "interrogate the obvious" (McNeill 1996). *Tribal Warfare* aims to contribute to this task by using textual analysis and survey research to probe the political content of *Survivor*. One way to do so is through Fredric Jameson's "political unconscious," which at the simplest level is defined as the collective repression of a "historical nightmare," mediated through varied texts. The historical nightmare is the set of class struggles that critics such as Karl Marx have said permeate human history: the haves vs. the have-nots. Buried in the "unconscious" of novels, plays, and other texts are ideas about these struggles, according to Jameson, born in Ohio in 1934 and now a professor at Duke University. His theory will be thoroughly explored in Chapter 2.

Survivor as Allegory?

Tribal Warfare, then, will explore *Survivor* through the lens of the political unconscious by probing examples of Jamesonian repression on the show, the intent being to determine whether it functions as a political allegory reflecting society's hierarchical nature. As will be seen, on *Survivor*, repression falls into two categories that often overlap:

- Repression that springs from contestants withholding information from competitors.
- Repression that springs from editors/producers withholding information from the audience.

As will become apparent, much of this repression involves hiding the presence and makeup of voting alliances, which form the core power structures on *Survivor*.

To further support the investigation of class politics on *Survivor* and attempt to test Jameson's theory in some way, online survey research was conducted. This study compiled responses from two comprehensive surveys of 1,000 viewers each, conducted in spring 2004 and spring 2005 regarding their expectations, desires, and reactions in viewing the first ten seasons of the program.[6] For the 2004 survey, questions dealt with the seasons of the show especially important to this project, particularly Season 1, *Borneo*; Season 4, *Marquesas*; and Season 6, *The Amazon*. These seasons were stressed because they were the first of their kind structurally: In *Borneo*, one bloc of players maintained power throughout and eradicated their opponents; *Marquesas* was the first season where one full bloc of players wrested power from another; and *The Amazon* was the first where no bloc of players was able to maintain power, resulting in strategic chaos.

Respondents to both surveys were asked to think back to their viewpoints at the time the shows initially aired.[7] They were asked whether they had felt certain groups of players would prevail or be voted out, whom they had wanted to win, and their reaction to certain outcomes.

The 2005 survey was far more comprehensive, containing a host of questions regarding various aspects of the program. Most critically, it had respondents rate randomly determined contestants from the first ten seasons using one of three instruments, with photos of contestants provided.

First, considering a contestant's "overall depiction" on *Survivor*, the respondents were asked for their "overall attitude toward each of these contestants at the time their season aired," taking into consideration their personality; behavior at camp; physical abilities and challenge performances; mental and emotional makeup; game-play and strategy; and treatment of other players. For contestants who also appeared on *Survivor: All-Stars*, respondents were asked to primarily consider their first season on the show.

Respondents rated them on a seven-point scale from "very positive" to "very negative." These ratings were averaged and later adjusted to account for apparent biases that may have been the result of certain seasons being more recent than others and therefore fresher in respondents' minds, as well as skews in the survey population sample (the adjustment formula is detailed in Appendix C). The resulting ranking of all 150 contestants is referred to in this text as the adjusted audience attitude index, or AAAI. The unweighted raw audience attitude index also is cited whenever the mean of several contestants' rankings is being discussed.

Second, for a different set of contestants, the respondents were asked to briefly describe the first thing they remembered about them, be it a specific incident that occurred on the show, a personality trait, or something in their biography. Respondents were, however, asked not to simply list what place the contestant finished.

Third, for yet another set of contestants, the respondents were presented with three drop-down menus, each with a list of nine adjectives, then asked to pick the adjective from each menu that best described that particular contestant, as depicted on *Survivor*. If none did, respondents could select "none of these." Definitions of each adjective were made available.

The surveys also asked for a number of demographics, including both standard queries (age and gender) and one particular to *Survivor*—level of fandom. With Jameson's theory in mind, these questions enabled testing whether social class, income, education level, political orientation, and other class-related factors affect how one reacts to *Survivor*. The results provide evidence that this may indeed be the case.

Chapter 1 reviews the literature on reality television and examines why *Survivor* is best suited for political analysis compared to other, more derivative reality programs. Chapter 2 examines the political unconscious, defines "repression" as used herein, and differentiates it from simple suppression. Chapter 3 contains a textual analysis of how *Survivor: Borneo's* Tagi alliance became a repressed element and presents corresponding survey results. Chapter 4 examines repression among contestants and Chapter 5 repression by producers/editors; both also include corresponding survey results. Chapter 6 examines how gender hierarchies are handled on *Survivor* by contestants and editors; Chapters 7 and 8 do the same with issues of age and race. The conclusion sums up the role of class in *Survivor* as well as the overall survey results, and revisits the concept of the political unconscious.

Notes

1. Adapted from Baker 2003, 58.

2. See Raphael (2004) for a discussion of the political and economic dominoes that helped lead to reality television's resurgence as viable alternative programming.

3. Contestants are virtually always strangers, the exceptions being members of *Survivor: All-Stars* (spring 2004), nearly all of whom already knew one another; and certain contestants on *Survivor: Guatemala* (fall 2005), in that two players, Bobby Jon and Stephenie, had also been on the previous season, *Palau*. Therefore, they already knew each other, and most of the other contestants already "knew" them from having watched them on TV, and were "star-struck" by their presence (CBS, 11 Dec. 2005). An interesting future research project could entail to what degree players in the heat of the game in *Guatemala* felt that the pair's actual personalities matched their edited personas from *Palau*, keeping in mind the potential for moderate fame to change them in some way.

4. To keep contestants on their toes (and the audience from growing bored), producers have tweaked this formula in varying ways—for instance, forcing contestants to swap tribes, bringing ousted players back into the game, or delaying the merge.

5. See Magder (2004) for a discussion of the high-stakes *Survivor-Friends* duel and the reality show's impact on the TV business.

6. Surveys could only be taken once from the same computer, and results had a normal distribution. However, the survey was a convenience sample, rather than a random sampling such as those conducted by the Gallup organization, something impossible to perform with the resources available. As a result, despite the large sample size, the data cannot be assumed to represent the opinions of all 20 million or so *Survivor* viewers. However, the statistically significant cross-tabulations and regression results still reveal patterns in key demographics that may well be embedded in the larger population. Additionally, many of those who took the survey were attentive *Survivor* fans with extensive knowledge of the program, giving the results additional merit. For details, see methodology (Appendix C). Basic results and selected cross-tab and regression analysis charts also appear throughout the main body of the text and in other appendices.

7. At this point, *Survivor* had not yet begun to air in syndication, nor were any full seasons available on DVD. *Borneo, All-Stars,* and *Australian Outback* had been released on DVD by the time the spring 2005 survey was launched.

Chapter 1

"You Cannot Talk to the
Guys in the Boat"

Survivor *as the False Real*

THE EMERGING LITERATURE on reality television—a small number of academic books exist on the subject, with scattered other essays to be found in
journals and online—demonstrates that these programs in fact project a mediated, manipulated, contrived "reality," to varied degrees. For instance,
documentary-style shows such as *Cops* may be less mediated than *Queer
Eye for the Straight Guy*, which is presented as taking place during a single
day, when in reality it occurs across several. Even more mediated are highly
packaged shows such as *Survivor* and *The Real World,* which, as Hugh Phillips Curnutt explained, "shows us a place not based in any arguable reality"
(2002, 4). To his credit, Mark Burnett, executive producer of *Survivor*, has
argued from the beginning that his show is not reality but rather "dramality,"
a contrived, unscripted drama (McDaniel 2000).

Indeed, the notion of "reality TV" is ironic on its very surface. The
phrase connotes truth, everyday experience, and perhaps most importantly, a
lack of mediation—that what you see on video is as it happened. But the
genre obscures or makes viewers "forget" cameras, time compression,
editing, contrivances, packaging, and sound and lighting instruments.
Consider *Survivor*: Each 44-minute episode is culled from 72 hours of
footage from multiple cameras.[1] Burnett and his editing team only have to
show what they want to. They can make anyone look bad. They can make
anyone look good.

Journalist Peter Lance appears to have been the first to document *Survivor's* "unreality" in his 2000 book *The Stingray: Lethal Tactics of the Sole
Survivor*. He describes a number of occurrences where footage was aired out
of order—or simply left out—to boost suspense. For instance, although a big
deal was made out of contestant Richard shedding his clothes in Episode 6
of *Survivor: Borneo*, he had been stripping all along, and others had joined
in (Lance 2000, 69). Also, several contestants told Lance they had been un-

fairly portrayed, victims of biased editing[2] (Lance 2000, 18), something that has become a running theme in the literature since.

An e-mail interview the author conducted with *Survivor: Thailand* (fall 2002) contestant Helen Glover shed light on how the show is constructed. For instance, in one episode, we watched as Helen and tribemate Jan got lost at sea in their tiny boat. Obviously, for this to have been filmed, a "camera boat" had to have been with them. As audience members, we are lulled into forgetting this. Glover wrote:

> There is *always* a camera boat that follows you everywhere. In fact, a few times we were yelled at for not waiting for the camera boat to follow. They're afraid that you'll say something pertinent to the game and they won't have it caught on tape. That being said, you cannot talk to the guys in the boat, get any help from the guys in the boat, ask questions, etc. It's as if they're not there. And, believe me…it's useless to try! They won't answer you. (Glover 2004)

Most intriguing is Glover's statement that "it's as if [the camera boat is] not there." This, apparently, is the desired effect for both contestants and, eventually, viewers. One thinks of theorist Walter Benjamin's notions of history and reproduction—that is, his definition of history as things documented, through photography or otherwise (Benjamin 1968, 220). However, that which secures history is pushed off the stage of history. As a simplistic example, say you photograph a person eating an apple. You wind up with a piece of glossy paper featuring an image of that person eating an apple. Is this "real"? Perhaps a close approximation—but the angle, the lighting, and so on, all were subjective choices on your part. Also, a truly real real, as it were, also would have to include you in the image, taking the picture with your camera. But then, a real image of that would have to include the second cameraman taking a picture of you taking a picture of the man eating the apple. And so on and so forth—context inevitably would be left out of the picture (Tinkcom, 2002).

Beginning in October 2001, this writer contributed a series of articles to the cultural Web magazine *PopPolitics.com* that discussed sociological and other aspects of *Survivor*. A motif of these involved heavy-duty selective editing the program employs, particularly with stereotyping and "character development" (an odd term to use, since these are real people, but accurate nonetheless). Given that producers must introduce sixteen "characters" to America in little time, perhaps it is unsurprising that they fall back on stereotypes in choosing what footage to air. So we repeatedly see the Whiny Woman (Lindsey, Shawna); the Bossy Older Man (Frank, B.B., Sarge); the Devout Christian (Dirk, Joanna); and the America's Sweetheart (Colleen, Elizabeth, Stephenie in her *Palau* depiction only) (Wright, 22 Oct. 2001).

For instance, consider *Survivor: Africa's* Linda, a 44-year-old African-American who was portrayed as obsessed with African spirits and even mentally unstable:

> As always, editing plays a big part in our perceptions. For example, after CBS aired the episode where she was [voted out], Linda complained in interviews that her portrayal was skewed: Every time she opened her mouth onscreen, she said, something about African spirits came tumbling out....Linda claimed the editors chose to air every such comment she made, but left out 99 percent of her other dialogue, which had nothing to do with Mother Africa. This complaint is reminiscent of former [African-American] Survivors Nick and Gervase, who claimed they were portrayed as being much lazier than they actually were. (Wright, 26 Nov. 2001)

Scholar Steven Vrooman read these incidents another way. Several contestants, but especially *Australian Outback's* Nick, were portrayed as primitives, he argued. Certain tribemates dubbed Nick lazy, and because "[w]e hear almost nothing from Nick in these early [episodes, there] is no temptation to identify with him and see him as other than a primitive racial other.... At Tribal Council, the host asks, 'Anyone here not pulling their weight?' and the camera cuts to Nick" (190-91).

Race and culture have played a factor, too, in portrayals of *Survivor's* settings. Jennifer Bowering Delisle makes a fascinating case that *Survivor* simulates 19th-century imperialistic fiction. She compares the "staged authenticity" of tourism—the idea that a "host culture," aware that visitors seek interaction with an "other," exaggerate elements of local culture while keeping their real lives "back stage"—with the way "native lands" are portrayed on *Survivor*. Before *Survivor: Marquesas* began filming in the fall of 2001, for instance, the crew demolished a house, dock, and freshwater-gathering system on a bay to be used for filming, and sprayed the beach daily with insecticide. The house's longtime resident, who gave permission for it to be torn down, was moved inland (Delisle 2003, 47, 53).

Additionally, "On *Survivor*, continual emphasis is placed on ancient traditions and myth and a sense of universal origin" (2003, 43-44). Several seasons' official Web sites have featured selected histories of the lands in which the shows were filmed. They "chronicle only the colonial history [of the areas]. The indigenous peoples are barely mentioned; instead the events cited are moments of Western discovery and conquest" (2003, 45). Similarly, in *Africa*, bustling cities are not shown; instead, contestant Lex visits a needy AIDS hospital to deliver supplies. "Thus the image of the benevolent colonizer entering Africa to save the morally diseased Other is repeated in a contemporary context" (Delisle 2003, 46). These issues will be further explored in Chapter 8.

Elsewhere, Mark Andrejevic argues that "*Survivor* neatly epitomizes the paradox of reality TV by offering a 'well-produced' version of reality, apparently more convincing than the transparently manipulative episodes of *Big Brother*" (2004, 196). This, among other factors, helps bridge the gap between reality and fiction, he writes. "Perhaps the hallmark of the reality format is its incorporation of a variety of genres: fiction, soap opera, and documentary." Reality remakes of *Green Acres* or *Gilligan's Island*, which transpose recycled fictional works into the real, "promise to rejuvenate exhausted formats by overcoming the abstracted relations of the industrial production of culture" (2004, 69).

The Digital Paradox

Arild Fetveit tackles another reason that reality television isn't real: Just as we are seeing the rise of purportedly real video, so, too, are we witnessing an increase in digital manipulation of photography and video. "[W]e are experiencing a strengthening and weakening of the credibility of photographic discourses at the same time" (2002, 119). On the one hand, in shows such as *Cops*, a one-camera unit rides with the police. It captures a chaotic scene, featuring white noise from the scanner, ragged camera movement, extraneous environmental noise, and often, citizens at their disheveled worst. This creates authenticity, which is further enhanced by an opening voice-over that states, "*Cops* is filmed on location with the men and women of law enforcement" (Fetveit 2002, 124).

On the other hand, "the development of computer programs for manipulation and generation of images has made it, at times, very hard to see whether we are looking at ordinary photographic images or images that have been altered" (Fetveit 2002, 125). Appropriately, lodged in the middle of this paradox is *Survivor*. Occasionally, the producers of this reality show have used manipulated footage to throw off viewers or tell a better story. Midway through Season 1, "opening-sequence footage—showing only Colleen, Rudy, Sean, and Gervase seated at a Tribal Council—was aired," leading the thousands of viewers who "gathered" online at Web sites such as SurvivorSucks.com to guess they would be the final four players remaining. As it turned out, however, this was a digital creation—only Rudy made the actual final four[3] (Wright, 10 Jan. 2002). During *Survivor: Africa*, it appeared that contestant Brandon's tribal buff—a bandanna whose color signifies tribal membership—was temporarily digitally changed from green to red, in order to disguise the fact that his tribe had merged with the other. Similarly, in a promotion for a *Survivor: All-Stars* episode, Shii-Ann's buff color apparently was digitally altered to hide another such twist.[4] It takes a keen eye to notice such details, and the world of online *Survivor* "spoiling" has been explored by several authors.[5]

Such manipulations remind us of the fact that, unlike reality shows such as *Big Brother* and *American Idol*, *Survivor* is filmed entirely in advance (except for the live finale). We may forget this, however, and to producers' advantage—for thinking of these events as happening in real time makes them seem *more real*. On *Survivor*, host Jeff Probst sometimes describes prior events as having happened "last week," even though, as filmed, they usually had occurred three days ago. "Viewers are asked to accept the *Survivor* time frame as if the events were occurring in the present and not in the past," according to Mary Beth Haralovich and Michael Trosset (84). "In this regard, watching *Survivor* is like watching the Olympics or Emmy Awards in tape-delay." Indeed, viewers who wish to circumvent the "tape-delay" can turn to the online spoiler boards, though predictions found there do not always come to pass.

Others have also written eloquently about TV's authenticity, and not just in terms of reality programs. According to Jane Feuer, TV has in many ways been institutionalized as "live" and "real": "By postulating an equivalence between time of event, time of television creation, and transmission viewing-time, television as an institution identifies all messages emanating from the apparatus as 'live.' The live program is thus taken as the very definition of television" (14).

Lynn Spigel has struck a similar tone, arguing that "television at its most ideal promised to bring to audiences not merely an illusion of reality as in the cinema, but a sense of 'being there,' a kind of hyperrealism. Advertisers suggested that their sets would deliver picture and sound quality so real that the illusion would come alive" (1992, 133). Spigel also has detailed the historical and social role television has played in the family; Anna McCarthy, meanwhile, has examined how television affects public areas such as bars and shopping malls (2001).

Elsewhere, John Fiske and John Hartley argue that the medium in general is convincingly real. "Television realism, then, following the pattern of language at large, 'naturalizes' the way in which we apprehend the world out there [and says that] the world is, naturally and of itself, what the mind-originated conventions of realism say it is" (161-162, 1978).

This naturalization theme is followed up by Tarleton Gillespie, who writes that "according to [one] argument, television 'trains' the viewing public to observe the world in ways that support dominant interests" (2000, 36). For if ideological content is presented as natural—that is, as transforming history into nature, in the words of Barthes—the danger is that content in "reality" programming will be seen as more natural still.

Survivor as Society?

With so many "reality" programs to choose from, the question inevitably arises: Why use *Survivor* as a vehicle for exploring political content in the reality genre? The answer is two-fold. First, *Survivor* is the "granddaddy" of the current reality crop, has now gone into syndication, and remains a major hit, with the potential to air for years to come—and is therefore most relevant. Second, *Survivor* in its very structure is overtly political, often self-descriptively so.

Although *The Real World*, as noted earlier, paved the way for *Survivor*, the latter's giant success—51 million viewing the first season finale, 20 million or so viewers on average since then—has caused other reality programs to flood the market. Many of these have borrowed to varying degrees from *Survivor*, in terms of the use of physical and mental competitions, terminology, being "voted out" in some fashion, editing style, a host who banters with contestants, and so on.[6] ABC's *The Mole* is especially noteworthy for its use of *Survivor*-like terminology. The program features twelve or so strangers who trek around Europe together[7]; one person is a "mole" charged with sabotaging various competitions, while the others (and viewers) must determine the mole's identity. The players, some of whom form "coalitions" to help one another out, take part in "games" and "tests" that win them money and sometimes allow one person to obtain an "exemption" from the "quiz" that occurs at the end of each episode, during which the players must answer questions about the mole's identity. The players then proceed to the dramatic "Execution," where the player who scored the lowest on the quiz is "executed" and escorted from the game.

So, where *Survivor* has its challenges, *The Mole* has its games and tests. *Survivor* has alliances; *The Mole* has coalitions. In *Survivor*, players who lack immunity risk being voted out; on *The Mole*, players lacking an exemption risk execution. This use of similar terminology by *The Mole* (which also features a talkative, charismatic host, like *Survivor*) accomplishes dual, dialectical objectives: It links *The Mole* to *Survivor* at the same time it separates the two. In this way, ABC's show, and others, take on their own identity while still using similar lingo to keep an intertextual link to the most ballyhooed reality program.

The great majority of these "duplicate" programs have fallen by the wayside, and excluding *American Idol*—which is more a talent show than anything else—none have had the sustained ratings success of *Survivor*. Shows that looked promising—*Joe Millionaire* for one—tailed off dramatically when sequel seasons aired; others, such as *The Bachelor* and Burnett's own *The Apprentice*, have had some staying power, but at a lower wattage than *Survivor*'s. And although *The Apprentice* and *American Idol* have each taken their turn in the national spotlight, neither has been a cultural phenomenon to the extreme degree *Survivor* was in the summer of 2000, when "Tagi alliance" seemed to be the first words off of anyone's lips. The show's status as cultural touchtone, then, coupled with its long-term high ratings and having both spawned and outlived most other reality programs, makes *Survivor* the first show of its genre to turn to for academic investigation.

When the topic being examined is politics, *Survivor* is all the more an appropriate target. Politics—the struggle for, and exercise of, power—is at the heart of any society. And as it turns out, *Survivor* frames itself as a natural, primal society. As host Probst has told viewers at the start of most seasons' debut episode, *Survivor* contestants, upon being deposited in the remote wilderness, are "forced to work together to create a new society." *Survivor* insists it depicts a society that is natural—i.e., "real," including the formation of "tribes" and the use of forced primitivism. Then there is the democracy echoed in Tribal Council voting. That voting leads to power plays and cuts off any sense of utopia among *Survivor's* contestants. Certainly, Karl Marx saw things as such, with his assertion that every society is based upon economic relations and therefore class-related hierarchies—that is, the haves and the have-nots, the powerful and powerless, the dominant and dominated. Since *Survivor* purports to be a "new society," is it too structured as Marx envisioned?

Executive producer Burnett certainly appears to think so. Speaking of *Survivor: Borneo's* dueling tribes, he writes, "If Tagi were the island's 'haves,' Pagong were definitely the 'have-nots.' Instead of empowering themselves by working harder, like Tagi, the Pagong victimized themselves" (2000, 89).

Yet despite all this—Burnett's statement, Tribal Councils, and the self-proclaimed conceit of *Survivor* as society—rarely has class politics been discussed in existing literature on reality television. The main exception is Jennifer Thackaberry's essay "Manual Metaphors of *Survivor* and Office Politics: Images of Work in Popular *Survivor* Criticism," in which she notes that "producers cast across levels in the social and occupational hierarchy, lumping the haves and have-nots, the powerful and the powerless together in order to incite conflict" (2003, 155).

However, what of social status *on* the show? Thackaberry also succinctly discusses the popular metaphor of "*Survivor* as the workplace," something that perhaps more appropriately describes *The Apprentice*. Yet why not expand that metaphor to "*Survivor* as society," as the show insists at the opening of most seasons? Indeed, does *Survivor* reflect the hierarchical nature of society?

This is where Fredric Jameson's *The Political Unconscious* comes in.

Notes

1. Occasionally, an episode will be longer than 44 minutes or take place over a smaller time period than 72 hours.

2. Additionally, *Survivor: Borneo* contestant Stacey sued the program in 2001, claiming executive producer Mark Burnett had pressured contestants into voting her off. The charges were never proven, and no one since has alleged anything similar. Only 19.6 percent of respondents to the 2005 survey believed Stacey.

3. The footage apparently was created from the final seven Tribal Council, which featured Colleen, Rudy, Gervase, Sean, Sue, Rich, and Kelly. The latter three were apparently digitally removed to throw off fans. This followed the discovery of a CBS Web site "glitch," suggesting Gervase would win, that made national headlines, as well as legitimate video that aired in Episode 3's opening sequence. This video showed nine players around the Tribal Council campfire, who proved to be the final nine remaining. Viewers who spotted this were able to accurately predict many of the next to be voted out of the game.

4. See www.londyscreations.com/survivornetwork/spoilers_ep9.asp.

5. For instance "Spoiler Sports," "Spoiled Rotten?," and other articles by this writer, as well as Derek Foster's essay "'Jump in the Pool': The Competitive Culture of *Survivor* Fan Networks," part of the anthology *Understanding Reality Television*, and a forthcoming work by Henry Jenkins III, author of *Textual Poachers*.

6. Note that *Survivor* itself is based on a European version, while the American *Big Brother* is also based on a program from across the Atlantic.

7. Two seasons with "regular" people aired; later editions have featured minor celebrities competing in Hawaii and other locales.

Chapter 2

"Apparently Reprehensible Material"
The Political Unconscious and Popular Culture

ONE OF FREDRIC JAMESON'S great accomplishments in *The Political Unconscious* is uniting Karl Marx's class-related theories of societal structure with Sigmund Freud's psychoanalytic ideas of the individual's mind. As such, he links the psychological with the political, the individual with the collective (Schwab 1993, 87), albeit with Marxism as the dominant force. In other words, *The Political Unconscious* slips Freudian thought into a Marxian context more than the other way around.

Before Jameson, others had tried to link Marx's thoughts with Freud's. Pierre Macherey (1966) had attempted something similar, as Adam Roberts notes (2000, 54). Joining them also appeared counterintuitive, however, since Freud believed that one's consciousness is shaped by personal events, while Marx felt that "each individual is determined by society" (Roberts 2000, 54). How to reconcile such an apparent incompatibility?

Several parallels between Marx and Freud suggest themselves, according to Roberts. The Marxism model claims that an economic- and class-related "base" *determines* the cultural, legal, political, and above all ideological "superstructure" of society. Similarly, in Freud's model, an unconscious "base" of desire (the id) determines one's "superstructure" of ego, which the super-ego also affects (Roberts 2000, 57). Furthermore:

> A therapist looks into the conscious mind and tries to read the hidden and coded manifestations of the unconscious that has shaped the ego in order to bring them to the surface, where they can be rationally dealt with. Jameson proposes looking into aspects of the superstructure [such as books and films] and to try and read the hidden and coded manifestations of the economic and political base that has shaped them.... They can be recovered by concentrating on literary and cultural analogues of [Freudian slips] or the irrationality of dreams. (Roberts 2000, 57)

Yet one must remember that Freudian theory cannot be simply stirred in with Marx's ideas. As Jameson warned about previous attempts to link the two theories, there is too easily just "'a kind of supplementary social psychology' where 'repression and the damaged subject' are seen as the direct 'results of the exchange process and the dynamics of capitalism'" (Roberts 2000, 72). Marxism, not Freudian thought, is the center of his theory. Marxism "is the ultimate method under which other methods can be subsumed" (Hestetun 1993, 179).

Class as the Uber-narrative

In *The Political Unconscious*, Jameson claims that narrative exists in countless forms outside the conventional realm of the novel, and is not just a literary type, but an "epistemological" category. In other words, the idea is not that we create stories to understand the world around us—much like the Aesop's fables of childhood—but rather that "the world comes to us in the shape of stories," according to William C. Dowling (1984, 95). Some scholars may find Jameson's ideas about narrative as radical as the once-astounding notion that the Earth revolves around the sun—for Jameson sees such things as recipes, math problems, and sporting events as narrativistic. Indeed, all exhibit elements of plot and denouement. One must follow the step-by-step "plot advancements" of a recipe to arrive at the resolution of a fully cooked dish. A logic problem or algebraic equation require steps that lead to a proof or solution (Dowling 1984, 96). Teams in the NCAA basketball tournament must win six games to claim a championship—and each game is preceded by announcers reviewing "storylines" of the game, such as match-ups between players or defensive tactics.

Linked to the concept of narrative is that of interpretation: "[N]arrative, by just being narrative, always demands interpretation" (Dowling 1984, 96). Jameson rests his theories of interpretation on medieval "exegesis," as well as on the work of Marx and Althusser, whose notions of causality are especially useful. Althusser saw three types. The first, mechanical causality, is direct cause and effect, such as a pool cue striking the ball. Although not often useful, Jameson stresses we must not dismiss this type, especially because the Marxian notion of base/superstructure—that is, economic relations determining the rest of societal organizations—fits it (Dowling 1984, 25-26). The second is expressive causality, which to Jameson belies "a vast interpretive allegory in which a sequence of historical events or texts and artifacts is rewritten in terms of some deeper, underlying, and more fundamental narrative.... They reflect a fundamental dimension of our collective thinking and our collective fantasies about history and reality" (Dowling 1984, 28, 34). Note the importance of collectivity.

Yet Jameson finds neither form of causality adequate. He envelops them into Althusser's third form, structural causality, which is the notion that the interrelations of societal segments themselves *cause* structure. "This is an adept fusion of Marxism's drive to totalize. . . with...mistrust of a present or transcendent cause underlying our unavoidably textual experience," writes Roger Bellin (1998). "The structure in its totality is the cause of each element; but the elements, the multiplicitous texts or levels of society, themselves produce the structure" (Bellin 1998). Turning toward a text, "interpretive mission of a properly structural causality will . . . find its privileged content in rifts and discontinuities within the work" (Jameson 1981, 56).

This causality leads into Jameson's theory of interpreting narrative via three "concentric frameworks" of generality that give way to a "master code" and a view of the historical totality (1981, 75). His first level focuses on the text itself, which houses a symbolic/imaginary resolution of a real contradiction (76). Here, a text "represents a response to a concrete historical situation, as an effort to resolve 'determinate contradictions,'" according to Oyunn Hestetun (1993, 202).

As an example of the first "horizon," Jameson cites Claude Levi-Strauss' account of the Caduveo Indians in *Tristes Tropiques* (1961). They bear elaborate oblique facial decorations not seen in neighboring tribes; the Caduveo also are divided into castes that feature domination systems based on gender and age. Restrictions are placed on marriage patterns, whereas the neighboring tribes, while also hierarchical, have a more free-flowing social structure (or at least the appearance of one). But the Caduveo do not— instead, they bear facial paintings not matching the vertical axis of the human face, much like placing the 11 and 5 at the top and bottom of a clock rather than the 12 and 6. "The visual text of Caduveo facial art constitutes a symbolic act, whereby real social contradictions, insurmountable in their own terms, find a purely formal resolution in the aesthetic realm" (Jameson 1981, 79; see also Dowling 1984, 119-124). We can also, however, see examples in popular culture. One is rather simple: the use of a stake in *Buffy the Vampire Slayer* (Hurt 2002). Fraught with Freudian meaning, the stake Buffy uses to defeat demons also, it could be argued, operates as a symbolic and *powerful* phallus that resolves the contradiction inherent in male-female relationships—the idea that men and women are equal citizens, when history, pay grades, and the like teach us otherwise.

On Jameson's second level of interpretation, the social order comes into play. Here, the object of analysis is "dialectically transformed, and is no longer construed as an individual text or work in the narrow sense, but has been reconstituted in the form of the great collective and class discourses of which a text is little more than an individual" utterance (Jameson 1981, 76). Or, as Hestetun puts it, here "the hegemonic relationship between dominant and dominated social classes or groups is most pronounced" (1993, 202). Again, then, we have elements of contradiction and conflict. "A ruling class ideology will explore various strategies of the legitimation of its own power position, while an oppositional culture or ideology will, often in covert and disguised strategies, seek to contest and undermine the dominant 'value system'" (Jameson 84). The object of study becomes an "ideologeme," which is the "smallest intelligible unit of the essentially antagonistic collective discourses of social classes" (Jameson, 76). Dowling compares this to a word being the smallest intelligible unit of a language—the word, especially when part of a sentence, is only understood when viewed in the context of the totality. Or, as Clint Burnham writes, the "text is seen as an utterance of a class relationship"—the ideologeme (1995, 199).

Finally, in the third level, "the ultimate horizon of human history as a whole," the text and ideologeme "know a final transformation" and must be read as *ideology of form*, or "the symbolic messages transmitted to us by the coexistence of various sign systems which are themselves traces or anticipations of modes of production" (Jameson 1981, 76). Here, we speak of oppression and revolution over human "history":

> [Analysis centers] on "code, sign system, or the system of the production of signs and codes." What could be distinguished as oppositional class dialogue in the second semantic horizon is "focused in such a way that what emerges is rather the all-embracing unity of a single code," shared by these different oppositional voices. (Hestetun 1993, 203, quoting Jameson 1981)

Ideology of form is critical to Jamesonian analysis. Like Theodor Adorno, Jameson believed that the form of a work (its structure, genre, style) was most important, while content (plot, character, setting) was secondary (Roberts 2000, 43). As such, "the novel was the dominant form of literature in the 19th century precisely because it embodies—formally—the qualities of fragmented sprawl, of ironic disintegration of vision and reified experience present in 19th century lived experience.... Cinema and TV are the dominant forms of art today because it is in these visual media that the conditions of postmodern society are most thoroughly expressed," according to Jameson (Roberts 2000, 45). Television may be especially relevant here because of its serial nature, featuring characters we have grown to know and love (or hate), such as *Survivor's* cute Colleen and conniving Richard. Related to this need for attention to form is a need to historicize. Indeed, Jameson opens his book with the declaration, "Always historicize! This slogan...will unsurprisingly turn out to be the moral of *The Political Unconscious*" (1981, 9). A failure to historicize—that is, to simply look at the text alone, in an imminent analysis, without regard for the context—can allow ideological content to escape unnoticed.

From these layers of interpretation springs Jameson's notion of allegory: "the opening up of the text to multiple meanings, to successive rewritings and overwritings which are generated as so many levels and as so many supplementary interpretations" (1981, 30). From this allegory, we cast light on the political unconscious, the collective repression of a historical nightmare, in a history filled with class struggles. The bourgeoisie represses any thought of a revolution, while the proletariat represses the reality of its situation and the social contradictions of capitalism. Hence, through the political unconscious we can find, locked latently into virtually any narrative work, "repressed" ideas about class, and this is Jameson's master code. With some thought, it is difficult indeed to pinpoint any narrative that has *nothing* to do with class and therefore history. Some examples are patently obvious. James Cameron's *Titanic* is a class-based love story and "upstairs/downstairs" drama, right down to the fight over who could board the lifeboats in the end. The film *Gosford Park*, directed by Robert Altman, is clearly upstairs/downstairs as well.

Other examples are more subtextual in nature. For instance, *The Lord of the Rings* books and films have been subject to allegorical interpretations involving class and political ideology, with noted scholar Douglas Kellner writing that "the novel and film cycle suggests that only a few individuals are moral enough to resist the temptations of power (i.e., the Ring) and that superior individuals will rise to leadership and eventually produce a King and stable social structure" (forthcoming). Kellner has previously argued that the 1980s horror film *Poltergiest* reflects "a very average middle-class family in a house that constantly gives them troubles and is eventually taken away from them," among other themes (1995, 131); he also posits that the seemingly lowbrow concoction *Beavis and Butthead* "presents the revenge of youth and those who are terminally downwardly mobile against more privileged classes and individuals" (1995, 148). Additionally, a story arc in Season 4 of the TV program *Angel* features a demon goddess named Jasmine who uses mind control to convince everyone in Los Angeles they are perfectly happy and that she is their leader; those who see through her spell are hunted down, and she literally feasts on followers to maintain her strength. This could be read either as a warning about blindly following religion—or about the dangers of a totalitarian government where everyone loses their free will.

Elsewhere, Tennessee Williams' celebrated play *A Streetcar Named Desire* features a fading, upper-class Southern belle at the mercy of a bullying working-class oaf. The 1980s television show *Cheers* involves the relationships of people from all walks of life, together in a place where "everybody knows your name" (and so things were happy on the surface, at least). The J.K. Rowling *Harry Potter* series involves much sniping between "pure-blooded" wizards and witches and "mud-bloods," those with ordinary, non-magical parents. Even the 2003 animated film *Finding Nemo* features sea creatures imprisoned in a tank by a "powerful, controlling" human dentist. Other examples may not be so apparent, yet "history [is] present in every text but rarely evidently so . . . the surface narration usefully mediates the unconscious reality of the text's relationship with history" (Roberts 2000, 75-76). As will be seen, *Survivor* is not immune to this interpretation.

Jameson's Other Works, "Prickly" Writing, and Critics

Jameson's earlier works hinted at what was to come. *Marxism and Form* (1972) posited that "critics need to concentrate on the *form* of literature as much as the content, that form is not a mere trapping of the work of art, but embodies powerful ideological messages" (Roberts 2000, 3-4). Other works, such as his 1979 *Fables of Aggression*, a critique of writer Wyndham Lewis, elaborated how "Jameson could find interesting and valuable things in apparently reprehensible material. [This was] an influential critical position that opens up the possibility of reading *through* the surface of any text into hidden depths" (Roberts 2000, 4). Additionally, his *Global Aesthetic: Cinema and Space in the World System* (1992) examines movies that embody capitalistic, totalizing world systems (Roberts 2000, 5), and his *Postmodernism, or the Cultural Logic of Late Capitalism* (1991) helped revolutionize how that school of thought is viewed.

Jameson may be as well-known for his difficult writing style as he is for his ideas. As an example, Roberts quotes a sixty-word sentence from *The Political Unconscious*, then spends more than a page explaining what it means. Jameson, however, has said that "dumbing things down" doesn't make people think and even can be alienating. His writing is unique, he has implied, rather than mass-produced, humanity-free boilerplate (2000, 7). Furthermore, "by deliberately making his writing prickly and undigestible, Jameson is calling attention to the form of his own writing"; the writing is not a window onto his essays' subjects, but "is part of the way they produce their meaning. . . . By extension, all writing is like this" (2000, 10).

For this and other reasons, however, Jameson has come under fire. Hestetun has compiled many of these comments. Some academics, for instance, believe that Jameson's synthesis of Marxism with other critical approaches comes at Marx's expense. "Accordingly, he has been challenged for not having given the politics of class struggle first priority in his analysis" (1993, 179). Hestetun quotes James Iffland, who asks whether Jameson's attempt to amalgamate such a range of methodologies results in "a confusing mélange, full of communicational noise which has its consequence of weakening the book as a Marxism project" (1993, 179). Additionally, Terry Eagleton has argued that *The Political Unconscious* lacks "the impetus or consolation of a militant working-class movement, [which] leaves its scar on the study" (1993, 179).

Others question whether class struggles are the center of all narrative:

> Given contemporary poststructuralist discourses' general suspicion of "grand narrative types of theory, it is only to be expected that Jameson's historicism, with its totalizing perspective and his gesture of invoking "history" as the ultimate ground for interpretation, is radically challenged. Ironically, however, even a repudiation of Jameson's master narrative presupposes an alternative "narrative," even if it is one that privileges skepticism and negation rather than affirmation. (Hestetun 1993, 182-3)

Elsewhere, deconstructionists protest Jameson's attempt to assimilate their interpretative method. Hestetun quotes Jerry Aline Flieger: "One has a choice of either accepting the rules of the deconstructionist's game—the premise or ground rule that no totalized solution may offer an access to Truth—or of rejecting that premise, and refusing to engage in that particular game" (1993, 184). Jameson, meanwhile, seems to be *re*constructing the text's historical moment via the political unconscious (1993, 185).

Finally, Jameson has even been his own critic: "The dialectical 'narrative' of history is a good deal more complicated and reflexive than my own slogan may have suggested," he said in an interview (Hestetun 1993, 181). The great collective story may become a "much more inclusive story of struggles...where the notion of cultural hegemony is related to several 'marginalized or oppositional cultures in our own time,' which would include . . . 'black and ethnic cultures, women's and gay literature . . . and the like'" (Hestetun 1993, 181, quoting Jameson). This extension of Jameson's theory will be discussed in Chapters 6, 7, and 8, following extensive examination of struggles between classes as allegorized on *Survivor*. First, though, fine-tuning is necessary, in order to better grasp how to unearth "collective repression" on the program.

Survivor Alliances and the Unconscious

The role of repression and denial in *Survivor's* narrative is crystallized by a short scene in Episode 8 of *Survivor: Marquesas*, the show's fourth season (spring 2002). At this point, nine contestants remain, with four of them part of a secret voting alliance. These four intend to string along tribemates

Neleh and Paschal in order to dispatch outsiders Sean, Vecepia, and Kathy—
then get rid of Neleh and Paschal using what would then be a four-on-two
advantage (see also Figure 4.1, p. 46).

Kathy, however, has caught wind of this plan. Realizing the secret alliance is still a numerical minority, she approaches Neleh in an attempt to
sway her vote:

> Kathy: [T]his alliance stuff is what's killing us here.
>
> Neleh: Yeah. . . . just know there's gonna be alliances, no matter what. . . .
> [T]he bigger stink you make of things, the more vulnerable you are . . .
> (CBS, 18 April 2002)[1]

Neleh, of course, believes she is part of a six-person alliance with the
aforementioned four and her close friend Paschal. Put off, Kathy confides to
the camera that Neleh seems fine "with being booted out fifth.... She thinks
if you make too many waves [it's bad]. She said, 'Kathy, if you talk any
more about that, you're gonna get voted off.'"

Kathy next talks to Paschal, saying she does not want to be a pawn in
the four-person alliance's plan. But he also rebuffs her:

> Kathy: I want it to be fair. It should be fair.
>
> Paschal: Well, this game's not fair.

The outcome of all this politicking will be discussed in Chapter 4, but
the dialogue reveals an underlying, repetitive message to *Survivor's* allegorical "underclass": *Don't talk about alliances. Don't bring them up. Forget you ever thought such a thing. Keeping quiet will ensure you last longer.
Piping up will lead to an early exit.*

The repetitious denial of alliances—often in the face of overwhelming
evidence—only serves to demonstrate just how critical they are to the structure of the game. Alliances are feared, yet desired. Hated, yet necessary.
They are a central tenet to every season of *Survivor*, and how the narrative
deals with them leads directly to allegorical issues of class politics.

Is It Repression, or Merely Suppression?

Much information is withheld on *Survivor*, both by contestants and producers, but not all of it would reasonably be seen as repression in Jameson's
theory. Banal occurrences, such as uneventful trips to the water hole or a
game of checkers, remain on the proverbial cutting room floor. Other elements are also merely suppressed, left out, ignored: Extra votes at Tribal

Council that only pad the majority, or the answer to the question of whether *Australian Outback's* Kel really snuck beef jerky into camp. On *Survivor: Africa*, the less-than-smart (or so we are to believe) Brandon failed to tell his close friends of a last-minute switch in his Tribal Council voting plan, which infuriated them and led to his ouster three days later. For *Survivor: Borneo*, producers elected to edit out the first reward challenge, which would have aired during the first episode. Such instances of suppression do not rise to the level of repression.

However, at times suppression by editors or contestants transforms into repression when presented to the viewer. A key trait here is that, in the narrative, the repressed item often becomes a *repeated* element, such as contestants' dismissal of Kathy's concerns about alliances. Freud contended that repetitive words or objects in dreams often pointed to repressed fears and anxieties, especially when the patient dismissed their importance—*denial* is another trait of repression. For someone to affirm the presence of an alliance, thus revealing the apparent truth of the situation, would cause even greater anxiety. As Roberts describes, the economic and political features "hidden in literature...can be recovered by concentrating on literary and cultural analogues of things like 'Freudian slips' or the irrationality of dreams" (2000, 57).

Yet by not at least *hinting* at Kathy's concerns through the editing, later events in the episode would pack a less powerful punch, or even confuse viewers. It is therefore necessary to at least bring it up. Indeed, something is repressed when it's structurally necessary to acknowledge and then discredit it—thus, in narratives at least, creating suspense for the reader or viewer. Something seems a little "wrong" to us, a little off, but we can't quite put our finger on it. If at the end, however, the repeated, denied element is brought out into the open for all to see, this resolution sparks *pleasure or displeasure* for the audience.[2]

In other words, the text suppresses things so that spectators' wishes (or fears) can be played out, and therefore takes on the form of repression though repeatedly hinting at, then disavowing, the truth—a truth that in Jameson's view, the bourgeoisie and/or proletariat cannot stand to think about. Instead, we continue to pretend that everyone on *Survivor* is equal, even when dialogue such as "this game isn't fair" reminds us of a painful truth, one that players hardly dare to speak of. (Indeed, on *Survivor: The Australian Outback,* "villain" Jerri's torch was extinguished soon after she complained about the game's unfairness.) For the audience, all this may lead to extreme pleasure or displeasure, once an outcome is reached, especially if it is a surprise. The suspense of seeing what happens next keeps us engaged, as Haralovich and Trosset also have written (2004).

Generally, then, the three "symptoms" to look out for in the repression of information on *Survivor* are repetition, denial, and intended audience (dis)pleasure. Much of this repression deals with alliances, which directly involve questions of power and, therefore, class politics.

However, one could argue that, because viewers are usually plainly shown the development of alliances on *Survivor*, such information is *not* suppressed to them, though it may be to some contestants. Yet this is not quite the case: Alliances *are* unsaid in the text of *Survivor*, because any alliance is merely a promise until contestants hit the voting booth—and we viewers are not privy to each player's vote during the course of the episode. To put it another way, contestants give their word all the time that they will ally with one another, but often do not, so we aren't necessarily being told the "truth" when we see one person swear allegiance to another. "Though contestants discuss voting options openly, the voting is done individually and no one is assured that any other contestant will honor an agreement to vote a specific way" (Boone 2003, 103). From a viewer's perspective, we still view repression among contestants as mediated by the television, seeing only what the editors let us.

For instance, in the opening episode of *Survivor: The Amazon*, contestant Rob[3] promises two competing blocs of players that he will vote against the other bloc. Obviously, he can only hold true to one deal—but the audience is not told in advance with whom he will ally, and can only guess what he does in the text that is presented, because his vote is not shown. When contestant Ryan narrowly is voted out, we can surmise Rob had voted against him, but only if we watch the extra-textual closing credits, during which each person's vote is shown, can we know for certain.

We'll return to the character and actions of Rob in Chapter 4, in a discussion of suppression-turned-repression by contestants onto others, before proceeding to Chapter 5's analysis of repression through editing. However, the interview with *Thailand's* Helen allows a peek beyond the curtain at the level of suppression during filming. Helen, who won fourth place on *Thailand*, lasting thirty-seven out of a possible thirty-nine days, said she knew who would be evicted at every Tribal Council but two (those unfamiliar with this particular season need not worry about keeping straight the names of contestants below—the key here is Glover's experience of the "real"):

> The only Tribal Council where I had no clue who was getting voted off was the very first one. (Not counting the one when I was voted off!) The first Tribal Council, I thought Ghandia was likely to go, but I didn't like Clay from the start, so I voted for him. John voted for Ghandia, because he thought she was a weak link. *However*...everyone else voted for John, leaving me to wonder, "Where was I when this was decided?" And I felt very vulnerable after that because John and I were close. Before [Ghandia

was voted out at a later Tribal Council], I *knew* I was the swing vote, so knowing that I controlled whether she stayed or whether she went, there was no doubt in *my mind* of the outcome. (Glover 2004)

Therefore, although most aired episodes consist of editors trying to mislead and distract viewers from the outcome, the contestants are more likely to know what will happen. Consider, however, that Helen was a member of *Thailand's* dominant alliance. Indeed, the exception to this rule, Helen wrote, was that targeted tribemates—herself included, when it was her turn to go—were often clueless:

Rarely does the person know that they're getting voted off that night. Often, they have a "feeling" because of things that have happened, but the game changes rapidly, especially as numbers dwindle. When Jake was getting voted off [in sixth place], he knew he was because he was the only remaining player left from his original tribe [Sook Jai]. He didn't stand a chance and he knew it. Right before Tribal Council, he pulled me aside and said, "Helen, I think I'm going tonight." And I thought it fair to let him know then, that, yes; he's going off tonight. But they'll never show that on TV because that would ruin the suspense.[4] Often, what they'll do is show some tension between players to make you think someone else is going, again, to add to the suspense and make it more climactic. (Glover 2004)

Clearly, then, *Survivor* as a cultural product involves suppression of the truth by both contestants and editors. Both types of suppression were most notably combined during the show's first season, *Borneo*—and they became repression through repetition, denial, and audience (dis)pleasure.

Notes

1. Unless otherwise noted, all dialogue herein has been transcribed by the author. For clarity's sake, extraneous words such as "um" and "like" generally have been omitted. Because of the quality of the audio available, an occasional word may be inaccurate. Also, the airdate is cited only when the episode being quoted changes.

2. This way of looking at *Survivor* and the unconscious was developed primarily in conversations with Matthew Tinkcom of Georgetown University.

3. Not to be confused with "Boston" Rob from *Marquesas*, who also will be discussed in Chapter 4.

4. Occasionally, we see one contestant telling another he or she will be leaving that night—Lex, from *Africa* and *All-Stars*, for instance, has been shown doing this. However, it is never certain that will be the actual outcome. On at least one occasion, meanwhile, editors have made it abundantly clear who will be voted out, an instance that will be explored at the close of Chapter 5.

Chapter 3

"If It Happens Again . . ."
Repression and the Tagi Alliance

BOTH THE PLAYERS AND VIEWERS of *Survivor: Borneo* were innocents; neither had any idea of what to expect from contesting and watching the first edition of *Survivor*. So, given the game's rules—vote out one player every three days—it was perhaps inevitable that the majority of contestants would become susceptible to the secret plans of a few.

Those plans famously came in the form of a four-person voting bloc or alliance put together by the game's eventual champion, corporate trainer Richard, and also consisting of his Tagi teammates Kelly, Sue, and Rudy (see Figure 3.1). We first hear of Rich's plans as his tribe bickers over how to build an S.O.S. signal for a challenge. This occurs in Episode 4, some ten days into the competition. Rich is frustrated with certain team members, and the implication is that they are inferior to him in some ways. Implicit in this are issues of class and power—he finds certain people unworthy, based in part on their behavior during the challenge preparation. As he tells us, while out of earshot of the others: "Here comes the conflict. . . . Here come the people that just shout and don't listen . . . " (CBS, 21 June 2000).

We watch as teammate Sean, a young doctor, argues with Rich over how to build the signal. Sue and Rudy look on, apparently annoyed, as Sean interrupts Rich. Then it is back to a voice-over:

> Rich (to camera): [I'm] actually planning something . . . that might benefit me, and it's a little sneaky. I think I'm gonna handle this by beginning to develop alliances with some folks to ensure that I move into the next round.

So begin the allegorical, Jamesonian hierarchies of *Survivor*. Kelly and Sue join up in Rich's alliance; we soon see the trio plotting in the water, but the scene ends before we hear their plans—a bit of suppression by the editors, showing who is *really* in charge here. In Episode 5

Figure 3.1: Final ten contestants
on *Survivor: Borneo,* members of the Rattana tribe

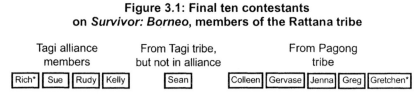

Tagi alliance members	From Tagi tribe, but not in alliance	From Pagong tribe

| Rich* | Sue | Rudy | Kelly | | Sean | | Colleen | Gervase | Jenna | Greg | Gretchen* |

* Apparent leaders of their respective blocs. Rich eventually won the game.
Note: See Appendix B for contestant descriptions.

(CBS, 28 June 2000), we see more misdirection by the editors[1] when Rich tells the camera his alliance's target will be either Dirk or Sean. Sean "yesterday was talking about how he doesn't want to form an alliance," Rich tells us. "Boy, Sean, it's time for you to go, bud." However, at episode's end, the audience finds that Dirk is the alliance's first victim. This demonstrates that as the show airs, suppression by contestants often coincides with that by producers (assuming that a camera crew at some point caught Rich, Sue, and/or Kelly discussing dispatching Dirk).

All this soon mutates into repression. In Episode 6, septuagenarian Rudy joins the alliance; then in Episode 7 (CBS, 12 July 2000), as the tribes—five members remaining in each—prepare to merge into one group, Jenna, member of the rival Pagong tribe, visits Tagi's beach as an "ambassador," while Sean takes a trip to Pagong's camp. The narrative finds Jenna asked of any rumors she has heard regarding Tagi. She tells them of rumors that Tagi has formed " an alliance against us." Replies mastermind Rich in mock amazement and shock: "*Really?*" Denial is clearly the order of the day.[2] We see a similar conversation at Pagong as Sean visits:

> Gretchen (based on what she has heard, it seems): So they're planning on . . . picking us off one by one?
>
> Sean: I think they've changed their minds. . . . [T]hey have very nice warm, touchy feelings for you guys.

Sean's denial, however, is contradicted by extra-textual information contained in Burnett's book *Survivor: The Ultimate Game*, which features many "behind-the-scenes" goodies. In a drunken conversation with Jenna at that night's "ambassador's merge summit"—at which the two, among other things, create the combined tribe's name and flag, among other things—Sean discloses to her that his "conniving" tribemates "put together a voting bloc against Dirk. . . . The least they could have done was told me what was going on. I mean, you should have seen the look on Dirk's face. He was stunned. It broke my heart" (Burnett 2000, 122). However, the TV viewing audience sees none of this, and is left to believe that Sean either truly thinks there is no long-term alliance, or is hiding its presence to help his Tagi tribemates, even though they did not invite him into the fold. Or maybe his statement that "they've changed their minds" is correct, and the editors just want us to *think* the Tagi alliance remains strong.

In any case, there are plenty of repetitious hints that something is going on here, and they continue to pile up over the next several episodes: Despite at first holding a voting majority, the unallied players seem to catch on to Rich and company's plans, then back off or disregard their concerns, or make no discernable effort to do anything substantial about it, so far as we are told. Then, another of their members is voted off, and the cycle repeats. The remaining Pagong at the merge—Colleen, Gervase, Greg, Jenna, and Gretchen—along with Tagi's odd man out, Sean, are portrayed as collectively unable or unwilling to make a move to improve their status. Rather, they merely tread water, waiting to be picked off, pretending that the game of *Survivor* still has its moral compass.

Taking Control

Taken in bits and pieces as America originally viewed it—one week at a time—it may be harder to notice this back-and-forth on the part of Pagong and Sean. However, in viewing each episode one on top of another, it becomes abundantly clear that many of them follow the same pattern, with Sean and most members of Pagong essentially saying, *That was a suspicious vote last night! I wonder if there really is an alliance? Probably not—after all, we are all supposed to vote our conscience. If it happens again at the next Tribal Council, though, I may have to rethink my strategy.*

These moments when we are shown *Survivor's* facsimile of an underclass, Pagong/Sean, momentarily worrying about an alliance but then disregarding it, form a classic case of Jamesonian repetition and denial. As an audience, we are more aware of their naïvete, but thanks to suppression on the part of the editors, we can't be *sure* that the alliance will prevail. Maybe, as the editing later suggests, Kelly really *will* abandon Richard, Sue, and Rudy. Maybe Rich's arrogance really *will* get the better of him. Maybe, most importantly, Pagong/Sean really *will* figure out the truth before it is too late and their subordination becomes a mathematical certainty.

Certainly, the group of six has enough opportunities. At the Episode 7 Tribal Council, just after the merging of Pagong and Tagi, Sean explains to host Probst that contestants are "concerned about alliances" or an intertribal "boodbath. . . . But I don't think that's going to occur." So, either he is lying to save face among the Tagi four, or he really thinks the alliance that took down Dirk six days prior was a one-time shot. Meanwhile, Greg and Jenna swear off alliances, with the latter player wanting to vote based on "who should really go," not tribe of origin. Thus, Pagong and Sean ignore the rumblings of an alliance and *split their six votes six ways*, entirely diluting their numerical strength. The Tagi four vote as a bloc, all for Pagong leader Gretchen—thereby cutting the head off of the enemy and stunning their competitors.

In this way, Pagong and Sean—too naïve and unorganized to unite or even care—resemble the splintered underclass of Western and particularly American culture, from which *Survivor* springs. For instance, those with the lowest income are least likely to participate in the political process via the ballot box—that is, the route to true power in America. In 2000, people with an annual household income of less than $15,000 made up 15.9 percent of the U.S. population, yet only 7 percent of those voting in the presidential election; on the other end, those with annual household incomes of $75,000 or more made up 22.5 percent of the U.S. population, but 28 percent of the voting population (CNN.com 2000, CensusScope.org 2001). The reasons behind this trend are too complex to investigate here, but nonetheless demonstrate intriguing parallels between *Survivor's* faux society and the real society that produced it.

You Will Deny This Three Times

Following the Tribal Council, Pagong and Sean are more suspicious, but the Tagi four still play innocent. Early scenes of Episode 8 (CBS, 19 July 2000) feature the following dialogue:

> Sean (walking alone on the beach): . . . Last night was a very strange vote.
>
> Jenna (to camera): It looked like there was a conspiracy. And maybe I'm being paranoid . . . but four people from Tagi voted for Gretchen I think.
>
> Gervase (to camera): I really don't know what happened last night. At first sight it looked like, just pick Gretchen off.
>
> [Cut to Greg, Gervase, and Sean around the water hole]
>
> Sean: I think that my former team, Tagi, probably formed an alliance against [Gretchen]. . . . The duplicity of the whole thing was pretty bad . . .
>
> Greg: It's sleaziness, if you want to play it that way.
>
> Gervase: I think that if it happens again, then you can say for sure there's an alliance. If it does, then I'm more determined than ever to bust that plan up and kill 'em all and win.[3]

Figure 3.2: Recollected desires of survey respondents as to fate of *Borneo's* Tagi alliance

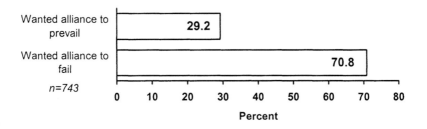

Later in the episode, just before Tribal Council, the non-allied players converse again, with Gervase arguing to Sean that alliances are "fair game." Colleen tells the camera that Pagong "has the upper hand" since it has four players who could unite. Things, then, may be looking up for Pagong and Sean. Have they learned their lesson? Do they recognize the truth of the situation? While they still hold a majority, can these five unite to dispatch an alliance member?

In a word: No. The truth that rises to the surface at the episode's start is again buried, beginning with Gervase's tell-tale "if it happens *again*" line. Jenna becomes convinced she must ally with the other women, and as we learn in *Survivor: The Ultimate Game,* is even told by Sue and Kelly that they did not vote for Gretchen. Instead of calling them on it and using it as evidence to bring Sean into the fold, Jenna protests not, perhaps comforted by this reassurance—as well as by Sue's promise that only men will be leaving the island in the near future—and Sue changes the subject (Burnett 2000, 138-39). Elsewhere, Greg says that "fear-motivated self-preservation" does not interest him. Even Colleen says at Tribal Council later that she is unwilling to do "whatever it takes" to win or to "play both sides." None, then, appear interested in playing the "dark side" of the game.[4]

Survey respondents, it turns out, viewed the Tagi alliance as "the dark side" by wide margins. More than seven in ten wanted the Tagi alliance to fail, while only 29.2 percent wanted it to prevail in the end (see Figure 3.2).

Similarly, of those who saw Tagi as good or bad, 78.1 percent saw them as "the bad guys." A mere 6.4 percent said the same of Pagong and Sean.[5] Averaging the adjusted audience attitude index of these ten players finds that the Tagi four had a mean AAAI of 3.561 (out of 6.0) and mean rank of fifty-fourth (out of the 150 contestants); Pagong and Sean fared better, with a mean AAAI of 3.877 and rank of thirty-seventh.[6] Sean was rated lower than any of the Pagong five; including him instead with his original Tagi teammates substantially widens the gap between Tagi and Pagong. As a whole, these statistics clearly show that through a combination of editing and perhaps actual personalities, the Tagi alliance became framed as collectively antagonistic (despite the popularity of member Rudy), something that reflects the tendency in our culture to root for David against Goliath, where underdogs like the "Hoosiers" become heroes and even horses such as Smarty Jones and Funny Cide are framed by the media as "working class" or "blue collar" champs.

As Tribal Council looms, both sides weigh their possible fates. The first strands of a developing theme for Kelly appear, with her comment that Tribal Council "gets worse every time. I feel like a backstabber. . . . The truth is, I like [Pagong]."

Sue and Rich, meanwhile, are at least mildly nervous, reflecting the bourgeoisie fear that Jameson argues creeps up at the thought of the masses seizing power:

> Rich (to Kelly): Right now, we're not invincible.
>
> Sue (to camera): [The alliance will succeed] as long as everybody can keep their mouth shut. . . . [T]here is some fear about [a counteralliance from Pagong], because we haven't gotten enough of them voted out.

When the next Tribal Council convenes, the idealistic, naïve Pagong/Sean again decline to dirty their hands. Despite the overwhelming evidence that something is afoot, the Tagi continue to deny the alliance's existence—facilitating its continued repression in the eyes of the others. Directly asked by host Probst whether an alliance exists, Sue stammers in reply.

> Sue: Nooooo. . . . I vote people off that I don't care for, you know, that really would irritate me if I was working with them at a job . . . and, uh, here I got a chance to vote them off. I can get rid of 'em!

Despite the awful delivery, this apparently convinces Jenna, who claps at Sue's last statement, likely somewhat in relief. Kelly also denies there is an alliance. Yet any relief this double denial gives worried Pagong members evaporates once more when Greg is voted out minutes later. The pact that dares not speak its name strikes again, and Pagong/Sean's best chance to derail the alliance is gone. Amazingly, Sean and Jenna actually vote for Greg, while Colleen, Gervase, and Greg vote to oust Jenna. *None* of the non-allied players votes for a member of the Tagi alliance:

> None of the other contestants [appear] to doubt the lies of these alliance members [at Tribal Council]. This interrogation [takes] place at a critical juncture; if all the remaining contestants [were to band] together . . . the al-

liance would have remained vulnerable and the outcome may well have been different. (Boone 2003, 104)

Yet they do not band together. *Survivor's* unified "bourgeoisie" is now even with the splintered "proletariat," yielding a class allegory that provides pleasure for the former and distress for the latter.

The Emergence, and Fall, of the Hero(ine)

Colleen is *Survivor's* heroine, and had the highest AAAI of all 150 rated contestants, 5.031 out of 6.000. While Sue and Rich scheme, while Rudy makes his hilarious, if sometimes offensive, remarks,[7] while Kelly waffles and Jenna, Sean, and Gervase refuse to recognize the truth, Colleen emerges as the moral center of the show, telling it like it is to the camera in her sweet, charming way as Episode 9 (CBS, 26 July 2000) opens:

> Colleen: Those people flat-out lied [at Tribal Council about the alliance]. . . . They want a million bucks and they're gonna get it. . . . Rich opens his mouth and I just wanna be like, "Oh, be quiet over there in the corner. . . . Just go home and go get your liposuction and go catch more fish." . . . He thinks he's so above everybody . . .

Note the phrase, "he thinks he's so above everybody." Colleen is depicted as the one most perceptive of Rich's supposed position—and in the power structure on the show, Rich *is* above everyone, trumpeting the arrogance of power that is often associated with business, community, and political leaders. Marx wrote that the oppressed had to be taught their own self-interest; perhaps this is the beginning of *Survivor's* allegorical underclass learning that lesson. Later, enjoying a barbecue reward with Jenna, Colleen mocks Sean for something her own tribemates appear to be guilty of as well, then forms a plan. Until this point in the series, "Colleen had been treated like a kind of island Kewpie doll," writes Lance in *The Stingray*. "Suddenly, she showed that she had brains, grit, and substance" (2000, 108). To wit:

> Colleen: [Tagi] voted four against Dirk . . . and they voted four against Gretchen, and then . . . four against Greg. And [Sean says], "If it happens one more time, I'll know [there's an alliance]!" and I was like, what are you talking about? It's happened three times!

Jenna and Colleen then decide to form an alliance of their own. The obvious problem: Colleen, Jenna, and friend Gervase are only three votes in a group of eight. Right on schedule, however, the editors begin to assert that

Kelly's loyalties are wavering. Indeed, this episode features several shots of Jenna, Colleen, and Kelly happily socializing. Rich and Sue look on, upset, with Rich muttering that "I'm hoping that Kelly hasn't shifted trust . . ." The symbolic bourgeoisie nightmare begins to take form. But to construct such a storyline, deception is necessary: Spliced into one of these scenes, which occur on Day 27, is part of an argument between Kelly and Sue that actually took place on Day 36[8], in which Sue accuses Kelly of cozying up to the Pagong members. Then Kelly tells the camera that she is the potential swing vote. "Alliance or no alliance, there's two people that I have in mind to vote off." As she says this, the screen cuts to Sean and Rich.

The producers took at least one other step to shroud the truth of the proceedings and give those rooting against Tagi hope. As mentioned previously, the opening montage of Episode 8 featured a brief shot of only Rudy, Sean, Colleen, and Gervase at Tribal Council, leading some to believe the Tagi alliance would crumble; Chapter 1 also noted the discovery of a CBS Web site "glitch" that indicated Gervase would win, something that made national headlines. Burnett has denied doing this deliberately, but both incidents pushed the narrative of Tagi being "overthrown"; they offered the possibility of excitement and pleasure that, like Godot, would never arrive.

This apparent editing/propaganda strategy, however, appears to have worked to an extent. Just 29.2 percent of survey respondents[9] expected the four Tagi alliance members to become the final four. A plurality of 37.2 percent expected that the alliance would generally dominate, but that some combination of the other players would partially derail Tagi—while less than 6 percent predicted a total failure.[10]

This statistic might not be surprising, considering that any "coup" would be dependent on Sean—and the kind doctor, while urging everyone else to vote their conscience, is sticking to a cop-out strategy: voting alphabetically. He publicizes his plan to make Jenna next on his ABC hit list. However, he specifies to Gervase that, "If I'm going to be the swing vote, which I don't think I will be," then he'll vote for someone else. That is, Sean will only cast his ballot against Jenna if he doesn't think she is the target of a majority.

Sean is shown repeating this assertion and dismissal twice more during the episode, first at Tribal Council and then in the actual voting booth, where he has to perform to none of his competitors:

Sean (at Tribal Council, to host Probst and other players): I think [Jenna's] a safe vote tonight. If I thought she was in jeopardy, I would think twice at the very least of casting that vote.

Sean (in voting booth, to camera only): Jenna . . . I hope you don't get voted off. . . . You might have one vote or two votes or something like that, but nothing major I don't think . . .

Here again, then, we see an element—the idea that Sean's ballot against Jenna might be a swing vote—brought up repeatedly and then dismissed. And note that with three days' worth of footage to choose from, editors specifically decided to show all three of those denials. This is perhaps the purest example of Jamesonian repression *Survivor* has to offer, for Sean's repetitious statements and denials are prophetic: Rich, Rudy, and Sue take advantage and pile on with votes against Jenna, who is narrowly dispatched.[11] As Probst extinguishes Jenna's torch, the alphabetical mastermind looks floored as he, and we, realize he naively has been used as a tool by the allegorical elites. Once more, the bourgeoisie's nervousness subsides and the proletariat's amplifies; *Survivor's* rich get richer; the poor get poorer.

Even this, amazingly, barely affects Sean's sense of denial. The next day, as Episode 10 opens (CBS, 2 Aug. 2000), Sean admits he unwittingly led to Jenna's dismissal, yet contends, "I'm not 100 percent sure [that] there is an alliance," noting he has yet to be asked to "partake" in one.

Colleen again is the voice of reason: "Sean, come on! Open your eyes!" she tells the camera. Yet if Sean knows more, the editors have suppressed it. He appears clueless in the face of danger. In the narrative of powerful vs. powerless, it would make no sense for him to be a conspirator.

At the end of Episode 10, Gervase is voted out. Making this obvious, however, would be boring and yield no (dis)pleasure for the audience. So the editors continue playing up the Kelly-is-waffling angle, aided by the fact that she did not vote against Jenna in the prior episode. "I didn't want to be part of the alliance because it was conniving . . . and untrue to myself," she tells us, later adding, what "if something exciting would happen . . . that nobody expects?" Her contention that she is no longer in the alliance contradicts later events, but for now, Jameson would say that by shutting out whatever the truth is, this gives the proletariat hope and the bourgeoisie shudders.

Despite Kelly's wavering and Sean's lessons (sort of) learned, Colleen and Gervase appear to abandon all hope when they use white medical tape to modify their wardrobe for that night's Tribal Council. "My code name for tonight is 'Bull's-eye,'" Gervase explains to us, displaying his blue T-shirt with a large target taped onto the front and back, the word "TARGET" also on the back in large letters. Colleen tapes an outline of a mallard onto her shirt: "I'm otherwise known as 'Sitting Duck.'" This is perhaps *Survivor's* best use of a symbolic resolution to a real contradiction, not unlike Levi-Strauss' description of the Caduveo Indians' facial decorations discussed in Chapter 2. Colleen and Gervase are faced with a real contradiction—that although the remaining seven players are purportedly equal, in reality, they are not. The two are the outsiders, the doomed. Indeed, for all the talk about democracy and juries and voting, *Survivor* is just as much about exclusion. The editors let us watch the marginalized Pagong symbolically resolve this contradiction by expressing their condition via clothing, which they wear to Tribal Council, *Survivor's* "hall of justice." Through their clothing, they are saying that they aren't all equal; that there are classes on this island, like it or not. For all the denials, the truth again, for a moment, rises to the top.

Then Gervase is voted out by all five Tagi members. Kelly, despite her protestations, votes with Richard, Sue, and Rudy; Sean, despite his lectures about voting one's conscience, joins in as well. This leaves "five castaways and one scared little duck" in the game of *Survivor* (Burnett 2000, 181).

The last gasps of Jamesonian repression play out on Episode 11 (CBS, 9 Aug. 2000), as viewers cling to the hope that beloved Colleen will live to see the game's end. Our heroine—her legs being devoured and lived in by insects, in a sort of accidental symbolism—has become wistful, longing for the days of Pagong. "I miss my old team, I miss my old beach," she says mournfully as the screen cuts to dreamlike shots of her grinning former tribemates, their beach and shelter, their waving, yellow tribal flag—producing a sense of nostalgia not unlike our culture's tendency to yearn for the past, for "better times" when things were allegedly simpler, more innocent. "I am the last sole survivor of the Pagong tribe," Colleen reminds us. "I'm a dying breed."

The episode is filled with more Kelly waffling, and it seems even she doesn't know where she stands. It reaches the point where her angered Tagi teammates plan to vote her out rather than the lone duck, or so we are told. But then, in a showdown with Colleen on a plank over the furious ocean, Kelly wins immunity, forcing the alliance's hand. Sweet, innocent, yet wise Colleen is voted out, whispering "Play fair, be nice," to the remaining players as she exits. She gives a rueful half-smile as Probst snuffs her torch. The producers know that this is no ordinary ousting, that it carries more meaning—and indeed in the following episode it seems abundantly clear all along that Sean will be the one to go. So Colleen's departure serves as the true ending to the class allegory of *Survivor*. Indeed, it is telling that this episode does not feature the standard closing imagery of remaining castaways exiting Tribal Council with torches ablaze, as the show's theme music bursts forth. Rather, we watch in silence as the camera lingers on Colleen's darkened torch—representing the snuffed life of the Pagong, and with it the hopes of the underclass—then fades to black.[12]

A Dream Deferred

Much time has been spent discussing the process and outcome of *Survivor: Borneo*, but with good reason—it is the purest example of the political unconscious the program offers. This is, again, because this was the first season. Going into it, no contestant knew what an alliance was in terms of the

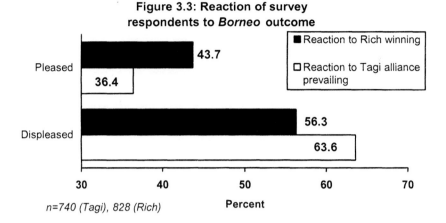

Figure 3.3: Reaction of survey respondents to *Borneo* outcome

n=740 (Tagi), 828 (Rich)

game (with the possible exception of Rich). This was going to be a game about surviving Mother Nature, not one another. This was going to be about classic Darwinism, rather than the social variety.

Or so we would have liked to believe. In the end, though contestants and editors alike tried to hide reality—staying hush-hush about alliances, denying their existence in the face of overwhelming evidence, manipulating audiences through selective or even deceptive editing—the form of the program (social interaction, winning/losing of challenges, voting at Tribal Council) necessitated that hints at the truth kept popping up. Members of the Pagong tribe (plus Sean), who just wanted to have fun, were systematically eliminated by a group who was at first numerically inferior, but who understood that to get ahead in this microcosmic society, one had to strategize and unite behind a common goal. Pagong/Sean's fantasy of voting one's conscience—which reflects the upper-class talking point of "we're all equal, let the cream rise to the top"—was trumped by Tagi's successful pooling of resources (i.e., votes) to create and maintain (political) wealth. In the second horizon of Jamesonian analysis, the first season of *Survivor*, allegorically, was about the triumph of an *intelligent*, dominant group. As will be demonstrated shortly, this class-based narrative is reflected in the 2004 survey results.

Certainly, contestants could have been completely honest with one another. Editors could have made it abundantly clear each episode what would occur at Tribal Council, could have telegraphed that Tagi would prevail in a landslide. Certainly, given the "45-minutes-of-airtime-for-72-hours-of-footage" situation, many banal moments are left out. However, items are also suppressed in order to make things *more interesting,* to hide the truth of this affair. This suppression indeed becomes repression when what producers choose not to tell us *generates excitement.* "Why didn't we know that?!"

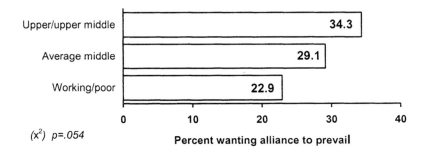

**Figure 3.4: Percentage of respondents wanting
Tagi alliance to prevail, grouped by social class**

(x^2) *p=.054*

we ask. The answer: Telling us everything would not only sap the show's intensity—and therefore ratings, and therefore advertising revenue—but put on full display the political allegory of the program that many would like to believe isn't there . . . not in a show that makes voting, a fundamental tenet of democracy, part of its core structure. Cynically, *Survivor* tells us that daily life is characterized by want, and everyone who is anyone is thirsty for money and power. Our culture isn't about pleasure and the American way, *Survivor* says—it's about struggling to have a chance at those pleasures, while the rest suffer.

So, as *Survivor* resolves itself, as the collective repression of a historical nightmare fades again into the background, audience members suffer great displeasure at Pagong's (and to a lesser degree, Sean's) ultimate vanquishing. Indeed, respondents who watched *Borneo* and had an opinion about its outcome were displeased by a 27-point margin when the Tagi alliance prevailed (see Figure 3.3). "We are left this week with five people who [we] all want to see covered with honey and tied to ant hills," wrote one viewer in an episode summary posted on SurvivorSucks following Colleen's departure (Lance 2000, 140). By a somewhat margin of 13 percentage points, viewers reacted negatively to alliance mastermind Richard's eventual win.

These numbers may not be surprising, in that Richard and company appeared to be framed as the "bad guys" by *Survivor's* editing all along. All this evidence—the selective (even manipulative) framing of characters and events, the purposeful repetition and denial, the survey frequencies described thus far—suggests reading *Survivor* as a class allegory as has been done here, with the Tagi alliance as the haves, pooling their resources and exploiting their strengths and others' weaknesses, and Pagong and Sean as the have-nots, unable or unwilling to recognize and/or do anything about their predicament—thus reflecting how our own culture functions, with more

**Figure 3.5: Percentage of respondents pleased
by Tagi alliance prevailing, grouped by social class**

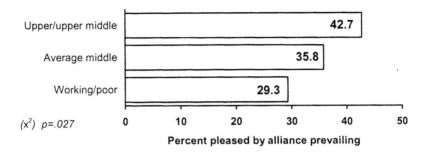

(x^2) $p=.027$

Percent pleased by alliance prevailing

people at the bottom of the income ladder than at the top, yet apparently oblivious to or uncaring about the political process.

If *Survivor* is indeed constructed this way, one would also expect it to be *consumed* this way, with upper-class audience members viewing more positively Tagi and working-class audience members viewing more positively Pagong and Sean. In fact, cross-tabulated survey results betrayed startling differences among respondents of different perceived social classes and related demographics. As Figures 3.4 through 3.6 show, respondents who identified themselves as upper class or upper middle class[13] were much more pleased with the Tagi alliance and Richard's eventual victory—with such respondents more pleased by a 16-point margin than working-class respondents with the final outcome.

These results are statistically significant, as indicated by the Pearson Chi Square values ("p") listed.[14] Also significant were results of questions that asked whether respondents had considered the Tagi alliance and/or Pagong and Sean as "good" or "bad." Just over 20 percent of working-class respondents perceived Tagi as good, compared with 29.3 percent of those from the upper classes. (p=.010) Conversely, a whopping 96.4 percent of working-class respondents saw Pagong and Sean as "good," as did 89.5 percent of upper-class survey takers. (p=.042) Another question asked respondents to name who, out of *Borneo's* ten finalists, they had wanted to see win. 17.4 percent of upper class/upper middle-class respondents chose Richard; only 5.9 percent of working-class, working-poor and poor respondents did so. 14.5 percent of upper-class respondents chose Kelly, while 21.0 percent of working-class respondents did. Perhaps they commiserated with Kelly's struggle to stay in the game, being forced to go on an immunity streak to keep from being ousted by her on-again, off-again alliance-mates. Fan favorites Colleen and Rudy were liked across the board.

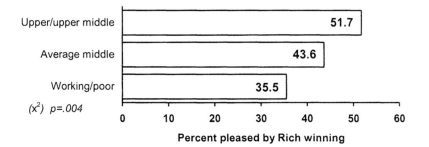

**Figure 3.6: Percentage of respondents pleased
by Rich winning, grouped by social class**

Upper/upper middle — 51.7

Average middle — 43.6

Working/poor — 35.5

(x^2) *p=.004*

0   10   20   30   40   50   60

Percent pleased by Rich winning

A clear pattern thus emerges from the survey's findings: Upper-class respondents viewed the Tagi alliance—the contestants with power—more positively overall than working-class respondents, and viewed Pagong and Sean, the symbolic proletariat, more negatively. This strongly suggests that *Survivor* indeed resonates differently among different social classes, supporting Jameson's theory. This pattern is further supported by cross-tabulated results of other demographic variables that significantly related to class (insofar as this survey is concerned).[15] Although statistically significant differences were not found for all questions, a number of them do have them. A sample of these results:

- **Education Level:** Among survey respondents, as education level rose, so did perceived social class. Of those with a high school diploma or less, 31.4 percent expected the Tagi alliance to be the final four, while 41.1 percent of those with at least some graduate or professional degree work correctly expected the alliance to prevail. (p=.041) On another question—whether the Tagi alliance members were "the good guys"—there were similarly stairstacked replies. Of those with graduate or professional work, 26.3 percent thought of Tagi as good. That number slipped to 22.8 percent and 21.0 percent for respondents with a college degree or some college, respectively . . . then dropped all the way to 11.7 percent for those with a high school education or less. These figures approached statistical significance (p=.076), as did those involving reaction to Rich's win: Nearly half of respondents—49 percent—with at least some graduate work were pleased with his victory. Compare this to 45 percent of those with a college degree, 41 percent of those with some college, and 34 percent of those with only a high school diploma. (p=.063)

**Figure 3.7: Percentage of respondents pleased
by Tagi alliance prevailing, grouped by political party**

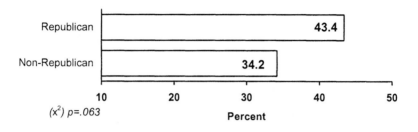

- **Independents:** Political independents—who in this survey were significantly more likely to identify as working class or poor—were more likely to want the Tagi alliance to unravel than those who identified with a party by a margin of 74.9 percent to 69.2 percent, and more likely to be displeased when the alliance prevailed, 68.2 percent to 61.7 percent. Both differences approached statistical significance. (p=.147 and .123, respectively)

- **Republicans:** GOP respondents—who were significantly more likely to identify as upper or upper middle class—were significantly more pleased when the Tagi alliance prevailed in Borneo than were non-Republicans, by a nine-point margin (see Figure 3.7). They also were six points more likely to have earlier wanted the alliance to win out, a difference that approaches significance. (p=.103) A full 35.9 percent wanted Rudy to win (picking from the list of the final 10). Just 21.2 percent of non-Republicans wanted the military veteran to prevail. (p=.002)

- **Household Income:** Members of higher income households were significantly more likely to perceive themselves as upper class or upper middle class, among survey respondents. On questions relating to *Survivor: Borneo*, those making $35,000 or less per year were far less likely to want the Tagi alliance to prevail than those making above that figure (see Figure 3.8). Similarly, 98.1 percent of those making $35,000 or less viewed the non-allied Borneo players (Colleen, Sean, etc.) as "the good guys," vs. 89.7 percent of respondents making $100,000 and up. (p=.049) Members of high-income households were also more likely to want Rich, Rudy, or Gretchen to win, and less likely to want Colleen, Kelly, or Greg to win; perhaps they saw the former three as leaders, and the latter as unworthy followers. (p=.026) Finally, when it came to Rich's ultimate victory, those

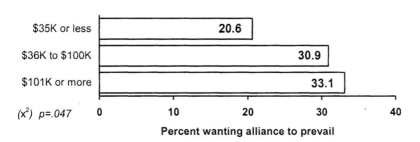

Figure 3.8: Percentage of respondents wanting Tagi alliance to prevail, grouped by annual household income

making $35,000 or less per year were less pleased than those making $100,000 and up by a 13 percentage point margin. (p=.076)

An ordinary least squares (OLS) analysis provides further supporting evidence; many bivariate relationships held up under multiple regression.[16] A regression equation with "reaction to the Tagi alliance prevailing" as the dependent variable was created. On a scale of 1 to 5, with 1 being "very pleased when Tagi prevailed" and 5 being "very displeased when Tagi prevailed," a respondent who was a member of an online *Survivor* community, a member of a union household, identified as upper class or upper middle class, and did not identify as Democrat or Independent, gave an average reply of 2.7, the most "pleased" response under this equation. Conversely, one who was not a member of an online community or a union household, identified as working class or lower, and identified as a Democrat, gave an average reply of 3.8, the least "pleased" under this particular equation. (p=.000)

As noted by this regression analysis, only one variable had perhaps unexpected results for any *Borneo*-related question. Labor unions are traditionally a working class, Democratic constituency. Yet intriguingly, members of union households responding to the survey were more than 10 percentage points more likely to want the Tagi alliance to prevail. When the alliance did so, respondents from union households were more pleased by a margin of 8 percentage points. (p=.103) Because alliances are analogous to unions—with the concept of strength in numbers prevalent—it is not surprising that members of union households rooted for the alliance to win out. This is, however, the only case where a typically working-class demographic was significantly more likely to view the Tagi alliance more positively among respondents.

In the end, then, the study found that respondents in upper class-related demographics were significantly more likely to support the Tagi alliance than those in the lower classes. This supports reading *Survivor* as being constructed, if not entirely intentionally, as a political allegory as envisioned by Jameson, reflecting the culture that created it—namely, a culture where members of the lower classes outnumber those in the upper classes, yet because of their disorganized, politically disinterested tendencies, lack power. However, overall Richard and the Tagi alliance were viewed negatively by wide margins in their tussle against those constructed as the "underdogs." No matter how one divided the data, most were displeased when the "bad guys," the ones with power bearing down on the helpless "sitting duck," prevailed. The disappointed masses, their dream deferred, found themselves looking to the future for a happier ending.

Three seasons later, halfway through *Survivor: Marquesas*, they got their wish.

Notes

1. However, there were also reports at the time that contestants tried to mislead producers by lying about strategy when cameras were present.

2. Left a mystery is how members of Pagong could possibly have heard about the alliance. The logical conclusion is that the production crew spread the gossip (Lance 2000, 69). This brings up ethical issues beyond the scope of this book.

3. For brevity, additional dialogue by Rudy, Greg, and Rich, among others, has been omitted from this section.

4. See also Burnett 2000, 144-46. This section of the book continues the mixed signals regarding Sean's awareness of the Tagi alliance; however, in the primary text, the aired television content, he is portrayed as utterly naïve to it all.

5. These figures disregard respondents who did not watch *Survivor: Borneo*, could not recall their opinions at the time, or had no opinion either way. However, when the latter group is included in the sample, about a third of overall respondents—33.0 percent—responded that Pagong/Sean were "neither good nor bad." Far fewer, 23.0 percent, said the same of the Tagi alliance.

6. This difference of means is not statistically significant according to a T-test. The raw AAI had a somewhat larger but still statistically insignificant mean difference between the two tribes of 0.453, versus 0.316 for the AAAI.

7. Rudy and Gretchen were also rated in the Top Ten of all 150 contestants through the first ten seasons.

8. Many online fans noticed when Episode 9 aired that Sue and Kelly's clothing in this part of the scene did not match what they were wearing in the abutting footage; moreover, Sue inexplicably had a large bandage wrapped around one hand. Three episodes later, she would be wounded by a sea creature, accounting for the injury but proving the deceptive, highly "unreal" editing. On Day 36, when the conversation actually took place, all the former Pagong had been voted out of the game and sat on the jury. Sue feared that Kelly's friendships with those Pagong would earn Kelly their votes should she reach the final two; in the context of Episode 9, it

appeared that Sue was angry that Kelly was on the verge of perhaps abandoning her alliance and taking up with Pagong.

9. The percentage listed is of survey respondents who watched *Survivor: Borneo* and said they could recall what their expectations of the game's outcome were as it progressed.

10. Discounting those who said they had no idea what would happen, the numbers are 40.4 percent that expected Tagi to prevail, 51.5 percent that expected a partial derailment, and 8.2 percent that expected a total failure.

11. Jenna is voted out 4-3-1. Colleen, Gervase, and Jenna vote against Rich, while Kelly breaks with her alliance to vote against Sean.

12. All this had such an effect on online *Survivor* fans that the verb "Pagonged" became part of the fan lexicon, referring to the process whereby one tribe or voting bloc systematically eliminates another. Contestant Shii-Ann even self-referentially used the term in this context on *Survivor: All-Stars*. Note, too, that occasional, later episodes of *Survivor* (finales aside) have ended differently—when *Pearl Islands'* Osten up and quit, for instance, the camera ended on his fallen torch, in a sort of show of anti-respect.

13. For brevity, generally these respondents will be referred to in the text as "upper class," although they include respondents who self-indentified as either upper class or upper middle class.

14. A p value of .05 or lower is considered statistically significant; one of .15 or lower is considered approaching statistical significance. To clarify, values are of those who had an opinion; i.e., since 51.7 percent of upper-class respondents were pleased with Rich's victory, 48.3 percent were displeased. However, even when "no opinion" type responses were included in the above Chi Square analyses, the results were still statistically significant for the below-mentioned "who did you want to win," Tagi/Pagong as good or bad questions and Figures 3.5 and 3.6, and approached significance for Figure 3.4, when computed against perceived social class.

15. Survey results indicated statistically significant correlations between perceived social class and several other demographic variables. For these "class vs. other demographics" tests, only results with a Chi Square p value of .010 or less are considered. Republican respondents ($p=.007$), non-full time employees ($p=.000$), those working fewer than 31 hours per week ($p=.004$), homeowners ($p=.000$), and white-collar employees ($p=.000$) were all significantly more likely to identify as upper class or upper middle class. On the other hand, politically Independent respondents ($p=.009$), full-time employees, those working at least 31 hours per week, renters, and blue-collar employees were all significantly more likely to identify as working class. (Democratic respondents were not more likely to identify as one class or another.) Furthermore, as education level rose, so did social class ($p=.000$); the same held for household income ($p=.000$).

16. Additionally, an OLS analysis with class as dependent variable found that several independent variable responses predicted social class. The regression equation showed that someone with at least some master's or professional work, who is Republican, makes more than $100,000 in annual household income, is not a member of a union household, does not work full-time, is a student, and is not a blue-collar employee, is most likely to identify as upper or upper middle class. ($p=.000$)

Chapter 4

"They're All Lying to Me"
Repression Among Contestants

LATER SEASONS OF *SURVIVOR* have generally featured contestants schooled in the trappings of the game, as well as an audience that has come to know the ins and outs of life on deserted beaches. Luckily for Mark Burnett and CBS, not all seasons have produced the exact outcome of the first, a Pagonging, though this has been in part thanks to twists such as tribal swaps, a battle of the sexes, or the return to the game of previously exiled players. Through a combination of contrived "plot twists" and contestant strategies, things usually have remained interesting.

The second season, *Survivor: The Australian Outback* (spring 2001), saw a mild power swing in its fourth episode, when three members of a six-person tribe used a tie-breaking rule to grab control of their group. Several episodes later, the season's "villain," Jerri, was ejected and sent to the jury even though her original tribe controlled the game, so apparently unliked was she among even her purported alliance-mates. This sent up cheers nationwide; Jerri had the sixth lowest AAAI of all contestants, 1.842. However, the central alliance of Tina, Colby, and Keith never lost control and sailed to the end.

On the following *Survivor: Africa* (fall 2001), the first season to involve a tribal swap, four members of the Boran alliance survived a close call and consecutively voted out the last four members of the Samburu tribe. The close call came when a "mystery vote" against him led contestant Lex on a witch hunt to determine who cast it. Everyone denied it, Lex targeted and voted out the wrong person, and it nearly cost him and his alliance the game. However, Boran prevailed, with Lex finishing third.

Viewers thus entered the fourth season of *Survivor,* which occurred on the Marquesan island of Nuku Hiva, without having yet experienced an outright overthrow. Here, however, one finally happened, and it was made all the more suspenseful through suppression-turned-repression among contestants.

Figure 4.1: Final ten contestants in *Survivor: Marquesas*,
members of merged Soliantu tribe

Rotu alliance members	Tightly aligned, think they are in Rotu alliance, but aren't*	On outside looking in	Voted out at merge
John Tammy	Paschal Neleh	Kathy*	**Rob***
Robert Zoe		Vecepia** Sean**	

Note: See Appendix B for contestant details.
* Paschal, Neleh, and Kathy began the game in the Rotu tribe, then were switched into the Maraamu tribe.
** Rob, Sean, and eventual winner Vecepia began the game in the Maraamu tribe, then were switched into the Rotu tribe.

"These Guys Brought the Game in With Them"

The first three episodes of *Survivor: Marquesas* are a wipeout as the Rotu tribe defeats the Maraamu tribe in every single challenge. Rotu's members declare themselves the "love tribe," and there is little conflict in sight. With no Tribal Councils looming, there is no need to strategize. Indeed, the Rotu beach is nearly another Eden.

Maraamu, meanwhile, is ripe with strife, with one sect taking control by voting out the self-appointed leader, contestant Hunter, and two others. Then, in Episode 4, the producers remind everyone who really holds the power by injecting a twist: The thirteen remaining contestants are randomly redistributed into tribes of eight and five. This ruptures Rotu, as three members are swapped into Maraamu and three new people enter, including "Boston" Rob[1], who had controlled Maraamu following Hunter's eviction.

This five-on-three advantage at the new Rotu causes anxiety for Rob and his fellow "swappees," Sean and Vecepia. Their fears begin to poison the Rotu camp, like the snake and the apple. "They're all worried about how long they're gonna be here," naïve Gabe tells us in Episode 5 (28 March 2002). "These guys brought the game in with them. It's started here at our camp now."

John, expecting he and the other four original Rotu members to stick together and evict the three newcomers as necessary, approaches Gabe to go over the plan again. Unfortunately, Gabe is now fully channeling the Pagong/Sean line from *Borneo*: He insists he isn't here to play the game, will vote someone off if he has to, but refuses to confirm that he'll only vote for Rob, Vecepia, or Sean.

John's reaction, to the camera: "I had to get rid of Gabe right away, and I started to devise a plan." In other words, Gabe's telling the truth, combined with his naïvete, is unacceptable, not unlike the world of politics, where semantics and "non-denial denials" rise to an art form and where the thin-skinned never last. John forms an alliance with Robert, Tammy, and Zoe, the tribe loses an immunity challenge for the first time, and soon Gabe is shown the door. This recapitulation of the Season 1 storyline jars the audience: *Here we go again*, we think. *Is this same plot really going to happen time after time?* John takes the comparison a step further in Episode 6 (CBS, 4 April 2002) when he strips in front of his allies and goes skinny-dipping in a lagoon, saying it has "cleansed him somehow," in a sort of resolution to the contradiction of inequality that his tribe has been forced to assume.

Yes, for the second time, we have an alliance led by a cocky, naked gay man. "Everyone knows I'm running the show," John says. Confronted by Boston Rob after Zoe lies about the obvious alliance, John openly admits it, but then proposes that the remaining Rotu seven will stick together at the merge and vote out whatever is left of Maraamu (Kathy, discussed briefly in Chapter 2, and who had been swapped out of Rotu and into Maraamu, is apparently picked as the first target). Rob, John, and Sean shake on it, but Rob tells us he doesn't believe John, adding that John shouldn't believe Rob, either. The secrets and lies begin anew.

A Thousand Lies

In Episode 7 (CBS, 11 April 2002), "ambassadors" Kathy and Rob meet for the merge summit, and over pizza and beer, Rob alleges that Kathy's gal pal Zoe, along with the rest of her old friends, plan to vote her out immediately. Kathy, already facing the reality of symbolic subordination by being the odd person out in her tiny tribe of three—Neleh and Paschal are very close friends—is floored. But should she believe him?

"She doesn't know if I'm telling the truth or lying," Rob tells us after he and Kathy pledge to be the final two. "Just like I don't know" if she is. Suppression is indeed at the core of *Survivor,* and the lies between and among Kathy, Rob, John, and Zoe directly relate to power—for whoever is most cunning, most able to convince the others he or she is telling the truth, stands the best chance of emerging holding all the cards. But no one dares speak openly about all this, and Rob is taking a major risk by coming clean (sort of) to Kathy. Clearly, though, she is affected by his words, making an observation after the merge that goes straight to the heart of the game:

> Kathy (to camera): The game faces are on full tilt, and nobody wants to talk about it. Nobody wants to talk to *me* about it. I think the game has changed in a sense that the Rotu loyalty has dissolved or has taken on a new shape. There's definitely some undercurrent alliance that's been formed . . .

The key phrases here are "nobody wants to talk about it" and "undercurrent alliance." Kathy is hinting at unspoken signals that the audience knows full well about. Yet Neleh and Paschal—the next targets after her according to Rob's faux pact with John—certainly suspect nothing. Judge Paschal disregards Kathy's paranoia, telling her he'll "listen" and will "let her know" if he learns anything, sounding much like a politician dismissing the concerns of a constituent he disagrees with. What has he been told? We don't know, and we can't be certain of John and company's intended targets. We may think the truth here is not repressed, but it very much is. The Jamesonian repetition throughout these episodes of *Marquesas* is the suspected presence of such an undercurrent alliance that no one dares speak of—sort of a *There's something going on here!* from Person A and a *Hush! No there's not!* from Person B. In other cases, denial takes the form of silence. All this creates suspense that will inevitably lead to audience (dis)pleasure.

The one person willing to violate this vow of silence is Rob. He forces the uncomfortable, socially awkward Zoe into conversation with Kathy present. Zoe takes on the tagline of Person B. Excerpts from the chat:

Rob: I thought that [us seven] had an agreement. . . .

Zoe: No. . . .

Rob: Unbelievable. Tell the truth, for once. . . . The other day, didn't you tell me that you were voting for Kathy? Yes or no.

(long silence)

Zoe: No.

Rob: There. You paused, *and* you lied. . . .

(Kathy stands up)

Kathy: I get a story from you and I get a story from Zoe, and people are lying through their teeth and I haven't lied once!

Kathy soon makes for the nearby waterfall and lagoon and dives in fully clothed. "Zoe's lying to me, they're all lying to me," she says, moaning. "And I am being played as a pawn." Everyone from old Rotu still wants to hug her, be the love tribe again, it seems. It's "this game of kissy and love, but guess what, when we go to next Tribal Council, you're out," she worries. Kathy's understanding of the game, lack of power, and status as a "central character" places her in the heroine position that Colleen occupied in *Borneo*. Indeed, survey respondents wanted Kathy to win *Marquesas* by overwhelming margins: A stunning 56.7 percent picked her from a list of the final ten players.[2] She also registered the fourth highest AAAI out of all 150 contestants measured. Again, then, we see the underdog figure favored by the masses, the sympathetic story playing out once more.[3]

Soon, Rob, John, and Sean have an explosive argument, with John suggesting their deal is done because Rob tattled to Kathy. By now, things have become so confusing, with layer upon layer of secrets and lies, that it appears that the editors barely have to suppress anything: The contestants simply do it for them. Kathy wins immunity, and at the first post-merge Tribal Council, Rob—he who dared bring alliances into the open—sees his flame extinguished.

Overthrow

As Episode 8 begins (CBS, 18 April 2002), the *Borneo*-like class narrative of *Marquesas* seems set in stone, and Sean's departure at the next Tribal Council appears assured. Having learned from the past, however, he refuses to go the way of the previous contestant named Sean. "I know I'm next," he tells us. "All I can do is go out trying." He continues with a variation on the Jamesonian, people-are-pretending-everything-is-fine line: "Everybody's like, 'we are family,' and I'm like, 'everything ain't hunky-dory over here! Things are going on, people are not to be trusted."

Kathy is saying the same things to Neleh and Paschal, the inseparable duo, insisting that John's alliance must be stopped; presumably, Rob told her about the four-way alliance that become obvious following Gabe's exit. But Neleh and Paschal aren't budging (as we saw in Chapter 2), telling Kathy that if she keeps bringing up alliances, she'll only get voted out sooner. They have good reason, it seems: Tammy reveals to the camera that Neleh and Paschal have agreed to vote out Sean, Vecepia, and Kathy. (What Neleh and Paschal don't know, of course, is that they would be next in the pecking order, and at a four-on-two disadvantage.) "If I could have formed the alliance with Sean and [Vecepia] and Paschal and Neleh and myself, I could have had a huge shot at it," Kathy laments. "But that's not going to happen." However, on *Survivor*, when someone says a certain event definitely won't happen, it usually does.

After four seasons of *Survivor*, viewers had begun to figure this out. The survey showed that just 15.4 percent of respondents expected the Rotu alliance to prevail.[4] This low number may also be thanks to heavy dislike for the Rotu alliance—after witnessing Tagi's dominance in *Borneo* and similar outcomes in *Outback* and *Africa*, viewers were clearly hungry for a change in *Survivor's* narrative. Of those who had an opinion about *Marquesas'* outcome, only about one in ten wanted the Rotu alliance to prevail, compared to 29.2 percent who had wanted the Tagis to win out (see Figure 4.2).

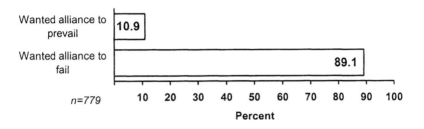

**Figure 4.2: Desires of survey respondents
as to fate of *Marquesas'* Rotu alliance**

Additionally, just 16.2 percent saw the alliance as "the good guys," versus 72.7 percent who saw the non-allied players as such.[5]

OLS regression analysis finds that memories of *Survivor: Borneo* may have affected consumption of *Marquesas*. An equation was created that featured perception of the non-allied *Marquesas* players as dependent variable. It showed opinion of *Borneo's* Colleen, Greg, and company to be the most significant predictor of how one viewed the *Marquesas* "underdogs" alliance (p=.000). A respondent who had viewed Pagong/Sean as "the good guys" was likely to think the same of Kathy and company.

Those fans who saw the doomed Pagong players as "the good guys" in *Borneo* are about to get some pleasure for their previous pain. Next on Episode 8 comes the immunity challenge, a quiz game about survival and the Marquesas. Each player has three bunches of color-coded coconuts strung over trees with rope. Each time a contestant gets a question right, he or she takes a machete and chops down one bunch of another's coconuts. Once all three of a person's sets have been cut down, they are out. The last person left wins immunity.

It is in this challenge that the unconscious strands about alliances and pecking orders come into open view, a bourgeoisie nightmare realized. Sean and Vecepia are immediately attacked; their bunches come down right away. "There's a conspiracy going on, y'all! I'm calling Johnny Cochran!" Sean shouts. Kathy is next: The three targets for eviction are cut out of the game at once.

Robert, John, Zoe, and Tammy focus the rest of their efforts on knocking down Neleh's and Paschal's coconuts. At this point, the alliance of four collectively has ten coconut bunches remaining, while Neleh and Paschal have six. Yet as the challenge continues, the four alliance members chop down all six of Neleh and Paschal's bunches—while only hacking three of one another's.

**Figure 4.3: Reaction of survey respondents
to *Marquesas'* Rotu alliance failing**

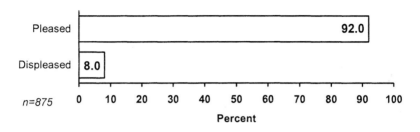

This does not go unnoticed by Sean, who mutters that this is the likely elimination order. Neleh and Paschal notice as well. The waifish young woman, 21, looks confused and concerned as John and Zoe chop down Paschal's bunches; the aging judge grins briefly before worry washes over his face. He looks even more concerned as Neleh's last coconuts drop.

Tammy wins immunity, but she, John, Robert, and Zoe have gone too far, become too cocky, and their secret alliance has bobbed to the surface. Neleh and Paschal finally see the light, as they discuss after the challenge:

Paschal: They were never gonna give us any consideration.

Neleh: No way!

Paschal: None.

Paschal (to camera): The way that immunity came down, it signaled that there was a pecking order and we were included in it, even though we'd been told that wasn't true . . .

Neleh (to Paschal): If me and you are going to get anywhere toward the end we have to do this. We would be fools not to. I'm not going to go out fifth or sixth.

These two clearly have learned from the mistakes of Pagong. Neleh, Paschal, Kathy, Sean, and Vecepia—despite their separate original tribes, despite their varied cultural backgrounds, despite Paschal's professed distaste for Sean—follow through and do what the allegorical underclasses who came before them did not. They unite while they still have a voting majority and cut off the head of the alliance, John. They realize that this is *indeed* about power, and do something about it. The Rotu four's behavior, particularly John's, illustrates the dangers of the arrogance of power and again reflects the culture that produced *Survivor*—and also Watergate, the Lewinsky affair, and countless other matters that have wounded or killed the careers of

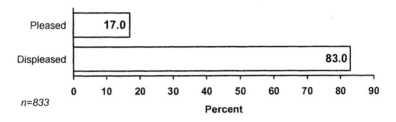

**Figure 4.4: Reaction of survey respondents
to Vecepia winning *Marquesas***

politicians. The existence or perception of power can make people think they
can get away with anything.

In ousting John, Kathy and company bring tremendous pleasure to the
audience, who have had hints of a power shift dangled in front of them so
many times before, most notoriously during the deception of Season 1. An
overwhelming majority of respondents—more than nine in ten—reported
that they were pleased when Rotu's alliance was defeated (see Figure 4.3).[6]
In addition, the four members had a highly negative mean AAAI of 2.791,
and an average rank of ninety-fourth; the members of the "coup," as it were,
had a 3.650 mean AAAI, good for an average rank of fifty-second. This difference approached statistical significance.[7] Clearly, John and his ilk received a negative edit, likely on purpose, and CBS certainly understood this
excitement: "It's the biggest power swing in *Survivor* history!" announced
promos for the following week's episode.

Of course, these five now become the symbolic bourgeoisie of their
tribe, with Zoe, Tammy, and finally Robert falling by the wayside, something that later ignites another power struggle that will be explored in Chapter 8. Yet the "coup five" contest that they aren't really an alliance; rather,
they want players "who don't try to manipulate others" to succeed, according to Paschal (CBS, 25 April 2002). Can he be believed? By grabbing control, does the new "Party of Five" lose the luster of protagonism? Are the
Rotu leftovers—Tammy and Robert—now sympathetic figures? Perhaps to
a degree, but at the final Tribal Council some of the vanquished alliance
members hurl venomous comments at the two finalists, Neleh and Vecepia,
and accuse them of lying or being immoral. This obvious hypocrisy lifts
much of any sympathy we may have, and reveals again that they are merely
deposed kings.

However, this did not help Vecepia's popularity as a winner. Fewer than
one in five survey respondents were pleased when "V" stood for victory (see
Figure 4.4), and only 1.9 percent picked her from a list of the final ten

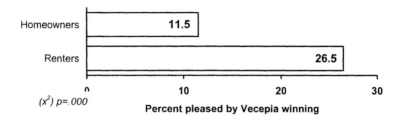

Figure 4.5: Percentage of respondents pleased by Vecepia winning, grouped by housing status

Homeowners   11.5

Renters   26.5

(x^2) p=.000

Percent pleased by Vecepia winning

contestants as the one they had wanted to win. This was likely due at least in part to the African-American office manager's quiet, undefined persona throughout the season. It seemed Mark Burnett wanted viewers to be surprised by her victory, so he made her an "invisible woman," a tactic that backfired (Wright, 29 May 2002). "Fans were stunned by the nearly invisible presence of the eventual winner, Vecepia," wrote a fan known online only as Garbotalk in an article for the site SurvivorFever.net. "It's not that she didn't deserve to win. But her scheming and planning were so well hidden from the audience through editing choices that it came out of nowhere" (2005).

As with *Borneo*, the survey revealed demographic differences in *Marquesas'* consumption. Other than working-class viewers being somewhat more likely to correctly expect the Rotu alliance to fail (p=.111), perceived social class was less of an indicator here, perhaps because of the overwhelming unpopularity of the Rotu alliance. Yet demographics that, as noted in Chapter 3, were associated with class among survey respondents did betray intriguing differences.

- **Housing status:** Homeowners were much less pleased with Vecepia's win than those who rent their home, by a 15 percentage point margin (see Figure 4.5). They were also less likely to see the non-allied players as "the good guys" than were renters. (p=.029) As noted earlier, home-owning respondents were significantly more likely to be upper class than renters, while renters were significantly more likely to be working class than homeowners.

- **Occupation:** Perhaps unsurprisingly, more blue-collar employees (15.7 percent) wanted construction worker Boston Rob to win than did white-collar workers (10.3 percent). A full 21.6 percent of respondents who have never held a job supported Rob. On the other hand, white-collar workers (59.3 percent) favored Kathy more than

**Figure 4.6: Percentage of respondents pleased by
Vecepia winning, grouped by annual household income**

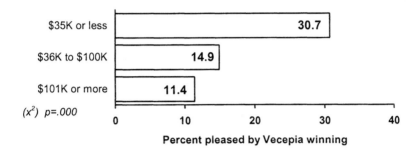

their blue-collar counterparts (52.4 percent). Kathy was especially unpopular among those who had never held a job. (p=.040) As explained earlier, white-collar respondents were significantly more likely to be upper class than blue-collar workers, while blue-collar workers were significantly more likely to be working class than white-collar employees.

- **Income:** Those in households making more than $100,000 a year were far less pleased by Vecepia's victory than those making $35,000 or less—the difference was nearly 20 percentage points. Compare this to *Borneo*, where those making more than $100,000 were more likely to be pleased by Richard's win by a 13 percentage point margin. Richard, of course, had come from the dominant alliance, while Vecepia rose from the group that wrested control of *Marquesas* midway through.

OLS regression analysis gives further evidence as to factors influencing reaction to Vecepia's win, with that issue as dependent variable. On a scale of 1 to 5, with 1 being "very pleased when Vecepia won" and 5 being "very displeased when Vecepia won," a respondent who was not a member of an online *Survivor* community, was female, nonwhite, 18 to 30 years of age, had an annual household income of $35,000 or less, was not a part-time employee and did not identify as politically Independent, gave an average reply of 3.1, the most "pleased" response under this equation. Conversely, one who was a member of an online community, was male, white, 51 years or older, had an annual household income of more than $100,000, was a part-time employee and identified as an Independent, gave an average reply of 5.0, the least "pleased" under this particular equation.

These data sets show again that respondents' reactions to *Survivor* alliances differed along class-related lines, buttressing the notion that the show reflects our own society's hierarchies.[8] Especially intriguing are differences involving Vecepia's win. If, as had been assumed by this writer at the time (29 May 2002), viewer dissatisfaction was based on her lack of character development or a perception that she had not done enough to "deserve" to win, why do class-based differences persist? Gender was not an issue, and although white respondents were less pleased with her victory than non-white respondents, race/ethnicity and class were not significantly related in the 1,000 person sample (race and *Survivor* will, however, be discussed in Chapter 8). One is left, then, with the suggestion that those from lower-class-related backgrounds identified more with Vecepia, her on-show struggles, and class-related stereotypes associated with her race, and therefore reacted more strongly to the first victory on *Survivor* by a member of a racial minority.[9] Again, then, we are left with the notion that *Survivor* is both produced and consumed as a political allegory, however unconsciously.

"An Alliance of One"

After the excitement of *Survivor: Marquesas*, some viewers found the next edition, *Thailand* (fall 2002), uneventful, as the Chuay Gahn tribe took control midway through and Pagonged the Sook Jai tribe. Because the structure was so similar to Season 1—with the exception of a delayed merge that caught contestants off guard, again reminding us who is really in charge here—*Thailand* will not be discussed much on these pages, although one particular incident involving eventual winner Brian will be discussed in the conclusion, because it involves the strongest survey results about how *Survivor* resonates among different classes. Ironically, the spring 2004 *Survivor: All-Stars*, which featured previous contestants returning to play again, nearly mirrored the plotline of *Borneo* (and *Thailand*). It seemed incredible that people who knew the game better than anyone—those who had played it before—would so easily fall prey to another Pagonging.[10]

Survivor: Borneo gave us a status quo game, power-wise; the plots of *The Australian Outback* and *Africa* tweaked that formula slightly, but did not completely reverse that first plotline the way *Marquesas* did. After *Thailand* reverted to *Borneo's* form and ideologeme, viewers were hungry for something new. They got it with *Survivor: The Amazon*, a thrilling season because one contestant, Rob[11], continually jumped from alliance to alliance, so much so that at some point in the game, every person in *Amazon's* final ten voted differently than he, usually multiple times (see Figure 4.8).

**Figure 4.7: Final ten contestants in *Survivor: The Amazon*,
members of Jacaré Tribe**

Began in Tambuqui tribe, then sent to Jabaru	Began in Tambuqui, remained there	Began in Jabaru, sent to Tambuqui	Began in Jabaru, remained there
Rob Matt Alex	Roger Butch Dave	Heidi Christy	Deena Jenna

Note: In Episode 5, six members remained in both Jabaru and Tambuqui; three from each tribe were switched into the other. Jenna was the season's eventual winner. See Appendix B for contestant details.

Rob's pattern of betrayals begins with the very first episode, where, as noted in Chapter 2, he promises two sects of his tribe that he will vote with them—then, of course, must turn on one. Ironically, one of those people he betrays, Matt, ultimately becomes a tool to bring Rob to the endgame. "I am an alliance of one," Rob aptly tells us late in the proceedings (CBS, 1 May 2003). "I am a lone wolf . . . a mercenary, if you will. I just pick up the bottom feeders as I go. They go with me because I promise them the dream of getting to the end." Rob's never-ending machinations give the audience great pleasure—in the survey, 91.7 percent of respondents said his alliance hop-scotching made *The Amazon* more exciting—as does the fact that repeatedly, contestants who think they control the game instead are voted out. This may have been the first truly unpredictable season.[12]

Amazon begins as a battle of the sexes, eight men vs. eight women. When six remain on each gendered tribe, the contestants are rearranged, resulting in the configuration depicted in Figure 4.7 by the time the two tribes merge. At this point, Roger, described as a "dictator" by Alex, is voted out, with Rob among those betraying him. This will be discussed further in Chapter 5. Next, Dave is ousted unceremoniously. Figure 4.8 depicts these and later Tribal Council results.

Now things begin to heat up, especially in terms of Rob's machinations. Deena has a final-two alliance with Rob and declares that she is "in control" (CBS, 10 April 2003). She targets Alex, which angers Jenna and Heidi, who are good friends with him. The three conspire with Rob to vote her out. Thus does Rob betray Deena, fearing her perceived power. With seven left, Jenna, Heidi, Alex, and Rob are allied—"as long as we control immunity, [we are] the final four," says Alex (CBS, 24 April 2003). However, Rob is the odd person out, and Alex even tells him he plans to vote Rob out at the final four. Unnverved, Rob turns on his three alliance-mates by reuniting with the other three players (Matt, Butch, and Christy). Alex is dispatched, 4-3, not long after he tells Jeff Probst, "I'd be pretty surprised if I got voted out." Matt, meanwhile, speaks of Alex being "dethroned." Thus does Rob betray Heidi, Jenna, and Alex.

Figure 4.8: Tribal Council results,
Survivor: The Amazon, Episodes 7-13

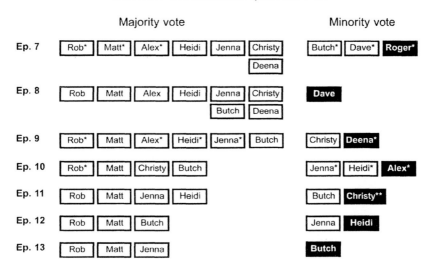

Note: Black indicates ousted contestant; only the first of three Episode 13 Tribal Councils is listed.
* Majority alliance the ousted person (and at times others in the minority) *thought* he or she was a part of.
** Christy thought she was the swing vote and had all the power.

Six now remain, three men and three women. Heidi and Jenna are absolutely furious with Rob, and try to swing Christy, the show's first deaf contestant, to their side. Meanwhile Rob, Matt, and Butch are trying to keep her with them. Christy speaks openly about her newfound status, repeatedly saying gleefully, "I've got the power." She refuses to tell anyone how she will vote, contending she will make up her mind as pen hits paper in the voting booth (CBS, 1 May 2003). "I make the final decision . . . for tonight's vote," she tells Probst at Tribal Council. With no one able to trust her, Rob secretly proposes to Heidi and Jenna that they make things easy on themselves and simply oust Christy. Despite their anger, Heidi and Jenna unite with Rob and Matt one last time and do precisely that. Thus does Rob betray an absolutely floored Christy.

As each person in power—having stated aloud his or her command of *Survivor*—successively is dispatched, the audience experiences pleasure. Never have so many supposed power players been kicked off so rapidly, and this again reflects the excitement over seeing an outwardly powerful figure in mainstream society go down in flames. The message here is that the person really in power is *Rob*. He has no long-lasting alliance, yet is the only

Figure 4.9: Percentage of respondents seeing Rob as "good," grouped by social class

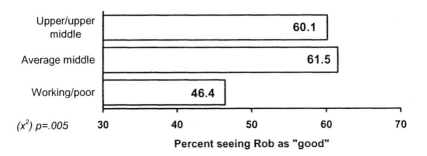

person to vote with the majority at every Tribal Council in which he casts a vote (see Figure 4.8; Matt had voted against the majority at two previous Tribal Councils). It seems that only Jenna, the eventual winner who also single-handedly votes out Rob at the final three, is wise enough to understand this truth.[13] She calls him a "puppet master . . . he's cutting the strings off [us] as he goes along." And he does this behind a wall of hilarious humor, using as a prop his "luxury item," a Magic Eight Ball. By keeping his comrades entertained, he distracts them from the truth.

Here, denial comes in, adding to the Jamesonian repetition and pleasure. Despite the bodies strewn in his path, despite the occasional line such as Matt's "Rob has betrayed a number of people," (CBS, 24 April 2003) *no one makes a serious move to vote him out*—not the way, for instance, Jenna, Gervase, and Colleen banded together late in the *Borneo* proceedings in a futile effort to take out Rich. Indeed, just before Matt says the above line, he tells us that "I appreciated [Rob's] honesty." Butch, similarly, has no problem re-aligning with Rob to get rid of Alex, even though Rob essentially betrayed him when he voted out Butch's friends Roger and Dave. Heidi and Jenna, furious at Rob for evicting Alex, turn right around and join up with him again to vote out Christy. This, not fifteen minutes in TV time after Jenna calls him a "slimeball" and a "snake" (CBS, 1 May 2003). Yet soon we see them together again, laughing and grinning. From our viewpont, the contestants collectively deny the reality of the situation—that Rob controls them all—despite the evidence to the contrary. Suspicions and anger fade as the hope to last three more days prevails. Rob, appropriately, puts it best himself: "I have told lies. . . . I have broken promises, and they all know that. Maybe that's why they still trust me. Everybody's [saying] how much they believe me. . . . Were these guys paying attention the first thirty-two days?"

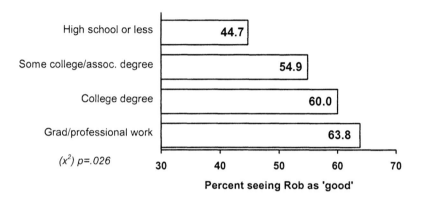

Figure 4.10: Percentage of respondents seeing
Rob as "good," grouped by education level

$(x^2) p=.026$

Percent seeing Rob as 'good'

By a moderate margin, the 2004 survey respondents found Rob to be a "good guy" despite his strategies—a direct reflection, perhaps, on his making the game more exciting and his sense of humor. Of those who saw him as good or bad, 57.8 percent saw Rob as good[14], and the 2005 survey respondents dubbed him the best player to not win *Survivor*, rating him twelfth in overall AAAI at 4.344. Similarly, more than six in ten respondents were displeased when Jenna voted out Rob in the endgame.

Initially, this writer expected that, if anything, members of the lower classes would see Rob more positively because of his "alliance-busting" nature. However, survey results show a starkly opposite effect (see Figure 4.9), with members of the upper and middle classes far more likely to see Rob as a "good guy" than working-class respondents.

This difference is also apparent across a handful of related demographic lines. Take, for example, one's level of education. The more educated respondents were, the more likely they were to see Rob as a "good guy" (see Figure 4.10) and be displeased when Jenna voted him out. Perhaps those with higher education appreciated his manipulations and intellectual strategy, but coupled with the results of the class question, it is most intriguing. White-collar respondents and members of non-union households were also more likely to be happy with Rob—in the latter case, by a nine-point margin over those from union households—although these particular differences only approached statistical significance.

OLS analysis again gives supporting evidence as to the role of class-related variables in one's viewpoint of Rob. A regression equation was created with perception of Rob as the dependent variable. On a scale of 1 to 5, with 1 being "Rob was a good guy, and very much so" and 5 being "Rob was a bad guy, and very much so," a respondent who was age 18-30; had at least some graduate or professional training; was not a member of a union household; and identified as a white-collar worker, non-Republican, and upper class or upper middle class, gave an average reply of 2.3, the most positive response under this equation. Conversely, one who was 51 or older; had a high school education or less; was a member of a union household; identified as working class, working poor, or poor; was a Republican; and identified as neither white nor blue collar (e.g., had never held a job), gave an average reply of 3.6, the most negative response under this equation. Of these factors, only identification as a Republican resulted in opposite results than one might expect, based on other questions analyzed earlier.

Perceptions of Rob also built on the past: On the same scale of 1 to 5, a respondent who was very pleased when Richard and Brian won *Borneo* and *Thailand*, but who wanted *Marquesas'* Rotu alliance overthrown and saw the non-allied *Marquesas* players as very good, gave an average response of 2.2, the most positive view of Rob under this second equation. Conversely, one who was very displeased at Richard's and Brian's wins, but wanted the Rotu alliance to prevail and saw Kathy and friends in *Marquesas* as the bad guys, gave an average reply of 3.5, the most negative under this equation.

The most intriguing item concerning Rob is that reactions of the upper class and of union household members have diverged—whereas both supported the Tagi alliance, only upper-class respondents view positively Rob's "alliance of one." Respondents from union households side with the rest of the working-class constituency in viewing Rob more negatively. Perhaps they see him here as an "alliance-buster," more than an "alliance-former," though in truth he is both. In a way, Rob is the allegorical embodiment of the American Dream—the dream that the upper class theoretically lives while the working class struggles to achieve it. Rob is at once pulling himself up by his bootstraps, the symbolic corporate dealmaker, and the autonomous agent taking full advantage of his limited resources. Perhaps the upper-class respondents, if only subconsciously, recognized him as such, while working-class members saw him as thinking only of himself, taking down everyone in his path without care—much, perhaps, as cynics among them may view the power players in real-life American society. Perhaps they are even more aggravated by the recognition that none of the other players seem to realize that he is in control.

In any case, these examples demonstrate that contestants regularly use secrets and lies to gain power and propel themselves further in *Survivor*. Sometimes it works, sometimes it backfires. A Jamesonian reading illuminates the political allegory of the program: *Marquesas'* Rotu alliance is overthrown by a diverse group of outcasts that has caught on to the truth, in a symbolic enactment of the bourgeoisie nightmare. *Thailand's* "ruling class," meanwhile, maintains its grip on power throughout the proceedings. And in *The Amazon*, supposed king after king is successively undone by a court jester who in reality holds all the cards—showing that at times, the only ruler safe from a coup is one who tricks everyone into believing he has no power.

Notes

1. Not to be confused with Rob from *Survivor: The Amazon*, discussed later in this chapter.

2. Boston Rob was second with 12.0 percent, followed by Paschal at 10.6 percent, Neleh at 9.3 percent, and Sean at 2.8 percent. Robert, a.k.a. the General, was the most popular member of the Rotu alliance, with 2.4 percent of respondents rooting for him to win.

3. Kathy had, in fact, begun the game in a terrible position, depicted as having poor social skills, etc., and forced herself to adjust. This only magnified her "underdog" image.

4. Forty percent expected it would be partially derailed and 33 percent thought it would fail, while 12 percent reported having had no idea what would happen. Discounting that last group, the numbers were 17.5 percent that expected Rotu to prevail, 45.3 percent that expected a partial derailment, and 37.3 percent that expected an overthrow.

5. Interestingly, the non-allied players in *Borneo* were viewed more positively than those in *Marquesas* by a 93.6 percent to 72.7 percent margin.

6. Again, this is of those who had an opinion about the overthrow. But even counting those with no opinion, 88.6 percent were still pleased at the turn of events.

7. A T-test found a p value of .099; using the raw AAI scores, the difference between the alliance and the coup group was even greater, with a mean difference of 0.942 (versus 0.859 for the AAAI) and a p value of .123 according to a T-test.

8. Note, however, that in regard to reaction to the "coup" itself, there were no statistically significant differences (or even differences approaching significance) along any class-related lines. This, again, may be attributable to Rotu's overwhelming unpopularity.

9. Note that Richard's status as a homosexual appeared to have little bearing on reaction to his win. *Survivor*, in fact, has had a diverse array of winners.

10. One member of the dominant *All-Stars* alliance had even been a member of Pagong—Jenna.

11. Not to be confused with the aforementioned Boston Rob of *Marquesas*.

12. Unpredictable, that is, for those not privy to the reports of a *Survivor* viewer who had happened upon the *Amazon* set while on vacation in Brazil. He did some sleuthing and suggested before the season even began to air that persons fitting Jenna's and Matt's descriptions would be the final two.

13. This despite an almost absurdly negative depiction by the editors—Jenna was the lowest rated winner of *Survivor* according to AAAI, placing 113th with a

2.541, and had an even lower raw AAI. She has, however, been more well-liked off the show and was more sympathetic on *Survivor All-Stars*, in part due to extenuating family circumstances, and has even been tapped by CBS to cohost an online radio show. Some have speculated that Jenna was purposely depicted negatively to throw off the scent of a detailed online spoiler that hinted she won (see previous endnote).

14. Taking into account those respondents who saw Rob as "neither good nor bad," the numbers were 44.3 percent good, 23.7 percent neutral, and 32.0 percent bad.

Chapter 5

"A Really Passionate Affair"
Repression Through Editing

AS DISCUSSED EARLIER, SELECTIVE EDITING is a major strategy employed by *Survivor's* producers. In whittling 72 hours of footage into 45 minutes of airtime, uneventful hours of laying around camp are excised, Tribal Council and challenges are compressed, and other unimportant, banal occurrences are suppressed. Yet now and then, editors appear to purposely create something from nothing, or make something look like nothing, in order to affect audience reactions. "Burnett is notorious for shrouding important information, showing conversations out of sequence, and editing dialogue and confessionals" to apparently mislead viewers (Wright, 18 Dec. 2001). Here things lead once again into repression and the Jamesonian unconscious.

Something from Nothing: Colleen and Greg

A major instance of this type of repression occurred in *Borneo*, where editors all but certainly constructed a false affair between contestants Colleen and Greg. This created the illusion of an alliance where there was none.

Much of Episode 5's plot revolves around the "affair." At this point, Tagi and Pagong still live on separate beaches and compete against each other as tribes. While Rich and company stealthily create their alliance, Greg tells us that he doesn't like sleeping in Pagong's shelter—he finds it smelly, and the presence of so many others makes it hard to sleep. So he goes to the forest, where he sleeps on a mat of branches and fronds. It's a bachelor pad, literally, and Greg's emphasis that he is "single" and a "bachelor" sets the stage for what is to come. We next watch, via a night vision camera, as Colleen and Greg leave the shelter and slink off together into the woods. Colleen "apparently finds [the forest] more comfortable as well," Greg says in a voice over (CBS, 28 June 2000).

Then comes the gossip, courtesy of Gervase and Jenna:

Gervase: They go off a lot. And sleep together. . . .

(Shot of Greg and Colleen in the dark)

Jenna (as we see Colleen and Greg return at dawn): [T]hey seem to be spending their nights under the stars and cuddling up. I think it's stepped up a notch . . .

This creates excitement for the audience, who will soon be viewing Tagi as the "bad guys" and Pagong as the "good guys." Adorable Colleen, who has not yet graduated to heroine status, confirms the rumors. "When we go off, it's all about sex," she says. "It's a really passionate affair . . ." She laughs, and we see a brief shot in the dark of the pair inside Pagong's shelter, appearing to lean in for a kiss. *Awwww*, we think.

Next, Greg, as we see evening footage of him handing Colleen her bag as they head for the trees once more, "reaffirms" that no romance is in bloom. Of course, there can be sex without romance, and this is seemingly what the editors want the audience to infer—that Greg's comments form a classic non-denial denial. Apparently, Colleen wasn't lying—it *is* all about sex. One could also interpret this as a stereotypical gender difference, with the man focused on the sex and the woman on the "really passionate" end of things. The segment concludes:

Colleen: [H]e reminds me of my friends back home. . . . [I can] be myself with him.

(Shot of the pair sharing a laugh)

Greg: We like to play together. . . . [S]leeping out there and the rest of it is great.

(Shot of them arm in arm walking along the beach)

This only reconfirms things for the audience: We really *do* have a budding romance on our hands. Sadly, however, in Episode 8—once the tribes have merged and Pagong leader Gretchen has been shockingly ousted—Greg decides he has to cozy up to Rich in order to stay in the game longer. He drops hints that he finds Rich attractive and apparently dumps Colleen, telling the camera, "It's like a kitten you find. . . . You pick it up, you take it home. . . . A week goes by and you haven't eaten, so you're starving. So you look right in the kitten's eyes and break its neck. Nothing personal" (CBS, 19 July 2000).

There's something bothersome about this speech, however, and not just Greg's unusually harsh language. Rather, as we watch Greg tell us this, on Day 23 or so, it appears that his beard growth is less than it is in surrounding scenes. What could this mean? Is it just the lighting? Or did this speech actually take place earlier on in the competition, and the editors saved it for now? Interestingly, in *Survivor: The Ultimate Game*, Mark Burnett mentions the speech during his discussion of Day 10 (2000, 70), a fact that Lance picks up on in *The Stingray* (2000, 54). This implies that it was indeed aired far out of order. Additionally, this is the kind of comment one would make after a relationship has ended. So why would Greg say it during Episode 4's time period, when the "affair" isn't even discussed until Episode 5?

Other things also repeatedly hint that something isn't right about this alleged situation. For instance, closely examining the aforementioned nighttime shot of Colleen and Greg "kissing," it appears a lip-lock may not be taking place after all. The camera angle is odd, and depth is hard to perceive because of the nighttime lens. We only see part of Greg's face; the back of his head is toward us. When Colleen leans up for the "kiss," it appears her jaw is moving, not as one's does during a kiss, but as during *talking*. Is that all this is, then? Are we being manipulated? Is the truth being stretched?[1]

Furthermore, why is the alleged romance not a heavy-duty plot point as *Survivor's* first season wears on? Why, when we see Greg making a back-handed come-on to Rich, do we not also see Colleen crying, shamed at being dumped? Why is there no conversation between buddies Jenna and Colleen, with the latter confused over Greg's sudden change in behavior? And why doesn't Colleen vote against Greg the first chance she gets—why does she vote against Jenna at the Tribal Council where Greg is dismissed?

These mixed signals and lack of new information hint that nothing is going on here at all. Indeed, in interviews following the show, both Colleen and Greg insisted they had not been involved. Colleen said she was only kidding around with her "really passionate affair" comments, hence the laughter. They were good friends, they told us, but that was all. As Colleen later told CBS: "We slept out in the woods together definitely, but nothing happened. . . . It looks good, you know, we sneak off into the dark and stuff like that. But more it just came down to, who wants to sleep in a hut with so many smelly people?"[2]

Assuming the contestants are indeed telling the truth, why did the editors create something from nothing? Three potential reasons spring forth. Most clearly, it made the show more exciting, and potentially could have generated headlines, higher ratings, and above all, money. *Romance on Survivor island! Is America's sweetheart, Colleen, in love with kooky Greg? Film at 11.* Second, the faux affair likely pushed audiences into rooting even more for Pagong, the kind, gentle romantics, rather than the emotionless Tagi who, in the words of *Survivor's* fifth champion, used car salesman Brian, were there only on "a business trip." Thus, the romance further differentiated Tagi and Pagong—by making the latter more likeable, the former became less so. Later, when the affair fell apart with the kitten remark and

Greg's ousting, it likely caused more displeasure for fans. Certainly, too, "casting" Colleen as romantic lead solidified her eventual heroine status.

Third, the illusion of sex and romance is also an illusion of the most powerful kind of alliance. Perhaps producers hoped audiences would expect Pagong to band together around Greg and Colleen—or even feel threatened by them. For as we saw most explicitly in the romance that blossomed between the victorious Amber and Boston Rob on *Survivor: All-Stars*, even a dyad has power, with the ability to string along others in order to get themselves to the final two. After all, in our culture, everyone loves a love story.

Nothing from Something: Ethan and "Mama" Kim

Speaking of the final two, this brings us to a second example of repression mediated through editing. In this instance, producers apparently attempted to make nothing out of something, rather than something from nothing. We'll focus here on events during *Africa*, the third season of the show, but must first review the ending of the second season, *Australian Outback*. As the author wrote in a *PopPolitics.com* article, editors hid the fact that contestants Tina and Colby were merely stringing along chef Keith to get to the end:

> [Burnett and his team] completely edited out the close relationship that Tina, the eventual winner, and Colby, the runner-up, built throughout the show. Viewers were led to believe Tina and Keith were the tight twosome, with Colby as the third wheel. Tina pulled together a last-minute strategy to save Keith from the jaws of Jerri early in the show, and, several episodes later, she dropped out of an immunity challenge to keep Keith from being threatened at the next Tribal Council. Late in the game, she and Keith saved the tribe's food supply during a flood. Meanwhile, Colby and Tina were almost never shown interacting one-on-one.

> Burnett did this, of course, to make it all the more shocking when Colby chose Tina over the disliked Keith for the final two—a decision that clearly cost him the million. After Colby voted off Keith, Tina's true feelings were made plain: She didn't think Keith deserved to win, and she and Colby had only dragged him along to the endgame to help them dispose of the other tribe members. Furthermore, we learned only in post-game interviews that Tina and Colby had had the tightest bond all along. Burnett had "cheated" by keeping this crucial information from us, and as a result posters on *Survivor* message boards dubbed Tina and Colby the "invisible pair" and immediately began wondering if a similar editing trick would occur in *Survivor: Africa*. (Wright, 18 Dec. 2001)

**Figure 5.1: Final ten contestants in *Survivor: Africa*,
members of Moto Maji tribe**

Began in Boran tribe, then sent to Samburu	Began in Boran, remained there	Began in Samburu, then sent to Boran	Began in Samburu, remained there
Lex* Tom* Kelly	Ethan* Kim J.* Clarence	Frank Teresa	Kim P. Brandon

* Members of the Boran alliance (Ethan, Lex, and Tom appeared to be the core members).
Clarence and Kelly were soon voted out, leaving eight people, two from each subgroup as listed above. Ethan was the eventual winner.
Note: See Appendix B for contestant details.

In fact, it did, to some degree. The editors in *Africa* obscured a close friendship between the eventual final two players, Ethan and Kim J., also known as "Mama" Kim. However, this time occasional pieces of evidence suggesting he was hiding something kept popping up, making this a prime example of textual repression.

Like the later *Survivor: Marquesas*, producers threw in a swap to keep contestants, and audience members, on their toes. In Episode 5 (CBS, 8 Nov. 2001), with six people left in both the Boran and Samburu tribes, the contestants receive "tree mail" instructing them to send three of their own on a "quest." This sounds like a standard invite to a challenge, but to everyone's shock, the six people sent off are forced to switch tribes. Hence, Boran now consists of three original members and three newcomers; Samburu has the same makeup. This severs a number of relationships, at least temporarily. After eight days of living like this, the tribes merge into one (now with ten players remaining). Soon two more are dispatched, leaving eight. As it happens, by now one person from each subgroup (Boran/Boran, Boran/Samburu, Samburu/Boran, and Samburu/Samburu) has been voted out since the switch, leaving two people from each of the four (see Figure 5.1).

This means that Tom and Lex have been the only constant presence in each other's lives the past twenty-some days—that is, both started in Boran, then were switched together into Samburu. The same goes for the pairs of Kim P. and Brandon, as well as Teresa and Frank. As one might expect, each pair has become good friends, and we are shown this. Tom and Lex, for instance, swear on their childrens' names to stick together until the end. Frank and Teresa are also clearly tight, having been part of the "older people's" alliance in Samburu after the tribe fractured along generational lines. Frank says at one point that he trusts Teresa more than anyone else in the game. Kim P. and Brandon, similarly, are always together, and were part of the "Mallrats" alliance in that split Samburu tribe (Wright, 18 Dec. 2001).

Oddly, the same does not go for Mama Kim and Ethan, the other pair that has been together the entire game. Unlike the other duos, they are not "*explicitly* portrayed as being close. We don't see them talk all that much, and we don't hear them gush over each other. In the clips selected for TV viewing, Ethan talks more about his friendship with Lex, whom he was separated from for eight days when Lex was swapped away" (Wright, 18 Dec. 2001). Meanwhile, Mama Kim, the eldest tribe member, is blandly portrayed as tribal mother, doing much cooking. This absence of information is tricky enough, however, that most viewers would likely not even notice.

Yet now and then, hints of Mama Kim and Ethan's close friendship bubble to the surface, then are denied, either by way of another contestant's dialogue or by simply omitting any other interactions, making those hints seem out of place and therefore more likely to be ignored by the audience. For instance, in Web-only, extra-textual "*Survivor* Insider" footage for Episode 3, Mama Kim singles out the Massachusetts native as her favorite, saying, "I relate to Kelly and Lex, but I'm really crazy about Ethan" (no longer available online). Later, in aired footage, Ethan soothes Kim's fears of being voted out after she loses a challenge for her team by repeatedly falling down (CBS, 1 Nov. 2001). He appears to truly care for her, in a mother-and-son kind of way, but again, oddly, little or nothing has gone on elsewhere in the *Africa* text to support such a contention. Then, in Episode 9 (CBS, 13 Dec. 2001), we watch as Kim rubs lotion on Ethan's back. When the two randomly are paired up for an obstacle course reward challenge in that same episode, Ethan boosts Kim over a wall, and they cross the finish line holding hands, grinning. When a desperate Teresa later suggests voting off Ethan because he is too nice, Kim tells us she is "shocked and pissed" (Wright, 18 Dec. 2001).

Yet that is all we see, and it doesn't add up. Ethan usually just interacts with Lex and Tom, or in a larger group that includes Kim. Kim talks much with the other women in the tribe. Ethan and Kim should be closer to each other than anyone else in the game, having spent so much time together, but only these occasional, seemingly out-of-place, repetitious visual elements hint at anything. Then we hear nothing more to confirm our suspicion—and by not letting us do so, Burnett and his team are denying them. *Ethan's and Kim's relationship isn't important, or we'd show more of it,* they are essentially saying. We also hear distracting dialogue from Lex, who at one point goes on about how close *he* and Kim are and how close Ethan is . . . to Tom, the fourth member of their alliance. Doth Burnett protest too much?

All this Jamesonian repetition and denial is building toward the endgame, when only Kim, Ethan, and Lex remain. Kim surprisingly wins the final immunity challenge, a test of endurance in the hot sunlight, and must choose whether to take Lex or Ethan to the final two. Here the entire reason for Burnett's charade becomes clear: He wants us to think she will pick Lex over Ethan—and since he has suppressed the soccer player's relationship with Kim, that is just what some of us expect. We think so even more since Ethan has been portrayed as a kindly soul all along, while the manipulative

Lex has been edited into a villain.[3] Therefore, we are stunned and delighted when Kim instead votes out Lex. As it turned out, Ethan was the one who held the power all along when it came to Kim, even if she and Lex were friends as well. In this way, we are not talking about a secret two-way alliance so much as a bond, one that, because of the way the game played out— Kim winning final immunity and thus *power*—led directly to the editors' need to repress it in order to bring the audience surprise and pleasure. Yet to completely omit it would only confuse viewers—which the Tina/Colby/ Keith revelation did to some degree—and so from a Jamesonian viewpoint, structurally the idea of their friendship must be occasionally brought up and then disregarded. Theirs is the most important relationship among all the sixteen castaways, and therefore it must be tucked away, out of sight.

Once Lex is voted out, however, Burnett lets the cat out of the bag. We see Ethan and Kim cuddle as Lex's torch goes out, hold hands as they leave Tribal Council, and—the clincher—kiss the next morning by the steel water tank. They then paint their initials onto it in a display of being the last two standing—the ones holding all the cards—in *Africa* (CBS, 10 Jan. 2002).

Something from Something?
The Strange Case of *Amazon's* Roger

The cases of Colleen and Greg and Kim and Ethan are two of the clearest examples of repression through editing on *Survivor*, but certainly many others exist. Every episode arguably contains elements of repression as contestants try to hide from one another who will depart from each Tribal Council, and producers do the same for the audience.

Something a bit backward happened, however, during the run of *The Amazon*. As we already saw in Chapter 4, this particular season was filled with unpredictability thanks to Rob's "alliance of one," but one week's installment stands out as especially intriguing from an editing standpoint.

In episode after episode of *Survivor*, a specific person is often complained about the most, then targeted for dismissal. This is almost always a red herring; Burnett likes to play with viewers' minds so they expect the unexpected. *Think Elizabeth is getting voted out? Gotcha! It's Jerri! Suspect Eliza is about to be tossed? Surprise—it's Leann.* On other occasions, we see contestants struggle to choose between two obvious potential "bootees."

However, on Episode 7 of *Amazon* (CBS, 26 March 2003), Burnett and his team make it blatantly obvious that nearly everyone plans to vote out bossy, sexist Roger, a company vice president—and for once, the "telegraphed boot" isn't a red herring. It's repression via non-repression. Barely a scene goes by that viewers don't hear things such as the following:

Figure 5.2: Percentage of respondents expecting Roger to leave in Episode 7, grouped by political party

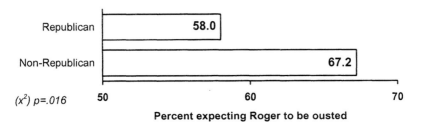

(x^2) *p=.016*

Percent expecting Roger to be ousted

- Heidi: Roger has got to go first.
- Deena: [Roger] has all these activities planned for [after Tribal Council]. Oops!
- Alex: He has no idea that he's going home tonight.
- Jenna: [Roger] thinks that he just has it in the bag.
- Rob: I'll be so happy [when he goes], and I'll just keep kissing his ass all the time so he doesn't suspect a thing.

We also see repetition and denial from Roger himself, who, as the merge occurs, is supposedly in an all-male majority alliance that plans to systematically eliminate the women. "It's just a little too easy, us six guys against the four girls," he tells ally Dave. "Something's probably gonna happen here. I'm not that confident yet, we'll see." But then it's back to being bossy again, telling everyone what to do and how do it. Then, later, to the camera, Roger says, "It looks like everything is falling into place. . . . I'm sitting here thinking, it's too good to be true." It is, of course—Roger's sneaking suspicions, which are largely forgotten (i.e., denied) in all his bossing around and the aura of male dominance, prove to be prophetic, as he is indeed voted out at episode's end.

All this only make things more exciting for the audience, who had a negative overall attitude toward Roger—he scored an AAAI of 2.541, good only for 120th place. These dueling acts of repression and anti-repression ensnared about 35 percent of survey respondents who remembered the episode, who felt all these comments were a red herring. Approximately 65 percent, on the other hand, correctly believed Roger would indeed be dispatched at Tribal Council. The survey did not ask a similar question for any other episodes, so it is hard to say if these figures are typical.

Surprisingly, even this seemingly innocuous survey question had divergent responses among those from different backgrounds. Those belonging to

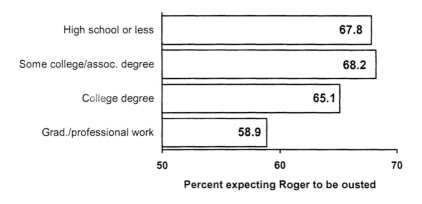

Figure 5.3: Percentage of respondents expecting Roger to leave in Episode 7, grouped by education level

demographics associated with the upper classes among respondents were *more* likely to erroneously expect Roger to be spared.

- **Political Party:** Nearly six in ten GOP respondents (who again, among survey takers, were significantly more likely to identify as upper class or upper middle class) correctly thought Roger would be voted out. However, nearly seven in ten non-Republicans thought so (see Figure 5.2). Among political independents (who, among survey takers, were significantly more likely to identify as working class or poor), 71.1 percent correctly thought Roger would be voted out. Yet just 62.7 percent of non-independents felt that way. (p=.030)

- **Job type:** 63.0 percent of white-collar respondents reported expecting executive Roger to be ousted, compared to 71.8 percent of blue-collar employees. (p=.099, approaching statistical significance)

- **Union membership:** Of those in union households, 71.1 percent expected Roger's dismissal, vs. 63.7 percent of those in non-union households. (p=.101, approaching statistical significance)

- **Education:** Generally, as level of education increased, respondents were less likely to think Roger would be voted out. Less than six in ten of those with at least some graduate or professional work incorrectly thought he would be ousted—about 10 percentage points fewer than those with less education (see Figure 5.3; approaches statistical significance).

From this intriguing data[4], it might be tempting to posit that when it comes to *Survivor*, those with only a high school diploma are somehow more perceptive than those with a doctorate. Far more likely, of course, is that those from backgrounds correlating with the upper classes—i.e., from where Roger appears to hail, and from where he symbolically operated as the Tambuqui tribe's bossiest member—viewed this episode with blinders on. That is, they saw Roger more positively than other viewers[5], and this bias bled into their expectations for the episode, much like political partisans in America who seem unable to grasp an obvious truth when it makes their party look bad. Indeed, perhaps such viewers were in denial as much as Roger was—Jameson might even expect such a thing. That said, these results demonstrate that apparently deliberate acts by editors to affect audience expectations *can* resonate differently among particular audience groups.

Overall, the three examples cited in this chapter are among many instances of repression through editing on *Survivor*, but they show the two main ways it occurs—constructing a falsehood and shrouding the truth—and how doing so hides the true nature of power on the show. Further, the unusual treatment of the Roger episode demonstrates that *Survivor's* editors realize that to keep the audience on its toes, every now and then they need to violate their own formula, and when they do, they ironically may be able to create repression through a sheer lack of it.

Notes

1. Colleen noted this in several interviews following her eviction from *Survivor*.

2. As quoted in a brief interview clip that aired on CBS in September 2000 during a rebroadcast of *Survivor* opposite the Sydney Olympics.

3. Burnett used imagery and other tactics, in fact, to help make the finish a battle between "good" Ethan and "evil" Lex. The 2005 survey found Ethan to be a "major hero" to respondents, Lex a "mild villain," and Kim somewhere in between.

4. As for the class question itself, 67.6 percent of working-class respondents believed Roger would be voted out, versus 61.0 percent of upper-class respondents. However, for this cross-tabulation, p=.301, so it is not significant.

5. Regression analysis of Roger's raw AAI results, in fact, found a very strong relationship between status as a Republican and positive feelings toward Roger.

Chapter 6

"These Three Girls Have All Been Riding Coattails"

Survivor's *Gender Wars*

AS DISCUSSED IN CHAPTER 2, JAMESON HAS ADMITTED that his "single great collective story" of historical class struggles is "a good deal more complicated" than he has at times suggested (Hestetun 1993, 181). The word "class," he says, may be an instance of "terminological slippage . . . leaving room for a redefinition of the term on a different historical basis when we come to modern society" (Hestetun 1993, 181, quoting Jameson). Even in the text of *The Political Unconscious* itself, he appears to hint at this briefly, noting that cultural hegemony relates to "marginalized or oppositional cultures in our own time [including] the oppositional voices of black or ethnic cultures, women's and gay literature, 'naïve' or marginalized folk art, and the like" (Hestetun 1993, 181; Jameson 1981, 86). On a related note, critical theorist Douglas Kellner has argued that "media culture provides social allegories which articulate class and *social group* fears, yearnings, and hopes. Decoding these social allegories thus provides a diagnostic critique with insight into the situation of individuals within various social classes *and groups*" (1995, 125; emphasis the author's).

What of it, then? Surely notions of class are implicit in the relations among other socially stratified groups of people: Men historically have dominated women; Caucasians have variously ruled over, discriminated against or enslaved members of other races; homosexuals have oppressed themselves and been discriminated against; and so on. In many of these cases, circumstances have improved via civil rights movements, but historically most of these sets of relations can be sorted into cases of dominant vs. dominated. This chapter and the following two will examine how *Survivor* can be read not just as an outright class-based narrative, but at times also as a related narrative regarding gender, age, or race—that in the end, still boils down to haves and have-nots.

Gender and Television

Countless studies have found that many gender differences are socially constructed rather than biological in nature, especially the activities deemed appropriate for one gender but not the other. Certain things, such as hunting, dairy operations, or weaving, are traditionally performed by men in some societies but women in others (Vander Zanden 1996, 225-26). Sex expectations and norms change over time within the same society as well—in Western nations, the "dashing cavalier [once] wore long curls and perfume," not something now associated with masculinity (225). Learning these roles is a crucial part of socialization—and children at an early age have demonstrated they know them. One study, for instance, found school-age children thought that most girls were gentle, obedient, quiet, weak, and followers; meanwhile, boys were viewed as rough, troublemakers, loud, strong, and leaders (Williams 1981, 45). Studies have found that television plays a large part in teaching these traits (Powell and Abels 2003, 14). As Nancy Signorielli writes with Aaron Bacue, "The young often turn to television, intentionally and unintentionally, to learn about the world in which they live" (1999, 542).

Ideas about gender-appropriate behaviors and television extend not just to TV programs themselves, but to discourses *about* TV. For instance, Lynn Spigel found that one early advertisement for television pictured a boy learning to play the saxophone, and a girl imitating a ballerina, via the television. Another, promoting having more than one television in the home, depicted a man watching a football game on a large living-room TV while his wife and daughter watch a cooking show on a small kitchen set (Spigel 1992, 51, 70).

Socialization via television now begins as early as age 1, with shows such as *Teletubbies* and *Barney and Friends* sending gendered messages, especially for females (Powell and Abels 2003, 21). This demonstrates how "it is in cultural fora like television that specific representations or significations of gender get generated day in and day out and circulated as tacit and not so tacit to millions of viewers the world over" (D'Acci 2002, 92).

These representations may include stereotypes, often related to gender. Stereotypes are generalizations about all members of a group that fail to take into account individual differences within that group (Schaefer 1996). For instance, the stereotype of "Southerners are prejudiced rednecks" may describe a smattering of Southerners, but certainly not all of them. But such a belief can cause a person to, upon meeting Southerners, jump to conclusions about them. Stereotypes can be applied to practically any groups—the Irish, Christians, librarians, liberals—but this project is most concerned with often-subordinated groups bearing obvious physical traits that leave them generally unable to shroud their status, namely racial minorities, women, and the aged. In these cases, especially, stereotypes pose a danger:

It has been typical for the media to either utilize stereotypes disparaging females and minorities and . . . perpetuate myths concerning their existence or . . . exclude them, implying that members of these groups occupy no significant social space. These representations are generally considered important due to the role they play in consumers' social construction of reality. More specifically, the media's practice of exclusion and stereotyping promotes a common sense view of reality that is oppressive and exploitative of groups with less power in society. (Eschholz et al. 2002, 300)

Indeed, regarding invisibility, television has been criticized heavily for giving more weight to men's roles over the years, although evidence suggests that gender gap may be shrinking somewhat (Elasmar et al. 1999, 20-33; Signorielli and Bacau 1999, 527-44). "Women are least likely to be cast in action-adventure programs and most likely to be cast in dramas and situation comedies. This sends a clear message [that] women are not as important as men, or are only important when viewed in the narrow confines" of the sitcom (Signorielli and Bacau 1999, 541).

Each season of *Survivor* thus far has featured equal numbers of men and women, but as noted in Chapter 1, if the program has been repeatedly guilty of one thing, it is negative stereotyping based on race, gender, age, sexuality, region (e.g., "rednecks"), military background, and other such factors.

In producers' defense, stereotypes are likely used on *Survivor* in part for simplicity's sake. Thanks to time constraints, many episodes lack "character development," instead featuring selective footage that constructs a contestant's personality based on existing perceptions of whatever subgroup he or she falls into. Never was this more apparent than in the opening episode of *Survivor: The Amazon* (spring 2003), when for the first time, contestants were divided into tribes of men and women. What resulted was a clinic in stereotyped representation that involved Jamesonian repression as well. As such, this chapter will first analyze this particular episode, using a close reading—as well as a content analysis of the episode performed by eight coders, four male and four female. The chapter will then note several other instances of gender-related suppression and repression by both players and editors on *Survivor*, primarily involving the seventh season, *Pearl Islands*.

Gossipy Girls and Sex-Crazed Boys: Stereotypes in the *Amazon*

When CBS announced that *Survivor's* sixth season would begin with tribes divided by gender, some saw the move as an ingenious twist—and others as another contrived gimmick. Whatever the case, it garnered a new burst of publicity for the show, with the move landing as the lead story in *USA Today's* Life section the day of the announcement (Levin 2003, 1D). The media (and CBS) framed the decision as risky given the show's reliance on sexual tension (Petrozzello 2003, 75). "It's a huge risk," Mark Burnett told the *Cleveland Plain-Dealer*. "But you have to be brave and just do it, and there's no way to know what the outcome would be. . . . Somehow it just always ends up better than we hoped" (Dawidziak 2003, E1).

In this case, Burnett and his team had given themselves a perfect opportunity to play up socially constructed differences between men and women, both for humor's sake and to get audience members to choose sides. And they took full advantage of it, portraying in Episode 1 the men as hard-working, cocky, and sex-starved, and the women as gossipy mavens who appeared to have never before spent one day outdoors. All this, however, was a buildup to the surprising, climactic first immunity challenge, an obstacle course where the "hapless" women found a way to outrace the "macho" men—thus fulfilling a modified bourgeoisie nightmare.

First Impressions

As *Amazon* opens, we see host Probst dividing the sixteen players into tribes as they sit on the deck of a tour boat in the river. (For those who did not see *Amazon*, there is no need to keep straight every contestant mentioned herein. Simply keep in mind the five key contestants described in Table 6.1, four of whom were already discussed in Chapters 4 and 5.) As Probst announces the name of each person—who then climbs down into a smaller rowboat marked with his or her tribe's color—it becomes clear that something unusual is happening. Heidi—a skinny blonde in her early 20s depicted as somewhat flighty[1]—is the first woman to speak to the camera: "When Jeff called the fifth girl [for the same tribe], I knew it instantly: This is an all-women tribe." (CBS, 13 Feb. 2003) Or as Deena, who later becomes her tribe's symbolic male, says next: "We can let our hair down. We can pee in front of each other." Such are our first impressions of the ladies of the *Amazon*.

Setting the tone for the men, meanwhile, is corporate vice president Roger. "The [women] don't have the strength," he says. "It's pathetic." Muscular Daniel next announces that the men will never even visit Tribal Council.

These sets of comments frame the rest of the episode, with the men shown as buff, gruff, and efficient, while many of the disorganized women worry more about washing their clothes. This is quickly reinforced when the women are unable to untie their rowboat from the larger tour boat. The men wind up reaching their camp first as a result ("That was easy!" one shouts as they arrive), and the editors point out via a screen caption that the women do not do so until "Later that day."

Table 6.1. Key contestants in Episode 1 of *Survivor: The Amazon*

Name	Age	Occupation	Notes
Jenna	21	Swimsuit model	Skittish, skinny, smart; uses "feminine wiles"
Deena	35	Deputy D.A.	Symbolic male
Roger	56	Company V.P.	Bossy "alpha male"
Rob	24	IT projects coord.	Horny, game-savvy geek; "stand-up comic"
Ryan	23	Model	Symbolic female

See Appendix B for more contestant details.

Fire and Fish

A ritual of any opening *Survivor* episode is the attempt at making fire. The *Amazon* tribes receive flint and steel to assist in this matter—and, fulfilling stereotypes, the men succeed almost immediately after pouring lantern kerosene on their kindling. "I wonder if the chicks have built a fire yet?" asks Matt.

The editors conveniently cut to the women's camp to show viewers that they in fact have not. The confused-looking ladies struggle with their flint and steel, getting a tiny flame going several times only to have it die away. Smoke is everywhere, with the women helplessly blowing at the wood.

Another *Survivor* staple is finding food—and when the women go fishing in their rowboat, things go no better. Swimsuit model and eventual winner Jenna catches only a leaf on her tangled line, while two others have a bit more luck, landing the Amazonian equivalent of a minnow. The women chow down on about a half-teaspoon each. The men apparently catch no fish at all—but crucially, we are not shown them trying and failing. Rob, ever the comedian, muses on how awful things must be for the ladies.

> Rob (to camera): [T]he women have got to be having a very difficult time. Especially [because] they're not gonna catch any fish. We have expert fishermen out there and we haven't caught anything yet. But I don't think [they knew] they'd be doing this on estrogen alone . . . in the camp of the vagina monologues.

The editors cut to the women's camp, where Deena confesses it took her team as many as six hours to start a fire. This, along with repetitive imagery and dialogue, couples with the smooth sailing on the men's side to reinforce gender stereotypes.

Creepy Crawlers

If the footage of fires and fishing didn't do enough to paint the women as clueless campers, other scenes certainly do the job. Eye-rollingly stereotypical is a sequence in which the women become frightened by a tarantula. Jenna introduces things for viewers as Day 2 dawns, explaining that the tribe is doing poorly, having spent the night on the earth itself. "We had bugs crawling all around us . . . crawling down your pants, or crawling in your hair." As if on cue, suddenly a tarantula is spotted near the food supply. "Oh my goodness!" and "I want it dead!" and "It probably climbed over all of us [in the night]!" various women shout. The tarantula soon climbs into the food container. Finally, the women crush the tarantula under a lid and throw it in the fire.

Later in the episode, soon after one older woman complains that her tribemates are dehydrated because it takes so long to boil water, we learn that the younger members are using the water not for drinking, but for *laundry*. As Jenna relates:

> Jenna: The flies are swarming us because we stink. So, we've boiled our buffs, we boiled underwear that wasn't clean. . . . I think it's a priority, because things can live on you, especially in *that* area, because it's dark.

Jenna then hangs the buffs and underwear to dry. All this after just 24 hours in the wilderness. The fact that this scene—along with the tarantula and the earlier struggle over the fire—is included from the 72 hours of footage available makes one wonder if *Survivor's* entire editing team consists of sexist men (although a more likely, Jamesonian rationale is clear by episode's end). At some point did a man squirm over a bug, or complain at having insects crawl over him in the night? Quite possibly, but as that doesn't fit the framework for which the editors are gunning, even if it did happen viewers certainly would not have been shown it.

I Dream of Jenna

While the ladies screech about bugs and do laundry—as well as gossip about the men—the other tribe is busy playing the role of horny schoolboys. This would come as no surprise to the women. "What are the boys talking about?" one posits early on. "How they get off!" someone replies, laughing. They picture the men as mad that young Heidi is not on their team since that means they cannot look at her breasts all day. Later, Jenna tells Heidi that to distract the men at challenges, she should "show them your boobs." All

these suspicions relate to an earlier assertion by Jenna that "womanly powers" are best used on men to "manipulate them better."

As far as viewers are shown, the women are dead on in their assessment:
"A lot of the talk around camp is centered around the girls' tribe," Rob tells
us, particularly Jenna, Heidi, and Shawna. In a surreal bit of editing, we then
are shown those three bathing together wearing only bikinis (this is actually
footage from a later episode), with the edges of the frame blurred away to
make it fantasy-like. This is an overt example of what sociologists call the
"male gaze," or the use of women in cultural creations as the objects of
men's sexual fantasies (Lorber 1994, 100). "Boys from 15 on, that's all they
think about," Roger tells us, grinning.

We also are shown an extended sequence where the younger men use
Rob's luxury item, a Magic Eight Ball, to tell them whether they will be
"hooking up" with any of the women. "I asked the Magic Eight Ball if I
would hook up with Heidi," says Daniel, grinning as he shows Rob that its
reply was "Definitely." This seems like something one would see with mid-
dle-school boys, not twenty-something men. "[Heidi] is so hot," says the
ever-horny Rob, "she could put Viagra out of business."

Even at Tribal Council, after the men lose the first immunity challenge,
they at Probst's prompting debate which woman is the most attractive. (If
one of the men on the team happens to be homosexual, surely this must be
an uncomfortable topic, filled with pressure to conform to gender expectations by talking up the wonders of cleavage.) "The quarterback doesn't
screw the cheerleaders at halftime," Dave warns soon after explaining how
sexy Shawna is. "We're here to play the game."

Host Probst chides them, saying that getting distracted by sex talk could
be their doom; however, in subsequent episodes the men are shown continuing to talk about the attractiveness of Jenna, Heidi, and Shawna, with little
reciprocation. This buttresses stereotypes that men think often of sex . . . and
think with something other than their brains.

Sharpening the Phallus

As discussed earlier in detail, the Jamesonian concept of the political
unconscious springs in part from the work of Sigmund Freud. Famously, the
basis of Freud's psychoanalytical theory is the Oedipus Complex, "in which
the young boy represses his emotional attachment to his mother and identifies with his more powerful father because he is afraid that otherwise, like
her, he will lose his penis . . . the symbol of masculine difference" (Lorber
1994, 100). In cultural products, phallic imagery is abundant—in Freud's
view, thanks to men producing the bulk of such products. "Penises are usu-

ally visualized as 'hard, tough, weapon-like,' making their owners potent, powerful, and authoritative. 'It is not [long objects such as] flowers that most commonly symbolize male genitals, but swords, knives, fists, guns' " (Lorber 1994, 98-99, quoting Dyer 1985, 30-31). Think of Dirty Harry's unnecessarily gigantic Smith & Wesson revolver—or in an aforementioned subversion, Buffy the vampire slayer's stake. The book *The DaVinci Code* prominently used notions of historic male cultural dominance and phallic symbolism. Alternately, the *Austin Powers* and *Naked Gun* film series have sent up such conventions through parodies, including a sex scene interlaced with footage of a rocket launching, a train rushing into a tunnel, and so on.

As it happens, a recurring visual element in this *Amazon* episode is the use and display of machetes, which, in a *Survivor* first, every contestant is issued along with a holster/belt. This ostensibly was done to help contestants traverse the jungle, but from a Freudian and semiotic perspective, the role these phallic symbols play is all too appropriate. Given the road the editors are taking us down—men as macho warriors, women as incompetent campers—it comes as no surprise when we are shown the men delighting over their blades, and the women struggling with how to effectively use them.

As soon as the men find the machetes and holster belts at their camp, Rob makes a comment—"This is so cool! My parents would never let me have a machete!"—that is amusing on both the surface and symbolically, given that he is repeatedly portrayed as sexually frustrated. We see a one-minute montage of the men busily chopping down trees for their shelter and fire—quite successfully, in fact, with Rob later remarking as he hacks away with his two-foot blade that he should have been a lumberjack, which is about as symbolically masculine and virile an occupation there is. Just before heading to the immunity challenge, we see the men stand in a circle, touch all their swords together, then snap them upward like musketeers, shouting their tribe name.

Contrast this display of power in wielding phallic weaponry with the women's situation. We are shown Deena struggling to split a twisted vine with her machete; Joanna cries "timber" only to have the narrow tree she had chopped down get stuck in the branches of another; Heidi's blade becomes lodged in a half-chopped tree, as does Jenna's—perhaps she is simply better at doing laundry, we are made to think.

Curiously, we have exceptions on each tribe to these actions. On the men's side, during the montage that shows the men felling trees, six of them are clearly recognizable as chopping down at least medium-size trees, with a seventh, Matthew, shown shimmying up a very tall tree. The exception? Young Ryan is shown hacking away at a tree—then coming away with only a small branch, while behind him, Dave hefts a large log. Certainly, Ryan at some point chopped down a decent-size tree, and certainly the others gathered leaner branches for kindling. But this is not what Mark Burnett and his team show us. In this way, Ryan is portrayed as the tribe's least "manly" man, or even its symbolic female—something reinforced by the fact that the screen labels him as a "model," similar to "swimsuit model" Jenna. Any schoolyard kid will tell you that being less than macho means being labeled a "sissy," a "girly boy" outcast, however discriminatory and stereotyped that may be—and indeed this begins the setup to Ryan's ouster at episode's end, when his tribe rejects him, implicitly over him not being man enough.

In fact, soon we see bossy, vaguely misogynistic Roger commenting that Ryan and his pal Daniel aren't up to snuff. "They're just useless," he tells us. "They're digging their own graves." The camera confirms Roger's point as we see the pair trying in vain to merely pull vines from a tree. Later, at the challenge, Ryan and Dan are to blame for blowing the men's lead on a balance beam. In fact, both are reduced to lying on the cylindrical beam, wrapping their bodies around it, then yanking themselves along it in order to make it to the end. Their inability to quickly conquer yet another phallic object is, in the end, what dooms the men's team—and therefore Ryan.

Conversely, Deena over the course of the episode becomes the symbolic male of the women's tribe. She is the sole woman in Episode 1 shown taking a leadership role—something that connotes masculinity in our society, for better or worse—bossing others around a bit, sending half of her tribe on Day 1 to build a fire, the other half a shelter. "We're having a difficult time getting our tasks in order," she tells the camera the following day, clearly frustrated. Someone says, "'I'm kind of feeling like I need to wash my buff now,' so we wash the buffs. I'm thinking shelter."

Fascinatingly, Deena's mildly masculine, gruff demeanor is accentuated by the fact that she is the only woman in Episode 1 who is semiotically linked in a positive way to the machete symbol prior to the immunity challenge. When the tarantula "attacks," it is Deena who announces, "Give me the machete!" While Jenna and Heidi do their "laundry," we are shown Deena calmly sharpening her blade.

Finally, it is most intriguing that of all the women, Deena is shown doubting her team's chances against the men. She tells the camera that although the women may win a few challenges, she expects the men to "dominate" overall. This confirms audience expectations for the first immunity challenge—and supports Deena's representation as symbolic male. Even some members of the media noticed her masculinization at the time, with one bluntly calling her "the textbook dyke" (Siri on Survivor, 2004).

However, Deena is merely the exception to the rule. Indeed, when the two tribes show up for their immunity challenge, the men bring along their machetes, brandishing them with scabbards and all—but the women do not. Here, the tribes have helped out the editors with their respective decisions,

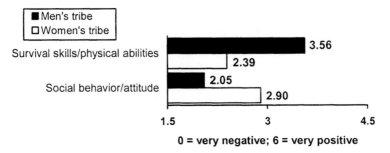

**Figure 6.1: Coded valence of tribes' depictions
in *Amazon* Episode 1, divided by depiction type**

0 = very negative; 6 = very positive

but it nonetheless reinforces the stereotypical notion of men as powerful, women as powerless. This repetitive imagery is also a symbolic resolution of a real contradiction in Jamesonian terms—the machetes have no real meaning, but the editors use them symbolically to play up the men's perceived power, which contradicts *Survivor's* (and society's) notions of everyone starting out equal. Of course, at the immunity challenge, all this is turned on its head, both in terms of the plot and symbolically. After the ladies win immunity, we finally see Heidi using her machete properly. And at Tribal Council, it is not a woman but a man—albeit the most "feminine" of the men—who sees his fiery, phallic torch extinguished.

The Social Construction of Reality (Television)

Results of the May 2005 content analysis performed by the eight coders—about half of whom had viewed the episode when it first aired in January 2003, but had trouble recalling its details before the experiment—generally found the men and women to indeed be portrayed stereotypically in Episode 1.[2] For instance, the eight respondents consistently labeled the women's tribe much more negatively than the men's in terms of physical abilities and survival and outdoors skills—especially in scenes preceding the immunity challenge. For these scenes, the men scored an average of 4.7 on a six-point scale, with 6.0 being a very positive depiction and 0.0 being very negative. The women scored only a 1.7, a statistically significant difference.[3] This margin narrowed significantly following the immunity challenge (see Figure 6.1). Coders also viewed both tribes negatively from a social attitude standpoint, with the women seen as whiny and the men as rude. The women's average score again improved after the immunity challenge, while the men's

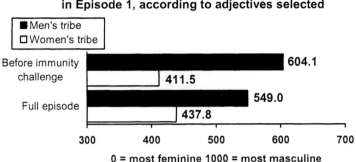

Figure 6.2: Codings of tribes' gendered depictions
in Episode 1, according to adjectives selected

dropped, leaving the women with an advantage overall in this category, though not a statistically significant one.[4]

Another part of the content analysis involved picking adjectives from a list of 36 that best described the tribe being considered. Each adjective had a value assigned to it on a scale of 0 to 1000, with 0 being most feminine and 1000 being most masculine, though coders were not informed of this.[5] Just before the immunity challenge, the adjectives selected by the coders yielded a mean of 411.5 for the women as depicted thus far, and 604.1 for the men, a statistically significant difference[6] that suggests the episode succeeded in portraying each tribe stereotypically (see Figure 6.2). At the end of the episode, the adjective test was again run, and the scores converged somewhat—the women's rating became 26 points less feminine, and the men's rating became 55 points less masculine.[7] Note that as the women became "more masculine," their corresponding valence (noted in Figure 6.1) became more positive; as the men became "more feminine," their corresponding valence became more negative. This would appear to reflect stereotypical gender hierarchies—for instance, women who take on professional work formerly the realm of men are often seen more positively in society, while men who become stay-at-home dads, the opposite of a "housewife," may be ridiculed.

Amazonian Repression

For the entire first episode of *Survivor: The Amazon*, executive producer Burnett and his team of editors set up the men's team as overtly masculine, powerful, and competent—and the women as clueless in the wilderness and more worried about spiders and dirty clothing than actual survival. To accomplish this, the editors relied on selective editing that reinforced existing, naturalized gender stereotypes via dialogue, imagery, and semiotics. At some point, aside from Deena's competence and Ryan's lack thereof, did one of the men commit a survival-related error, or did one of the women make like an Eagle Scout? We don't know, and the editors aren't about to show us, because they have expectations to build—expectations that, come the immunity challenge, the macho men will crush the clueless women.

Here again the Jamesonian unconscious rears its head. In this case, the repeated element is the men worrying that the women may beat them at challenges, despite their near-constant cockiness. Each male who is a focus of this episode is shown doing so aloud at least once. Rob and eventual "bootee" Ryan speak up early in the episode, separately:

> Ryan: Our butts are on the line right now. If we lose to the girls, it's gonna be rough . . .

> Rob (later): We've got everything riding on this. We look like the biggest asses ever if we go home.

Yet these comments are soon lost in the denial that is the continued boasting, sex talk, and phallic/dominance imagery, along with the confusion in the ladies' camp, detailed above. Lines such as Dave's "We're the favorites. . . . [W]e're just so much more adept" and Rob's "I [picture the women] panicking, trying to build a cell phone so they can call their boyfriends to come over to build their shelter" become the rule, not the exception.

However, just before the immunity challenge, Roger, essentially the men's leader, has the following to say to the camera: "We are confident we are gonna get through the first challenge. . . . If we lose to these women, we are gonna get ragged on big time."

Roger's note of fear, however, is immediately denied verbally as we cut to Deena's comment that she feels the men will dominate the challenges—as well as symbolically, when the men show up at the challenge with their machetes unsheathed. So, as we see, the rampant stereotyping has served a purpose after all, and a Jamesonian one at that—by pulling the men up, and pushing the women down, it has helped perpetuate notions of men as dominant and women as dominated that have permeated much of human history. In other words, this is an alternate form of bourgeoisie vs. proletariat, with the men in the former role and the women in the latter, and the men nervous that their worst nightmare—the women besting them—could come true.

It appears that this setup—build up the men as invincible, repeatedly hint at their losing then deny it, and finally shock the audience with a female

Figure 6.3: Percent of respondents pleased by Jabaru winning first *Amazon* challenge, grouped by gender

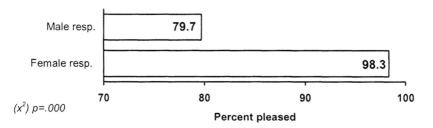

(x²) p=.000

victory—was specifically designed to create audience pleasure with the episode's outcome. The result of the 2005 fan survey supports this notion. An overwhelming majority of 90.4 percent recalled that they were pleased when Jabaru toppled Tambaqui in the first immunity challenge. Not surprisingly, a significant gender difference was also found, with female respondents more pleased than men by a 19-point margin (see Figure 6.3).

Were these viewers pleased as a result of the women receiving a more positive edit during the course of the episode? Not really, considering their much-reinforced outdoor ineptitude. More likely is that their defeat of the cocky men surprised, and overall delighted, audience members. This is all the more likely considering that based on the entire *Amazon* season, those originally from the Jabaru (women's) tribe had a far lower mean AAAI than Tambuqui, by a margin of 2.797 to 3.168—this was the second-lowest mean score among all 18 original tribes, and the lowest mean AAAI for a single season's female cast members, although not a statistically significant difference. Paradoxically, then, the women of Jabaru were not as well liked by these respondents (53 percent of whom were themselves female) even though these same respondents were overwhelmingly happy that the tribe won the first immunity challenge.[8] Fascinatingly, as will be discussed in more detail at the close of this chapter, female respondents tended to rate male contestants more highly, while male respondents rated up female contestants—something that cannot be explained merely by, say, male respondents finding Jenna or Heidi physically attractive.

A *Pearl Islands* Mutiny

The Amazonian season of *Survivor* was by no means the only one to feature gender-related dynamics. In the first season, *Borneo*, the women of the Pagong tribe banded together to vote out the athletic Joel before the merge after he and Gervase made what were seen as prejudiced comments; in the fifth season, *Thailand*, the last two women remaining, Helen and Jan, were hoodwinked by the final two men, Brian and Clay, into not banding together. As a result, Brian and Clay succeeded in ousting the two females. More recently, the ninth season, *Vanuatu*, again divvied the players by gender to start the game—and even featured a native ritual in the premiere episode that accentuated the women's symbolically inferior status. Later in the game, the women formed a solid bloc for several episodes, voting out all the men but one, Chris—who then managed to worm his way into the female alliance and ultimately emerged victorious.

However, most of the remainder of this chapter will focus on the penultimate episode of Pearl Islands, the series' pirate-themed seventh season (fall 2003), which has widely been viewed as one of Survivor's most successful outings. It had an ingenious beginning, in which the contestants were tossed overboard with only the clothes on their backs, rather than with the standard backpack containing a few days of clothing and bathing suit. It had a memorable (if eventually overexposed) hero in bearded, jolly Rupert, and an infamous villain in Jon, a.k.a. "Jonny Fairplay," who lied to his tribemates that his grandmother had died to generate empathy. And it had a controversial twist, in which two previously ousted castaways returned to the game. Those two contestants, Lillian and Burton, both survived to the final five along with Jon, setting the stage for an episode filled with repression among contestants that had at its core gender hierarchies.

As Episode 12 of *Pearl Islands* begins, the increasingly arrogant Jon and Burton—who have engineered several surprise ousters in prior episodes—are tightly aligned, and are pulling along Darrah and Lillian, with Sandra apparently on the outs. However, tired of Darrah winning challenge after challenge, Jon and Burton approach Lil about getting rid of the attractive mortician instead. The Boy Scout leader—who as a result of the opening-episode "clothes on their backs" twist has been stuck wearing her uniform for the entire game—is not pleased.

> Lil (to camera): I don't like this. What happened to our alliance of four people? First Burton promised me No. 2 spot, and now he's hem-hawing and saying that may not happen. Not only that, they talked about getting rid of Darrah before Sandra! We made a pact! So, I started thinking, if they can screw her over, they can screw me over. (CBS, 11 Dec. 2003)

Lil, who has been portrayed as emotionally exhausted and unable to strategize, suddenly has some wheels turning, realizing that Jon and Burton plan to be the final two players and leave the three remaining women in their wake. Burton then wins a reward challenge and takes Jon with him on an overnight camping trip. This is not the smartest move, since such rewards

Table 6.2. Final five players in *Survivor: Pearl Islands*

Name	Age	Occupation	Notes
Burton	31	Marketing exec.	Fourth person voted out, then returned in twist
Darrah	22	Mortician	Quiet winner of several straight immunities
Jon	29	Art consultant	Lied about grandmother's death
Lillian	51	Scout leader	Third person voted out, then returned in twist
Sandra	29	Office assistant	Somewhat sneaky eventual winner

Note: See Appendix B for additional contestant details.

cause jealousy among tribe members left out—and taking his closest in-game friend along only highlights their relationship. Burton clearly is confident enough in his faux alliance with Lil—and the women's perceived inability to execute a plan against him—to risk leaving the three ladies alone overnight. "Burton and I felt as if we could both step away from camp strategically and not overly worry," Jon explains.

Through this wall of confidence, however, doubt occasionally seeps through, providing the "repetition" element of the Jamesonian repression model. In this case, the conflict is unexpectedly framed as men vs. women—not as the result of a contrivance, as was the case in *The Amazon*, but thanks to the organic progression of the game. This frame is reinforced by the men's physical separation from the women during the reward. Furthermore, the imagery of the men enjoying a feast and riding in Burton's newly won car, while the women back at camp cook and eat a handful of mussels (as buzzards sit and watch), invokes hierarchical notions of gender.

Over dinner, Jon sounds the bourgeoisie's first faint alarm: "Are we worried about the girls strategizing against us?" (Note his use of diminutive gender marking, calling the trio "girls" rather than "women.") Burton, the season's longest-lasting alpha male, immediately denies this fear. "No," he says. "Not one of them has had a strategy yet in this game. I don't know why they'd start now." This appears to convince Jon, who mutters, "Yeah, yeah, exactly," amid Burton's comments, then tells the camera that even though the females are likely plotting an alliance back at camp, "we feel that we definitely have an intellectual advantage" over them. "These three girls have all been riding coattails the entire time they've been out here," Burton tells the camera.

This pattern repeats several times, as either Jon or Burton voices concerns that the women, who outnumber them, may be plotting against them (which in fact they are, having decided in the men's absence to ally and oust Burton). But the men's concerns are consistently denied by either themselves or one of the women.

Soon after the above conversation, Burton worries that, based on Lil's muted reaction to the dump-Darrah plan, "I don't know if I can trust anything she says from here out." He and Jon *again* change their strategy, deciding to ally with Sandra as a backup plan. Burton then supplies his own denial: "Jon and I have been running the show for the last twenty days, nearly. And those three girls? I don't think they could come up with a decent strategy if they had to."

Then, when Burton and Jon return to camp, Sandra hides under her blanket, pretending to pout, while Lil and Darrah—not all that convincingly—complain about her. Burton's suspicions again rise. He says that surely Sandra must have floated the possibility of voting him or Jon off, but the ladies deny this. "The girls seem to be putting up quite an act," he tells the camera, but "given enough time, we're going to catch them in some lies, because one, none of them are good liars, and two, none have any strategy." Note his near simultaneous raising and dismissal of his concerns. Translation: *The women may try something against us men, but we're better at this than they are, so we'll catch them at it and turn the tables.* Ignored is the fact that even if he and Jon *did* catch the women plotting, there wouldn't be much they could do about it, considering they are outnumbered.

Burton pulls aside Lil and confronts her directly, saying that he can't believe they didn't think up a "girl alliance." Lil denies this and protests: "Honey, Sandra's ready to leave. What do you want me to say? I'm tired, I'm worn out, I'm beat. . . . I just want to go home to my husband and children and dirty house and overgrown flower garden." Note the editors' decision to include Lil's reference to stereotypical gender expectations. Burton believes her—after all, she's a Boy Scout leader, and he himself is an Eagle Scout. "We'll go for Darrah," Lil reassures him. Intercut with all this is Sandra convincing Jon to trust her.

Darrah again wins immunity, and on the day of the "final five" Tribal Council, Jon worries to Burton about Lil's state of mind. "Lil looked all upset because I think she made a deal with [Sandra and Darrah] that if [Darrah] won, that you're gone," he says, prompting a "No, no, no, no," from Burton, who nonetheless worries to the camera that Darrah and Lil have become too close. "She's developed a relationship with Darrah that's making us nervous," he says, perhaps looking ahead to a potential 2-2 tie at the "final four" Tribal Council should Sandra be voted out that evening. After all, a defection by Lil and Darrah poses no threat so long as Sandra votes with Burton and Jon. "If we can get Sandra to go with us to get Lil off, I think it would be a pretty good move," he tells the camera.

Later, walking along the beach, Sandra convincingly tells Burton that Darrah is "bad for business" because she keeps winning everything. Burton bluffs, claiming Lil told him that the three women had talked about ganging

Figure 6.4: Percent of respondents pleased by Burton's second *Pearl Islands* ouster, grouped by gender

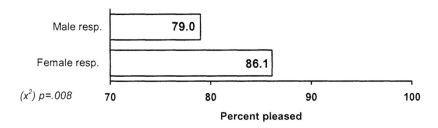

(x^2) p=.008

Percent pleased

up on the men. Sandra doesn't even blink at this, saying Lil must be making it up and that Sandra dislikes the other ladies: "I know they whisper about me. I don't care. . . . I wouldn't worry if I were you, because I'm going to write Lil's name down, big as sh*t." This lie assuages Burton's fears once more, supplying him with his denial. "The good thing about [Sandra] is that she would vote out her best friend," he tells us. "She'd go with five people she hated to get to that next level. . . . It's very cut and dry with Sandra."

After a final conversation at the campfire in which Sandra and Darrah again lie and say they will join the men in dispatching Lil, it's time to head to Tribal Council. But first, the thoroughly unlikable Jon delivers a final, over the top, misogynistic denial that again dredges up negative social constructions of women:

> Jon (to camera): All three girls are dumb. There's no "they share a brain." I don't think they even share a whole brain, or obviously they would have figured out, "Hey, we can get rid of these guys." They're foolish. The girls in this game have done nothing for women's rights or anything like that. . . . They've shown that they're nothing more than followers in this game. I think it's downright foolish that they didn't talk, but I felt and will continue to feel that I'm much smarter than they are anyway.

Over the course of this episode, then, the men—who have ruled the game strategically for several episodes running, and are thus even more so the symbolic bourgeoisie—channel the Jamesonian unconscious, momentarily worrying that the women may topple them and then dismissing those fears, over and over again. Furthermore, every time John or Burton denies their concerns, the given reason is some variation on the "girls" allegedly being unable to strategize on their own. They're inferior, Jon and Burton are saying (so far as the editors are showing), so what's there to worry about? All this reinforces both class- and gender-based hierarchies in one fell swoop—indeed, in this way the two combine to form an amalgam of stratification that lends itself well to a Jamesonian interpretation, complete with the audience pleasure that results at Tribal Council when the women vote out Burton, as Jon stares, stunned, and members of the jury celebrate. An over-whelming majority of 82.7 percent were pleased at Burton's ouster, even though Lillian herself had one of the lowest AAAIs among all contestants (Jon did as well). The male vs. female situation also resulted in statistically significant differences between male and female respondents (see Figure 6.4), although the margin was narrower than in the *Amazon*, which was much hyped as a gender war.[9]

Opposites Attract

As would be expected, the survey research conducted as part of this project found no relationship between respondents' gender and social class, but there were a number of intriguing differences among men and women's re-actions to various events. Returning now to the *Amazon*, take for instance expectations by gender of Roger's fate in Episode 7, discussed in the previ-ous chapter: Men were far more likely to correctly expect him to be voted out than were women, by a 14 percentage point margin. (p=.000)

These results are from the 2004 survey, and appeared puzzling indeed at first. Why would men be far more likely to have correctly expected Roger to be voted out (recall the "ideological blinders" argument from the previous chapter, where upper-class and white-collar respondents were less likely to expect his ouster)? Did men suspect it because they had already been stunned by the women's immunity win in Episode 1? Did female viewers find the chance of his being ousted too good to be true?

The answer appears to lie in a regression analysis of the 2005 survey's raw AAI results. When broken down by gender, a most intriguing situation became apparent: Whenever there were differences between male and fe-male respondents as to how they viewed a particular contestant, they rated contestants of the *opposite sex* higher nearly 75 percent of the time (see Ta-ble B.13, Appendix B). This is a statistically significant difference from an expected result of an even 50-50 split (p=.004 according to a Chi Square test). A SurvivorSucks message board contributor known only as Craig of-fered this astute analysis regarding these results:

> Each gender has a different bias. Men are more positive toward hot young females and are wary of dominant males, while women are more positive towards alpha males and feel threatened by young [hot women], especially those with spunk, like [Jenna from *Amazon*, Kelly from *Africa*] and Eliza. Isn't this the pattern of many marriages, where men tend to go for younger women and value beauty, while women tend to go for an older man with

wealth, power, success? The *Survivor* equivalent of such a man is Lex, Frank, Roger, Rupert, Andrew, and Sarge. No wonder [*Palau's*] Caryn couldn't bring herself to cooperate with the younger women and boot that specimen of a provider, Tom. The gap for alpha females (like Deena and Ami) and for young studs (like Colby, Ethan, [*Marquesas'* Rob], and Burton) is much less wide. (Craig 2005)

In addition to the Roger situation, where male respondents were more likely to correctly expect him to be voted out, female respondents were significantly more likely to correctly expect *Borneo's* Tagi alliance to succeed and *Marquesas'* Rotu alliance to fail. Men were significantly more likely to be pleased by Richard's victory, but were also more likely to have wanted Colleen to prevail—while women opted for Rudy. This suggests that much more than a contestant's gender is a factor in male and female viewers' expectations and desires regarding *Survivor*.

Female contestants also had a slightly more negative mean AAAI despite more women taking the survey, by a margin of 3.202 to 3.067 on a six-point scale. This was not a statistically significant difference.[10] An exercise similar to the adjective-selection used for the content analysis was also employed in the 2005 survey; as described in the introduction, respondents could choose up to three adjectives from a list of twenty-seven to describe a number of randomly determined contestants. The adjectives most often picked to describe women were weak, opinionated, and emotional; men, meanwhile, were most frequently called strong, honest, and self-confident (see Table B.20, Appendix B, for a full list). According to the gender-stereotype scale used earlier in this chapter, the mean value of all adjectives used to describe women (weighted by the number of times each was cited) was 484.8; for men, it was 522.7. Based on individual scores, the seventy-two contestants for whom adjectives were selected were also divided into seven groups ranging from "very masculine" to "very feminine." Not surprisingly, forceful, bossy women such as *Palau's* Jolanda, *Outback's* Alicia, and *Amazon's* Deena were the most "masculine" women, while Brandon from *Africa* and Coby from *Palau*, both openly gay, were the most "feminine" men.

Finally, respondents were shown photos of the thirty contestants who made the final four of their respective seasons but did not win, then asked whether each person deserved to make it that far. With 2.00 being "deserved" and 1.00 being "did not deserve," female contestants received a mean score of 1.52, while males got 1.73—again, despite more women taking the survey. When respondents were asked who the best player of the game of *Survivor* has been thus far, the top five responses (*Borneo's* Richard, *Thailand's* Brian, *Palau's* Tom, *Amazon's* Rob C. and *All-Stars'* Rob M.) were all men, although factors besides gender may have been in play

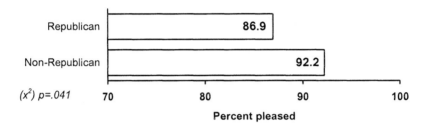

Figure 6.5: Percent of respondents pleased by Jabaru winning first challenge, grouped by political party

here. But apparently, women are portrayed slightly more negatively on *Survivor* and despite having won six times to the men's five in the first eleven seasons, also are seen as less strategic and worse at the game.

The Gender-Class Nexus

This chapter has argued that in addition to making rampant use of gender stereotypes, *Survivor* at times uses a modified political allegory in which gender takes the place of, or is mistaken for, class, fulfilling an altered bourgeoisie or proletariat nightmare. At least two statistical measures support this idea in addition to the textual analysis employed above. Because of concerns over deploying a similar survey twice to the same potential pool of respondents[11], many of the socioeconomic questions, and in particular the class question, were not included in the 2005 survey. But recall that Republican respondents were significantly more likely to identify as upper class or upper middle class, politically independent respondents were significantly more likely to identify as working class, and Democratic respondents were no more likely to identify with one class or another. As it turned out, Republican respondents were more likely to be *displeased* when the women of Jabaru—the symbolic proletariat, the underdogs—defeated the seemingly dominant men of Tambuqui, by a somewhat narrow but nonetheless statistically significant margin (see Figure 6.5). This was confirmed by a multivariate ordinary least squares regression analysis, finding that nonwhite, female, non-Republican respondents were most likely to be pleased by Jabaru winning, while white male Republicans were most likely to be displeased. Gender was, not surprisingly, the bigger predictor of a respondent's reaction, with status as a Republican the second biggest and race the third biggest. This finding suggests that even when the main surface storyline is one of *gender* differences, the historical role women have played as socially "below" men renders them as have-nots on *Survivor*.

Respondents from high-income households were also much more likely to identify as upper or upper middle class; this and political affiliation come into play when one looks at raw AAI differences for contestants from the entire pool of 150. Republican respondents tended to rate up men and rate down women; non-Republican respondents and those from low-income households exclusively rated up women and rated down men (see Tables B.17 and B.19, Appendix B). And note that respondents' gender was not associated with their political orientation or income. This evidence suggests that gender and class are, if unconsciously, linked, with respondents from backgrounds relating to the lower classes giving higher marks to those of the subordinate gender, women.

In the end, however, is it a question of gender, or of power, when class enters into the equation? That is to say, the men of Tambuqui and *Pearl Islands'* Jon and Burton were perceived to have power, and audience members were pleased when they were toppled. But on *Survivor: Vanuatu*, it was the women who gained power, and near the end game the lone remaining man banded together with three of those women to oust the "alpha female" of the tribe (the fact that this player, Ami, was a lesbian, a population subset stereotypically seen as "masculine," only complicates things from an allegorical gender hierarchy standpoint). The survey did not ask for reaction to this event, but if it had, it would have been most intriguing to see whether class-related differences were present; such a finding would provide further evidence, or contrary evidence, as to whether or not cultural notions of gender trump on-show displays of power on *Survivor*.

Notes

1. Despite having, as we find out later, the highest IQ of any contestant on her season (CBS, 11 May 2003).

2. For methodology, see Appendix C.

3. According to a T-test, p=.000. For the full episode (as depicted in Figure 6.1), the differences in coded physical abilities approached significance, p=.121.

4. p=.164 for the full episode.

5. The adjectives and values were taken from the U.S. list of gender-stereotype scores compiled by Willaims and Best, 1982, and had a mean of 498.3; their corresponding positive-negative score was 309.8 according to Anderson's 555-word list.

6. According to a T-test, p=.000.

7. The change in the men's mean score was statistically significant according to a T-test, p=.002; the change in the women's score was not, p=.285. However, the

difference of means between the men and women's post-immunity challenge scores remained statistically significant, p=.000.

8. The AAI questions came well before the Jabaru vs. Tambuqui question in the survey. The difference between the mean raw AAIs of the two tribes (2.806 and 3.212) was 0.406 to the AAAI's 0.371.

9. One other finding of note regarding an episode heavy in gender relations: Respondents sided with *Thailand's* Ted when it came to Ghandia's sexual harassment allegations against him, 64.3 percent to 35.7 percent. Ted was believed by 68.3 percent of men vs. 60.8 percent of women (p=.038).

10. According to a T-test, p=.313. The raw AAI showed a greater mean difference between men (3.278) and women (3.104) with a T-test p value of .262.

11. Especially given the priming issues explained in Appendix C.

Chapter 7

"Thrashing Around Like I'm Thirty-Five"

Paradoxes of Aging on Survivor

REPRESENTATIONS OF—AND ATTITUDES ABOUT—AGING in America reveal a fundamental ambivalence toward the process. Older people are revered for wisdom and life experience, yet derided for physical weakness and stubbornness. These conflicting images—the "Greatest Generation" on the one hand, a feeble woman shouting "I've fallen and I can't get up!" on the other—help cause the general public to simultaneously hold both ageist stereotypes and positive images of older people (Thorson 2000, 49). This is thanks to ageism, "a structured, historically formed set of myths or discourses that endorse the subordinate or marginal positions and qualities of the old" (Coupland 2004, 80), leading to specific aging stereotypes such as the despondent, the curmudgeon, the golden-ager, and the perfect grandparent (see Table 7.1). As it goes in "real life," so it goes in the contrived reality of *Survivor*: Older people are consistently on the outs socially and lack power early on in the game—but if they can advance past the first four Tribal Councils, they are much more likely than younger players to be part of the symbolic bourgeoisie—a winning alliance. Even though this is a game where physical strength and survival skills are allegedly important, statistically, *older* contestants are most likely to dominate.

"Invisible" Indeed

Clear patterns can be seen from a brief look at existing literature on televisual representations of older people, the definition of which varies from age 60 and up to age 75 and up, although on *Survivor*, people in their 40s may be considered "old" since most contestants are in their 20s and 30s. A British study published in 2002 found that when older people were interviewed about how those their age were portrayed on television, the topic of negative stereotyping in the medium was brought up repeatedly; only a very few were

**Table 7.1. Stereotypes of older persons, with corresponding
Survivor contestants age 50 and up**

Negative stereotypes	Applicable contestants	Positive stereotypes	Applicable contestants
(Severely) impaired Incompetent, feeble, incoherent, bizarre	Sonja, *Borneo* Kim J., *Africa* Jan, *Thailand* Scout, *Vanuatu* Wanda, *Palau* Jim, *Guatemala*	**Perfect grandparent** Kind, loving, grateful, trustworthy	Sonja, *Borneo* Rodger, *Outback* Kim J., *Africa* Butch, *Amazon*
Despondent Depressed, hopeless, lonely, afraid	Lillian, *Pearl Islands*	**Golden-ager** Lively, adventurous, active, capable	Maralyn, *Outback* Jake, *Thailand*
Shrew/curmudgeon Complaining, ill-tempered, prejudiced, stubborn, demanding	Rudy, *Borneo* B.B., *Borneo* Roger, *Amazon*	**John Wayne conservative** Patriotic, religious, determined, proud	Rudy, *Borneo* Paschal, *Marquesas*
Recluse Quiet, timid	Willard, *Palau*		

Note: Stereotypes based on Hummert et al. (1994) as quoted in Hummert et al. (2004, 93); Contestant lists based on adjective questions in 2005 survey and author's impressions from depictions on *Survivor*. See Appendix B for details on these contestants.

unconcerned with it (Healey and Ross 2002, 110). Another study, published in 2005, found that greater exposure to television yields more negative beliefs about aging—ironically, among the aged themselves (Donlon et al., pp. 307-319). "As television viewing replaces lost social contacts for older viewers, the likelihood increases that they will develop a reliance on television to construct their social reality," the authors write. "The problem is compounded by individuals tending to initially internalize negative age stereotypes from their culture in childhood" (2005, 308).

Additionally, older persons—especially those 65 and older—are an "invisible generation" on prime-time television (Robinson and Skill 1995, 111-119), something that doesn't help to combat negative stereotyping. Indeed, the most obvious fact about older persons on *Survivor* is that they are barely there. Of 150 people to appear on the first ten seasons of *Survivor*, just fifteen were age 50 or older.[1] Just one, *Borneo's* Rudy, was 65 or older. The mean age of all contestants is a mere 33.7 years old. *Survivor's* proportion of

Table 7.2: Age distribution of 150 contestants
appearing on *Survivor* seasons 1-7, 9-10

	Age 21-29	Age 30-39	Age 40-49	Age 50 and up
Number	69	42	24	15
Percent	46.0%	28.0%	16.0%	10.0%

Table 7.3: Age of contestants appearing on *Survivor* seasons 1-7, 9-10,
vs. TV characters in 1975 and 1990 and subset of U.S. population

	Age 20-49	Age 50-64	Age 65 and up
1975	76.5%	19.0%	4.5%
1990	80.9%	16.3%	2.8%
Survivor (2000-2005)	90.0%	9.3%	0.6%
U.S. population	61.8%	20.8%	17.4%

Note: 1975 statistics according to Greenberg, Korzenny & Atkin 1980, 23-33; 1990 statistics according to Robinson and Skill 1995, 111-119; U.S. figures based on the 2000 census (CensusScope 2001). Percentages listed are the proportion of all those age 20 and older; persons 19 and younger were left out since they were not applicable for this comparison.

contestants aged 50 and older is less than those studies found for television programs airing in 1990 and 1975, respectively, and far less than the actual U.S. population (see Tables 7.2 and 7.3). As a result, someone who is "old" on *Survivor* would be seen as merely in the upper reaches of middle age in regular society. Only when surrounded by 20-somethings in an intensely physical environment would a 50-year-old seem "old."

The reasons for the dearth of *Survivor* contestants age 50 and older are twofold. The first involves marketing. Advertisers like to showcase their wares for a younger audience, and CBS may have pushed for a younger cast, thinking that young men and women strutting on the beach in swimwear would attract younger demographics, ergo more money.

The second potential reason is that producers may feel older people cannot handle the physical demands of the contest. Consider that the three oldest *Survivor* contestants ever—Rudy, age 72; B.B., age 64; and Sonja, age 63—all appeared on the first season of the show. Since then, only two contestants, *Thailand's* Jake and *Guatemala's* Jim, have even been in their 60s. It's as if producers decided after Season 1 that the program was too difficult for contestants over 60, something reinforced by Jim being unanimously dispatched in Episode 1 of *Guatemala* after snapping his bicep in the second of two grueling challenges that left three younger men in agony themselves.[2] Alternately, it's possible that, after Sonja and B.B. became the first people voted out of *Survivor* and Rudy narrowly escaped being the third to go, Mark Burnett decided it was too big a public relations risk to have people in that age group—that they would, season after season, wind up being cannon fodder, voted out immediately. Perhaps, by limiting the show to only an occasional person 50 or older and virtually none at all over 60, he ironically hoped to avoid negative stereotypes. However, the lack of older contestants also implies older people aren't cut out for the show. It may be a no-win situation.

The paucity of older contestants and their often negative depiction makes them appear at first to be the symbolic proletariat. The treatment of these contestants is most apparent in viewing the premiere episode of the series—the only one to include three people age 60 or older, the aforementioned Sonja, B.B., and Rudy. For this episode, a content analysis involving eight coders also was conducted, in which, among other things, the valence of a contestant's depiction was coded as positive, neutral, or negative for each of sixteen scenes.[3]

"I Gotta Fit In, Not Them": The Acculturation of Rudy

Rudy receives *Survivor's* first "confessional," where he says his tribemates were stupid to row to shore while towing heavy crates, instead of placing them on the raft itself. Kelly tells the camera that he "was yelling at everybody" (CBS, 31 May 2000). Coders rated Rudy as being depicted *negatively* in this scene, where we see a stubborn old man, something that 28 percent of survey respondents recalled about him (see Table 7.4).

However, coders rated Rudy *positively* in his next scene, where he tells the camera: "The hardest part is hanging around all these young kids. I don't even know what 'MTV' means. . . . I gotta fit in, not them. There's more of them than there is of me." Later, we see his willingness to adjust and a *positive* rating as he explains that before he left the mainland, he formed opinions about the others, but then changed his mind. He cites Rich as an example: "He's strong, he's smart. . . . He's fat, but he's good." Foreshadowed here is Rich and Rudy's eventual bond; indeed "loyal," "honest," and "trustworthy" were most often chosen to describe Rudy. Nonetheless, he is nearly ousted in Episode 1, receiving three votes, and also is targeted in Episode 3.

Through this depiction, then, we see contradictory sides of Rudy, one adhering to stereotypes and the other countering them. He's stubborn, yet willing to bend his ways. (Although by saying he needs to "fit in," he evokes stereotypes of older people being out of touch.) This also relates to what sociologists call "acculturation," or the learning of a culture. Usually, this refers to society at large, but in the *"Survivor* as society" allegory employed in this text, a microcosmic approach applies. "If people know and understand the culture and the social system built upon it, they can potentially put the system to use. If they do not understand the way of life of the society in which they live, their lives can be confusing and unpredictable" (Atchley 1994, 159). Rudy now lives in a society called Tagi, and realizes that if he doesn't make an effort, he will quickly be on the outside looking in. To his credit, he perseveres, joins a winning alliance, and lasts thirty-eight out of a possible thirty-nine days. By forcing himself to fit in, he becomes part of the symbolic bourgeoisie. The same cannot be said for the opposing Pagong tribe's eldest member, B.B.

"We Got a Lot of Lazy People": B.B., the Opposite of Rudy

B.B. has his first prominent scene while searching the jungle for the water hole with Ramona. Although the pair becomes lost for an hour, content analysis participants coded both *positively*, perhaps because of the humor both showed, including B.B. commenting that if only the two of them know where the water hole is, they can't be voted out.

The next day, however, things change drastically as viewers are treated to B.B.'s bossy side. In a long scene, the tribal elder complains that others are not contributing. "I'm a little irritated," he says as the camera shows the "youngsters" enjoying the surf, walking on the beach, or simply lounging. "We got a lot of lazy people." He barks to no one in particular that "we need five more of these!" while using logs to build the shelter. Mother hen Gretchen tries to get B.B. to rest, but he refuses. "I never get burned out," he says, continuing to work.

Based on this scene and others like it in Episode 2, it's not surprising that survey respondents called B.B. bossy, opinionated, and mean (see Table 7.4). Also not surprisingly, B.B. was rated *negatively* by coders for this scene, though they gave him a *positive* rating for a scene in which he and Gretchen start a fire with the help of his custom-made bifocals. This generational divide, however, continues into Episode 2 (CBS, 7 June 2000), in which B.B. argues with Gervase and Joel over work ethics and how to build the shelter, grumpily washes his shirt in a pot, then is voted out.

Table 7.4 shows that viewers had a decidedly negative recollection of B.B.—of the seven adjectives that at least 20 percent of respondents cited, the top six were negative: bossy, opinionated, narrow-minded, forceful, quarrelsome, and egotistical. Unlike Rudy, B.B. maintains his narrow-minded ways and engages in conflict rather than attempting to circumvent it. He's the stereotypical old man shaking his fist, shouting, "those meddling kids!"

**Table 7.4: Common descriptions of *Borneo* contestants
over age 50, as cited by respondents**

Chosen from list of 27 adjectives	Percent citing	Open-ended question	Percent citing
RUDY			
Loyal	67.9%	Military veteran, SEAL, etc.	20.8%
Honest	48.8%	Tough, strong, resilient, etc.	19.5%
Trustworthy	44.4%	Old	18.2%
Stubborn	27.8%	Funny, entertaining	16.9%
Narrow-minded	21.0%	Cranky, crotchety, etc.	15.2%
		Loyal, honorable, etc.	10.4%
B.B.			
Bossy	53.4%	Bossy, controlling	22.4%
Opinionated	49.6%	Cranky, grouchy, etc.	22.4%
Narrow-minded	22.9%	Old	19.4%
Forceful	21.4%	Mean, rude	17.9%
		Washed clothes in cooking pot	10.5%
SONJA			
Kind	84.7%	Ukulele player, singing	36.5%
Weak	73.0%	Weak, fell down, etc.	19.1%
Honest	32.4%	Sweet, happy, kind	12.7%
Naïve	27.0%	Old	12.7%
Charming	21.6%	Cancer survivor	11.1%

Note: Percentages add up to more than 100 because respondents could list more than one word. Respondents were randomly asked the adjective or open-ended question for certain contestants, but never both questions for the same contestant. Adjectives chosen by 20 percent or more of respondents are listed; open-ended responses cited by 10 percent or more are listed. See Appendix B for more information on these contestants and Appendix C for methodology.

Indeed, B.B. mistakenly believes that the world of Pagong is equivalent to his real life, where, based on his status, he is a member of at least the upper-middle class. He's also accustomed to being in charge—and to being surrounded by people used to his being in such a role. But this is *Survivor*, where you have to earn respect all over again. B.B. lacks the automatic measure of respect that comes with being a military veteran. He does, however, have his background in real estate and construction. He could have used this to gain others' respect while building the shelter. Instead he only alienates his tribemates, coming across as a bossy, bitter old man.

"Thinning of the Skin": Sonja and Age Norms

Sonja perhaps has the most overtly stereotypical portrayal of the three older contestants, in both positive and negative ways: She's kind, but weak. This is shored up by her first scene, in which we see doctor Sean bandaging her slashed leg—and for which coders rated her as receiving a *negative* depiction. As Sean does this, Sonja gives a narration that sums up attitudes about aging that even the aged themselves often have: "I've been thrashing around like I'm 35 instead of acting my age. . . . One of the problems of aging is the thinning of the skin. . . . I may be getting a little more banged up than" the others. Most telling here is the phrase, *"acting my age."* By choosing to air this footage, editors enable older viewers to see one of their own repeat a negative belief about aging—on a "reality" show even. This illuminates a core idea noted throughout this book: By presenting programs such as *Survivor* as "real," any stereotypes and ideologies presented threaten to become far more convincing to viewers.

Sonja's statement also raises questions of role eligibility and appropriateness (Atchley 1994, 157). We saw Rudy struggle to find, and then adapt to, a role in his tribe; B.B. seemed to assume that his real-life role would be duplicated on the island, and suffered when it was not. By herself reiterating the physical "problems" of aging, Sonja reinforces the idea that there is no place for her on the island—no real role for which she is appropriate.

Sonja soon proves her point. At the strenuous immunity challenge, Sonja stumbles, helping Pagong win. "I really feel responsible. I was dragged totally off my feet," she says in a confessional, as the audience is again shown her fall—indeed, coders rated her *negatively* in all remaining scenes; her apparent physical weakness was frequently mentioned by survey respondents (see Table 7.4). She is voted out moments later, with Sue calling her "the weakest link" and Rudy saying "she's the reason we lost."

The first episode of *Survivor*, then, yields an ambivalent picture of older contestants—loyal but stubborn, hard-working but bossy, weak but kind—who face severe problems finding a role to fill on the island, and therefore lack political power. Yet older *Survivor* contestants in fact reach the endgame at a higher percentage than younger players—even if, paradoxically, viewers don't respect them for doing so.

The Importance of Being Eldest: Age and Alliances

Of sixteen votes cast in *Survivor's* first two Tribal Councils, thirteen—or 81 percent—went against players age 60 and over. Of the fifteen people 50 or older in their first appearance on *Survivor's* first ten seasons, five, or 33.3

**Figure 7.1: Game longevity of *Survivor* contestant
age groups, seasons 1-7, 9-10**

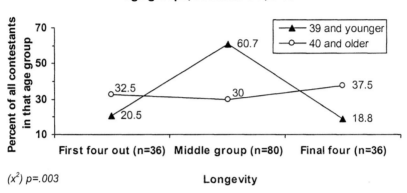

(x^2) p=.003

Note: For seasons 1-7 and 9-10. Lillian and Burton from *Pearl Islands* were counted both as "first four out" and "middle group" (in Burton's case) and "final four" (in Lillian's case), since both returned to the game after being voted out.

percent, were one of the first four players to leave the game. These factors, combined with the steady narrative of older players as physically weak and out of touch socially, creates an undercurrent of Jamesonian denial that these players have any shot at all. Repetitious remarks such as Rudy's "I've gotta fit in" and Rich's complimentary comments toward him are forgotten amid myriad storylines involving older players stumbling through challenge after challenge; needing to stop to rest on the initial walk to camp (which happened to Scout on the *Vanuatu* premiere); and spending time crying over dead bats and burying them in a "pet cemetery" (something *Thailand's* Jan did). Although older contestants generally were seen as honest, loyal, and kind by 2005 survey respondents, they were also described as weak, with older men frequently called opinionated, bossy, and narrow-minded, and older women called naïve, emotional, and absent-minded (see Table B.21, Appendix B). Rarely were players noted as being physically strong or shrewd, e.g., strategic.

Given all this, it's rather surprising that these same "weak" contestants are also most likely to reach the final four. Nearly half of 50-plus contestants have reached the final four; less than 20 percent of those aged 21-29 have done so. When groupings are collapsed into "39 and under" and "40 and older," this measure becomes statistically significant (see Figure 7.1). Additionally, contestants aged 50 and older are most likely to become part of a game-winning alliance—more than one in four such contestants have been in one, while only one in eighteen contestants from the larger pool of players

Figure 7.2: Percent of contestants included in game-winning alliances, grouped by age, seasons 1-7, 9-10

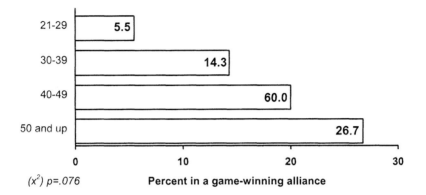

(x^2) *p=.076*   **Percent in a game-winning alliance**

aged twenty-nine or younger have been.[4] This also becomes statistically significant when collapsed into "39 and under" and "40 and older" (see Figure 7.2). Finally, original members of tribes that dominated the game were, on average, more than six years older than members of their opposing tribe, despite the apparent need for "physically strong" players who stereotypically would be younger.[5] The difference between the mean ages of contestants who reached the final four (37.4) vs. those who did not (32.5); between the ages of those who became part of a game winning alliance (40.4) and those who did not (32.6); and between the ages of those who were part of a dominant tribe (37.7) and those who were part of a dominated tribe (31.2), all were statistically significant according to a T-test[6], suggesting some reason beyond random chance for older players' success.

This data suggests that a few early boots aside, the older you are, the more likely you are to do well on *Survivor*. If you are over age 40 and survive the first four Tribal Councils, you have a much better shot of reaching the final four than your younger competitors, and to a statistically significant degree. Unlike most of the other things analyzed in this book, this isn't something taken from editing; this is just the way it is. The obvious question, then, is why? Do they simply slide by once the challenges become individual because they are perceived as weak? This may be part of it—but such an "immunity threat" theory fails to explain why tribes with an older average age tend to dominate those that are younger.[7]

Perhaps the answer is maturity and wisdom. Jeff Probst himself said as much at a press teleconference before *Palau* premiered: "The people who are parents in general are better equipped to deal with social situations. They've been through kids who have differences of opinions or are fighting.

Little squabbles about who gets the water. 'Oh, I'll go get it.' Older people are less likely to flip out" (SurvivorFever 2005). *Survivor* also depicts these contestants, according to survey results, as having good qualities for an alliance partner.

With older contestants, then, we see occasional early positive remarks—such as *Amazon's* Rob praising tribal elder Butch in Episode 1 of that season—overwhelmed by negative representations, such as Rob spending much more time bashing bossy Roger. Despite expectations that viewers would see successful older players positively, the surprising success of these early underdogs results in *displeasure,* completing a modified Jamesonian model. 2005 survey respondents were presented with the photographs and names, in random order, of the thirty *Survivor* contestants who lasted to the final four but did not win. They were asked whether or not each had deserved to reach the endgame. On average, 62 percent said that a given player had indeed deserved such a high finish. Broken down by age, these results were consistent across the board—except for contestants aged 50 or older, for whom the mean percentage dropped precipitously.[8] In every other age group, about 68 percent of respondents said such players deserved to go to the end. *For the oldest contestants, that figure plummeted to 42 percent.* This suggests that most of these contestants were seen by respondents as "riding coattails."[9]

Older, Wiser—and More Powerful?

The representation and performance of *Survivor* contestants age 50 and over reflects the double-edged nature of how society perceives aging. They are far more likely to be voted out right away than younger players—but also far more likely to last to the end. Older people are far more likely to be part of a game-winning alliance—yet are not respected for making it to the end, and are seen as just riding stronger players' coattails. In this way, such players are also seen as weak.

The fact that older players are more likely to partake of successful alliances is especially intriguing when examining how older *respondents* viewed specific contestants and situations, according to the 2004 and 2005 surveys.[10] Figure 7.3 shows a giant age gap regarding whether the Tagi and Rotu alliances were "the good guys" or "the bad guys." Since the five-person coup group in *Marquesas* was older than the four-person Rotu alliance, contestants' ages alone can't explain this chasm.

Similar results were gathered from the 2005 survey, which measured overall audience attitude toward every contestant, among other things. The only obvious "age bias" occurred with older respondents favoring contestants from the older halves of the *Vanuatu* and *Africa* generational conflicts,

Figure 7.3: Percentage of respondents perceiving Tagi and Rotu alliances as "good," grouped by age

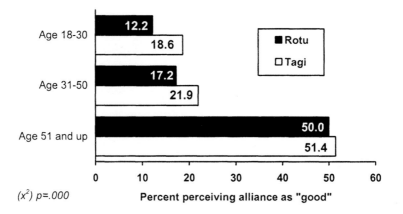

(x^2) *p=.000*

and giving low marks to the "young" people in those groups. Besides that, this part of the study found that respondents who were over age 50 generally rated more positively leaders, strategists and members of instigating alliances, successful or not. People such as *Africa's* Lex, *Palau's* Tom, *Outback's* Jerri, and *Amazon's* Deena received high marks; Sonja, *Outback's* Elisabeth, and *Palau's* Coby, meanwhile, were among those who were rated much higher among respondents age 18-30—and therefore more negatively with the older crowd (see Table B.14, Appendix B). Additionally, openly gay contestants such as Coby, Brandon, and Ami were rated more negatively by older contestants—with one notable exception.

Indeed, someone with one of the biggest "age gaps" was *Borneo's* Rich, leader of the Tagi alliance. Older respondents were far more likely to rate him highly than younger survey takers. Alliance member Sue was also rated more positively, as was outsider Sean, whose alphabetical voting strategy enabled the Tagi alliance to maintain dominance. Meanwhile, certain Pagong members were rated significantly more negatively by older respondents. Most members of *Marquesas'* fallen Rotu alliance were rated more positively; renegades Neleh and tribal elder Paschal were rated more negatively.

What this all adds up to is a tendency for older respondents to rate highly contestants with power, however fleeting, no matter their age, in a class-related undercurrent of sorts—perhaps, older respondents had come to respect those they saw as loyal and intelligent. This also is an interesting juxtaposition to the history of older players on *Survivor*, who are most consistent at becoming part of a powerful voting alliance and lasting most of the thirty-nine days. Certainly, elements of repression are inherent in the treatment of older players on the show itself, with a major surface narrative early on in most seasons being the physical weakness of the elder players, who consistently find themselves in danger of being voted out as teams seek to dispatch the "weakest link." Prime examples of this are Sonja, the first person ever voted out, *Palau's* Willard, and *Guatemala's* Jim. Other older players also are repeatedly portrayed as not fitting in with the young—B.B., *Africa's* Frank and Linda. These cases show older players as weak and therefore vulnerable. Any strong points they provide generally are disregarded as not compensating for overall weaknesses.

Yet the repetitive negative references belie a startling longevity, and in some cases, strength. Kim J., for instance—painted as physically and mentally weak all along, escaping Tribal Council by the skin of her teeth three times while blowing challenge after challenge for her team—turns around and wins the final two immunity challenges, one a memory game, the other a taxing test of endurance in the hot African sunlight. This ending is made startling by the fact that her mental and physical abilities had been downplayed in every episode before, through both challenge results and commentary (such as "Kim is feeling really vulnerable right now").

Age, then, comes to be both a positive (i.e., the wizened person) and a negative (i.e., the physically inept person) on *Survivor*, much as in society at large—no surprise there, given that life on *Survivor's* island mimics the political realities of regular society.

Notes

1. On their first appearance on the show. As has been the case for most of this book, *All-Stars* is disregarded here due to the complexities involved in trying to count the same contestant twice and in the very different dynamics in that season, in that it was not played among strangers, and was aired to an audience who had opportunities to view and interact with the contestants outside *Survivor's* version of reality. As for the fall 2005 season of *Guatemala*, contestant Jim will be mentioned briefly, but as the season concluded immediately before this book went into production, it was not possible to recalculate all the statistics included.

2. Though it is possible that the show has received no "quality" applicants above age 60, this is no excuse given that producers have been known to recruit contestants—the show's casting director, for example, spotted eventual *Pearl Islands* "villain" Jon "on a bus-stop bench smoking a cigarette" (Cohn 2005).

3. According to Scott's Pi, an intercoder reliability of 84.3 was reached; see Appendix C for methodology.

4. Alliances were termed game-winning for these purposes if they formed when at least five episodes remained in the season and if they succeeded in "Pagonging" all other players in the game, excluding immunity wins. The alliances in question are *Borneo's* Tagi alliance; *Outback's* final three; *Africa's* four-person Boran alliance; *Marquesas'* five-person coup; and *Thailand's* five-person Chuay Gahn coalition. *All-Stars* has been purposely ignored for much of this study, although such an alliance also occurred there; two of its six members were 40 and older, which would have widened the gap between success rates of the "older" and "younger" groups (to 30.8 percent for older vs. 13.5 percent for younger). Viewing the final six players of *Palau* as a game-dominating alliance also would have increased the gap between "old" and "young" success rates since their makeup was older than the entire pool of 150 *Survivor* contestants.

5. A dominant tribe is defined as one where a season's final four players are from the same original tribe, while a nondominant tribe is one that has no members reach the final four. Dominant tribes are Tagi, Boran, Chuay Gahn, and Koror.

6. For final four player age differences, p=.037; for game-winning alliance membership, p=.016; and for dominant tribe membership, p=.027.

7. For instance, it does not account for why *Palau's* Koror tribe, with a mean age of 36.3 years, would win every single immunity challenge over the Ulong tribe, with a mean age of 27 years. Nor would it explain *Thailand's* Sook Jai tribe being dominated pre- and post-merge by a Chuay Gahn tribe that was collectively more than eight years their senior, 31.1 vs. 39.6.

8. A chi-square test was run to test for the significance of a relationship between age of the *respondent* and belief that an older contestant deserved to reach the final four; the results were statistically significant for only one of the seven 50-plus contestants, Lillian. Therefore, there was no significant overall relationship between viewer age and perceived deservedness of older players reaching the final four. Lillian was also the only one with mitigating circumstances—she returned to the game after being voted out, something that for many must have disqualified her as deserving her placement.

9. Nearly one in three respondents to the open-ended question for *Africa's* Kim J., for instance, called her this or something similar. It is rather startling that of all the things that might pop into one's head about a former contestant, this did the most for her.

10. Contestants who older respondents rated more highly in the 2005 survey were on average about six years older than those they rated more negatively; however, those differences all but vanished when contestants from *Africa* and *Vanuatu*—the two seasons with overt, age-related conflicts and alliances—were left out. Also, when it came to rating specific contestants, older respondents gave higher marks to four contestants over 50, and lower marks to three of them (see Table B.14, Appendix B).

Chapter 8

"This Thing Runs Deeper Than a Game"

Survivor's *Troubles With Race*

IN JUNE 2005, TREVOR PHILLIPS—the chairman of Great Britain's Commission for Racial Equity—sang the praises of reality TV's ability to demonstrate diversity, saying the shows have helped ethnic understanding more than any recent media product. "What reality TV has done, whether you like it or not, is introduce the majority of the British public to people they would never normally meet," he said (Sheppard 2005, 9).

Unfortunately, Phillips' is a lone voice in the wilderness. Numerous other critics, this writer included, have chastised the genre for stereotypical depictions, especially of African-American men and women, as briefly discussed in Chapter 1. Other TV genres have been similarly accused, and just as representations of age and gender can influence political socialization, so too can those of race. This can be especially problematic for children. Research suggests that "lesser representation of nonwhites sends a message that children of color are not important"; minority children who are also heavy TV viewers are more likely to have more negative self-concepts (Van Evra 2004, 110).

Despite apparent progress, "minorities are still underrepresented on television and often misrepresented as violent or generally portrayed in less desirable ways, which perpetuates racism and stereotypes" (Van Evra 2004, 110). This chapter will demonstrate with survey results and other statistical analyses how *Survivor* in particular has done little to reverse this problem, and in fact may have compounded it. The chapter will first review literature on African-American representations in entertainment programs and news coverage, then relate that to how reality TV treats race in the eyes of scholars and journalists. The extent of negative African-American depictions on *Survivor* will then be detailed, followed by a close reading of the penultimate episode of *Marquesas*, which was filled with race-related confrontations as two white contestants and two African-American contestants each attempted to sway a fifth contestant, also white, to their side. The chapter then concludes by examining how race and class intersect.

First, a brief word about U.S. demographics vs. *Survivor's* "demographics." Like older people, racial minorities are underrepresented on *Survivor*—white people represent 85 percent of all *Survivor* contestants, yet only 69 percent of the U.S. population, according to the 2000 census. The proportion of African-American contestants, 10 percent, actually resembles their share of the U.S. population, which is 12 percent, though the series' eleventh season, *Guatemala,* included no African-American contestants at all. The problem for African-American depictions, it will be seen, is not quantity so much as quality.

For other minorities, representation is far less, rendering it pointless to draw conclusions based on their portrayals: The first ten seasons of *Survivor* included two Asians, two Hispanics, and four others clearly of mixed race, or 5 percent of the contestant pool—as opposed to about 18 percent of the U.S. population. *Survivor's* producers may argue this is because of the number of applicants rather than marketing, but since some contestants are "recruited" for the show, such a case holds little water. As a result, however, only African-American depictions will be discussed at length herein.

African-Americans on Entertainment Programs

Race remains a delicate topic in the United States—only exacerbated by the aftereffects of Hurricane Katrina, which flooded New Orleans in August 2005, leaving hundreds of thousands homeless and exposing the poverty that many African-Americans still face today. Stereotypes of African-Americans have been discussed in academic circles for some time. The landmark Princeton Trilogy study attempted to measure them, and found African-Americans to be most perceived as superstitious, lazy, and happy-go-lucky in 1933; superstitious, musical, and lazy in 1951; and happy-go-lucky, pleasure-loving, and lazy in 1969 (Madon et al. 2001, 1000). Researchers updated the study in the 1990s and found that the stereotypes had continued to change over time and had somewhat improved, commonly including loud, musical, tough, rude, loyal, humorous, and opinionated (Madon et al. 2001, 1000). A separate National Science Foundation study of 2,200 U.S. adults in 1993 found that about half of whites surveyed agreed that African-Americans are "aggressive or violent," while about three in ten agreed that "blacks are lazy" and about 20 percent said "blacks are irresponsible"— figures that differed only by a few points across conservative/liberal lines (Marable 1994, 15-16).

Such stereotypes finding their way onto television are nothing new; African-Americans have been shown to be quite concerned with this. "Almost

Table 8.1: Selected African-American stereotypes in entertainment media as described by Bogle (1989) and Jewell (1993)

Name	Traits (often have evolved)
Tom	Stoic, generous, kind; seen as heroes of sorts to whites (Bogle 1989, 6)
Coon	Clownish, unreliable, lazy; at worst, good only for "eating watermelons" (Bogle 1989, 8)
Buck	Angry, barbaric, sexualized; at worst, "out to raise havoc" or lusting "for white flesh" (Bogle 1989, 13)
Mammy	Aggressive toward peers, timid toward employers, fat (not so much today), masculinized, large-breasted (Jewell 1993, 50-53)
Aunt Jemima	Mammy variant; religious, jolly, good-tempered, more polite; at times tries to insert self into white culture (Bogle 1989, 9)
Sapphire	Sassy, verbose, opinionated, finger-pointing, loud; often appears opposite African-American male (Jewell 1993, 45)

all black interviewees commented on what they felt to be extremely negative portrayals of black people on television," write Jhally and Lewis (1992) in a major qualitative study of audience reaction to *The Cosby Show*, with one focus group participant telling them that "I've been brainwashed into thinking that the blacks have certain roles on television" (115). Sitcoms such as *227, Amen, The Jeffersons,* and *Good Times* "repeatedly came under fierce criticism for their stereotypical portrayals of black life. . . . Stereotyping is not just a minor problem, but one that affects [respondents'] everyday lives" (117-18).

Donald Bogle has for several decades tracked African-American stereotypes in entertainment media. He argues that even today, many depictions descend from stock character types originating with the birth of film. K. Sue Jewell has pinpointed other depictions. Some of these categories are explained in Table 8.1; later, Table 8.2 notes which types arguably apply to *Survivor* contestants *as mediated by the series*. "While there are individuals who conform to these traditional cultural images, such images are not representative of African American women as a collective" (Jewell 1993, 46).

Not everyone agrees with Bogle's assessment; African-American linguist John H. McWhorter, for instance, lauds Bogle's early work but argues that of late he has begun playing a "Can You Find the Black Stereotype?" game in which practically any depiction of African-Americans is grounds for criticism (2003, 104-137).

Herman Gray, one of the most prominent voices on the subject of African-Americans and television, also argues that recent portrayals of African-

Americans on entertainment shows naturally descend from those in the early days of TV, and before. "Our contemporary moment continues to be shaped discursively by representations of race and ethnicity that began in the formative years of television" (Gray 1995, 74). This has evolved from maids, cooks, deadbeats, and other "happy go lucky social incompetents who knew their place" on 1950s TV; depictions in the 1960s that rendered African-Americans "if not culturally white, invisible"; representations of what white, middle-class TV producers "assumed (or projected) were 'authentic' accounts of poor black urban ghetto experiences" in the early to mid 1970s; and in the late 1970s and early 1980s, a sense of "black upward social mobility and middle class affluence [replacing] black urban poverty as both setting and theme" (Gray 1995, 74-77).

Most notable in that decade was *The Cosby Show*, which depicted a successful, happy, upper-middle-class family—even as African-Americans continued to struggle economically overall, with median white incomes rising at a faster clip, for instance (Census.gov). The *Cosby* researchers and other critics, Gray among them, concluded that the program served as rose-colored spectacles, leaving the impression "that racism is no longer a problem in the United States. . . . If Cliff and Clair can make it, then so can all blacks" (Jhally and Lewis 1992, 71-72). Granted, this apparent damned if you do, damned if you don't argument prompts the question of what would satisfy such critics. According to them, shows such as *227* and *Good Times* present a stereotypical working-class view of African-Americans, and are therefore harmful. *The Cosby Show* presents a middle-class depiction, and that, too, is harmful. The implication is that an "acceptable" African-American depiction would fall into a narrow representational range indeed.

African-Americans on News Programs

That most "real" medium, TV news, has borne the brunt of criticism for negative depictions of African-Americans. "TV news, especially local news, paints a picture of blacks as violent and threatening toward whites, self-interested and demanding toward the body politic—continually causing problems for the law-abiding, tax-paying majority" (Entman 1994, 29). A study of local news in Los Angeles found that whites were indeed overrepresented on the news as crime victims, compared to actual government statistics; meanwhile, African-Americans were vastly overrepresented as crime perpetrators (Dixon and Linz 2000, 547-573). African-American respondents to the *Cosby* study fiercely criticized TV news "because it continually links blacks with the problems of crime and drugs" (Jhally and Lewis 1992, 114). As one woman put it: "I say to my husband sometimes, 'My God, don't white girls have babies [out of wedlock] anymore?' Or, 'Don't white girls go on the dope, and the boys too?' but they don't [show] that, it's always the black" (115).

Conversely, McWhorter—author of *Losing the Race: Self-Sabotage in Black America,* which posits, among other things, that African-American culture encourages nurturing a feeling of victimization rather than overcoming it—recently argued that from his perspective, "the problem, plainly, [is] not one of socioeconomic status—most of my black [college] students were in fact middle-class—but of culture, and lowered standards were likely to preserve and even intensify that problem, not to ameliorate it" (2004, 37-42). McWhorter in this instance, however, appears to overlook the probability that students who can easily afford college, no matter their race, are more likely to be at least middle-class anyway.

Overall, "stereotypes found in the news are harder to resist because the news is seen as real, whereas movies can be dismissed as make-believe" (Larson 2005, 83). This observation is especially worrisome for a society that now includes a number of popular "reality" television shows. News is presented as complete, objective fact—not unlike how "reality" television is put forth. This is particularly alarming considering that Jhally and Lewis found a number of white respondents who confused stereotypes as equaling reality. "You know, [on] *227*, the older woman hanging out of the window watching the neighbors walk by and stuff like that, which is reality in a lot of situations but . . . it just seems to be heavy into black stereotyping," one white interviewee said (1992, 102). Here, "stereotyping" and "reality" merge. As the authors explained, "a vague awareness of media stereotypes was combined with an equally vague assumption that perhaps these stereotypes were, after all, accurate" (103). If the obviously ficticious *227* can seem like "reality in a lot of situations," then TV news—and by extension *Survivor*, which combines entertainment with reality—could have a potentially damaging impact.

"A Gross Misrepresentation of Who I Am"

The *Washington Post's* Paul Farhi appears to have been the first to prominently note racial stereotypes on reality TV post-*Survivor*, writing in February 2001 of the genre's "bad black guy. He's the villain, the malcontent, the misfit, the jerk. . . . Misbehavior and character flaws come in many different colors and in both genders, of course. But on reality shows, they consistently come in the form of a black male" (Farhi 2001, C1).

Farhi's colleague Teresa Wiltz later noted the female side of this problem: "If you've ever seen a reality TV show, chances are you've seen her: a perpetually perturbed, tooth-sucking, eye-rolling, finger-wagging harpy, creating confrontations in her wake and perceiving racial slights from the flimsiest of provocations. . . . She's the Sista With an Attitude" (2004, C1).

The problem is not so much the existence of negative portrayals—it is that they are often the *only* portrayal. "There tends to be, on *Survivor*, an allotment of two blacks per show, one male and one female. Their faults stand out" (Wyman 2002, 8D). Or, as Farhi astutely explained:

> Some white men and women behave just as badly on these programs. . . . The key word, though, is "some." Other white characters plainly do not act this way. In fact, judging by the example of reality programs, white people seem to be a fairly diverse lot—some noble, some petty, some strong, some weak. You'd never make the same assumption about African-American men, for the simple reason that it's hard to see diversity when there's only one black man per show. The rigid tokenism of reality programs—call it the "one black guy at a time" rule—magnifies the behavior of [the bad black guy], giving him metaphoric power. (2001, C1)

Therein lies the rub. When it comes to white "characters" on *Survivor*, for every snarky Jerri, there's a sweetheart Elisabeth. For every manipulative Jonny "Fairplay," there's a straightforward Bobby Jon. But of the sixteen African-Americans to appear on the first ten seasons of the show, at most four received what could be described as a "positive" overall depiction.

This fact may be lost on producers of reality television—"We look for diverse personalities and interesting personas. . . . There's no mold or type we're trying to fit. It's very much intangible and subjective," CBS spokesman Chris Ender told Farhi (2001, C1)—but at least some reality contestants have realized the problem. Omarosa Manigault-Stallworth, who appeared on the first season of *The Apprentice* (which like *Survivor* is produced by Mark Burnett), was depicted as fiesty, rude, argumentative, holier-than-thou, lazy, and quick to accuse others of prejudice (see also Larson 2005, 3-6). Manigault-Stallworth defended herself to the *Post's* Wiltz:

> What you see on the show is a gross misrepresentation of who I am. For instance, they never show me smiling, it's just not consistent with the negative portrayal of me that they want to present. . . . It's all in the editing! . . . Minorities have historically been portrayed negatively on reality TV. These types of [shows] thrive off of portrayals that tap into preconceived stereotypes about minorities (i.e., that we are lazy, dishonest, and hostile). Reality television's "angry black women" portrayal strikes again! It's really unfortunate! (2004, C01)

Unfortunate—if Omarosa was indeed depicted unfairly on this and other programs on which she later appeared—and common. All this often leads to

African-Americans on reality TV symbolizing the underclass, reflective of their frequently subordinated position in society. Wages of African-Americans, for instance, have remained less than whites, even when controlling for education (Schaefer 1996, 83). Additionally, a June 2005 ABC News poll found 54 percent of African-American respondents had at some point felt that they "were being discriminated against because of [their] race," versus 19 percent of whites (Polling Report 2005). In a 2003 Gallup Poll, responding to the question, "How often do you feel discriminated against in public life or employment because you are black?" 39 percent of African-American respondents said at least once a month, 40 percent said less than that and 19 percent said never (Polling Report 2005). And among all respondents, a 2003 Associated Press poll found that 39 percent thought we are at least "fairly close" to "eliminating discrimination against racial and ethnic minorities in America once and for all," while 59 percent felt we are "not too close" or "not close at all" (Polling Report 2005). It is too early to tell as of this writing, but there would appear to be a chance that such attitudes will only grow in the aftermath of Hurricane Katrina.

On *Survivor*, meanwhile, African-American contestants overall perform much worse than their white counterparts.

Not-So-Sweet Sixteen

In order to present a complete picture of African-American depictions on *Survivor*, the following offers a guide to each of the sixteen to appear on the first ten seasons, with Table 8.2 (pp. 116-117) listing each contestant's placement and AAAI, as well as the adjectives and open-ended responses that survey-takers most often described them with. Using these results, the author selected details from their depiction that may have led to such viewer reactions, and when applicable, noted the historic stereotype (as described by Bogle and Jewell) that the depiction would appear to descend from, also based on survey responses.[1] As the chart summarizes, these contestants had consistently low ratings compared to all contestants, as well as consistently negative depictions as recalled by the 2005 survey respondents.

In the case of two contestants, one male and one female, a more detailed look at stereotypes follows (again, with the described scenes based on what survey respondents recollected most about the contestants). The contestants are *Borneo's* Gervase, who despite his stereotypical depiction is the highest-rated African-American contestant according to AAAI (which isn't saying much, since he barely makes the top third of all contestants) and *The*

Table 8.2: Summary of depictions for sixteen African-Americans featured on first ten seasons of *Survivor*

Player (AAAI/rank*)	Finish, season	Stereotypes depicted (See p. 111)	Top two or three adjectives cited in survey, from list	Top open-ended description	Situations likely responsible for respondent reaction
Ramona (108 / 2.579)	13th, *Borneo*	Coon elements	Weak 70.0% Lazy 34.5% Intelligent 28.2%	Got sick a lot 62.3%	Ill in early going, putting her at immediate disadvantage and leading her to rest often. Jenna: "I don't think Ramona's pulling her weight. . . . I don't think she can [handle this like] she thought." *
Gervase (49 / 3.564)	7th, *Borneo*	Coon	Lazy 72.1% Charming 45.7% Self-conf. 28.6%	Lazy 30.6%	See p. 118.
Alicia (61 / 3.326)	9th, *Outback*	Sapphire, Mammy elements	Strong 52.4% Opinionated 44.4% Forceful 40.5%	Kimmi fight, confrontational 49.6%	Personal trainer famed for shouting match with social outcast Kimmi over fate of tribe's chickens; quote: "I will always wave my finger in your face." *
Nick (83 / 2.971)	7th, *Outback*	Coon elements	Lazy 71.3% Unreliable 31.3% Weak 27.5%	Quiet, boring, bland 39.7%	Tribemate Jeff: "Nick is lazy. He won't pick up anything. He won't lift anything. If you ask him to help you, he'll act like he doesn't hear you." *
Linda (132 / 2.208)	13th, *Africa*	Mammy, Aunt Jemima elem.	Religious 30.9% Quarrelsome 30.1% Bossy 30.1%	Weird or crazy 26.7%	Regarding immunity idol after challenge loss: "Our idol goddess cannot live in a home with conflict. She went to find some peace! Mother Africa is a very spiritual place. Gods . . . are watching!" *
Clarence (123 / 2.402)	10th, *Africa*	Buck, Coon elements	Strong 63.0% Unreliable 56.5% Lazy 36.1%	Sharing/stealing beans, sneaky 61.0%	A can of beans goes missing, and it is unclear whether an ill player asked Clarence to open it and share it with her, or if he did it himself. He winds up apologizing to tribemates; their trust of him tears.
Sean (94 / 2.811)	5th, *Marq.*	Coon, Buck elements	Lazy 43.6% Complaining 37.6% Religious 27.1%	Angry, confrontational 21.6%	See p. 122.

Name (AAAI)	Placement, Season	Stereotype elements	Trait percentages	Short descriptor %	Description
Vecepia (94 / 2.811)	1st, *Marq.*	Aunt Jemima elements	Religious 78.2% Weak 37.1% Shrewd 33.9%	Invisible, quiet 40.0%	See p. 122; winner who remained "invisible" for much of the season, but demonstrated bubbly persona off the show. Chance for highly positive depiction of African-American wasted.
Ghandia (149 / 1.355)	13th, *Thai.*	Sapphire	Quarrelsome 72.0% Emotional 53.3% Complaining 48.7%	Grinding incident 32.4%	Accuses Ted of grinding against her in the night; wanders on beach, screaming at rocks.
Ted (85 / 2.932)	5th, *Thai.*	Tom elements	Strong 34.1% Naïve 20.2%	Grinding incident 54.3%	Accused by Ghandia of grinding against her in the night; first member of dominant Chuay Gahn alliance to be voted out.
Joanna (146 / 1.821)	13th, *Amazon*	Sapphire, Aunt Jem., Mammy	Religious 71.8% Narrow-mnd 30.2% Bossy 29.5%	Religious, fear of idol 44.4%	See p. 119.
Osten (150 / 1.203)	11th, *Pearl Is.*	Coon	Unreliable 77.9% Lazy 76.3% Weak 58.8%	Quit game 59.1%	Muscular, yet first to ever quit, and has lowest AAAI to show for it; struggled to swim during a water challenge; scared by pelican.
Tijuana (51 / 3.511)	7th, *Pearl Is.*	Not Applicable	Kind 36.4% Charming 30.9% Honest 25.5%	Nice, sweet 18.2%	Friendly contestant who often remained in the background; chance for highly positive depiction of African-American wasted.
Rory (90 / 2.856)	10th, *Vanuatu*	Coon, Buck elements	Opinionated 47.8% Quarrelsome 45.7% Stubborn 32.6%	Complaining, annoying 21.8%	Accused of not working enough, retorts, "I am a grown-ass man. I don't take orders real well." * Survives as lone man in women's tribe after threatening to not work unless guaranteed a place in the game.
Jolanda (110 / 2.56)	18th, *Palau*	Sapphire, Mammy elements	Forceful 51.9% Opinionated 51.9% Bossy 46.2%	Bossy, overbearing 45.9%	Wins short-lived individual immunity; makes bad decision during tribal challenge; declares that for every two hours that tribe members work, they must rest for an hour.
Ibrehem (67 / 3.154)	11th, *Palau*	Not applicable	Religious 65.0% Strong 45.3% Honest 40.9%	Quiet, silent 37.2%	Muslim; saved by opposing tribe at unique Tribal Council. Doomed more by his tribe's poor challenge performances than anything else; made final three of his hapless Ulong tribe.

* Episodes in order of quotation: CBS, 24 June 2000; 22 Feb. 2001; 8 Feb. 2001; 25 Oct. 2001; 30 Sept. 2004. See Appendix C for more on AAAI and descriptions.

Amazon's Joanna, one of three African-Americans in the bottom five according to AAAI.

Gervase: "I Haven't Done a Thing Out Here"

Gervase is part of the first season's doomed Pagong tribe and previously discussed in Chapter 3. His AAAI of 3.564 was the highest of all sixteen African-American contestants, placing him forty-ninth out of 150. Charming, friendly, and a poor swimmer, Gervase also has a self-proclaimed lazy side, highlighted in this sequence from Episode 6 (CBS, 5 July 2000):

> Colleen (to camera, amid footage of Gervase laying in a hammock): [Gervase] doesn't do stuff half the time.

> Gervase (to camera, amid footage of him on a raft with Joel, etc.): I haven't done a thing out here. . . . Joel does the fishing, he does the paddling, I'm just out there hanging on the raft with him. When they built that shelter on the beach, I was nowhere near there, I was in the shade somewhere looking for a coconut. I think everyone has been cooking rice at one time. I have yet to cook anything.

We then see Jenna and Gervase walking along the beach—with Jenna carrying a half-dozen canteens, and Gervase none. Gervase also rests in the woods during a critical tribal immunity challenge; respondents labeled him as lazy above all else, though he also was remembered for several positive qualities.

Additionally, although certain amounts of debate on *Survivor* center around the morality of alliances, questions of morality regarding a different topic—family values—take center stage for much of the *Borneo* episode where Gervase is ousted, discussed in Chapter 3. The tribe receives cigars with news that Gervase—never married and 30 years old—has just become a father for the fourth time. Rich, Sue, and Rudy question such a lifestyle choice, as the four children have two different mothers. Having children out of wedlock is a stereotypical circumstance of the under-privileged, as is an absent father. Gervase is obviously absent for his child's birth, a choice he must have deliberately made given the timing of *Survivor's* taping. We see Rudy calling such life choices "garbage" (CBS, 2 Aug. 2000).

All this reinforces Gervase's subordinated status, with his real life suddenly dovetailing with life on the island (note, however, that Sue in real life was a truck driver, showing that "class mobility" from real to faux world is possible on *Survivor*), and the suddenly morally superior Tagi alliance looking down on him, judging him.

Joanna: "I Am Gonna Shut You Down With My Hand"

Joanna—at the bottom of the heap in the AAAI rankings, with a 1.821 score and a rank of 146th—was depicted as essentially every negative African-American female stereotype rolled into one. She was overly religious, even superstitious; she was argumentative and holier-than-thou; and she was bossy and complaining.

We are shown during Episode 1 of *Amazon*—discussed at length in Chapter 6—that Joanna alone does not touch the immunity idol when host Probst offers it to the tribes before the first challenge. In Episode 2 (CBS, 20 Feb. 2003), we learn why in this nighttime scene, complete with eerie shots of the immunity idol and haunting music:

> Joanna (inside shelter): Thank you Lord. Cover us. And get that idol goin'. Put him out there. I'm serious! I'm not touchin' it.
>
> Deena (to camera): Joanna doesn't like the immunity idol because she thinks it *is* an idol. Idols are forbidden via the Ten Commandments. . . . She wants nothing to do with it . . .
>
> Joanna (to camera): That's why we got rained on last night, bringing the idol into our tribe.
>
> Another tribe member (inside shelter): That idol is the reason why we're all here right now.
>
> Joanna: [It is not.] We won before we had the idol. . . . I'm gonna talk all night about the goodness of the Lord and the land of the living.
>
> Deena: Can you do it in a whisper?
>
> Joanna: No.

Joanna earlier had been shown loudly singing gospel music, so put the two together and you have a negative stereotype alive and kicking. The next morning, Christy—who is deaf and therefore missed the nighttime conversation about the idol—is informed of what happened and says, "that's stupid," as Joanna happens by. The ensuing confrontation is nothing close to what transpired between Kimmi and Alicia on *Australian Outback* (see Table 8.2), but still has its moments, such as when Joanna thrusts her hand in Christy's face and remarks, "Don't interject in my conversation negatively, because I am gonna shut you down with my hand. . . . Leave me alone and get out of my face!" Christy may have started things with her overheard comment, but Joanna comes off worse, appearing overly aggressive.

Two episodes later (CBS, 6 March 2003), we see yet another "negative" side of Joanna. She is the first one up in the morning, begins sharpening her machete as others sleep, then works on the camp with Jeanne. "Can we not throw nut shells around the bed where we have to sleep?" she lectures to the younger players, still in bed. "Can we keep it clean, please? That's where our heads are laying at night!" Some of the other players don't come off well either, but the focus is on Joanna. Much like B.B., the workhorse who received a negative reaction to his complaining about others' lack of work on *Borneo*, this on top of everything else solidifies a highly negative depiction of Joanna, and she is soon voted out.

Well Below Average—But Why?

The sum of the above parts is that African-Americans on *Survivor* are consistently portrayed negatively and according to stereotypes. Figure B.22 (see Appendix B) shows that overall, African-American contestants were most remembered as lazy, strong, and quarrelsome; the forty-nine white contestants measured were recalled as honest, opinionated, and intelligent.[2] Seven of the ten adjectives most used to describe the white players were positive in valence, compared to only three of the ten most used to describe African-American contestants.

Many of the attributes chosen to describe African-American contestants also were consistent with the Princeton Trilogy studies and the "revisited" study. Respondents' frequency at recalling African-American men as "lazy" is especially worrisome given that the Princeton studies found laziness to decline in prominence as a stereotype since the 1930s (Madon et al. 2001, 1000). Other adjectives seen as African-American stereotypes in the Princeton Trilogy that the *Survivor* respondents frequently cited as applying to Gervase, Joanna, and company included (very) religious, unreliable, quarrelsome, opinionated, bossy, and strong. Still others, such as complaining, are similar in meaning to common Princeton Trilogy findings.

African-American contestants also had a far lower—and statistically, a significantly different—mean AAAI than did whites, with African-American women especially poorly regarded. Figure 8.1 illustrates this point.[3] The handful of nonblack racial minority members to appear on *Survivor* had a slightly lower mean AAAI than white contestants, but a far higher one than African-Americans.

In addition, a respondents' race rarely affected how he or she rated minority contestants, according to an ordinary least squares regression analysis. Out of twenty-three nonwhite contestants to appear on *Survivor*, nonwhite respondents (who were most often Asian, not black) rated only four of them significantly higher than white respondents did: *Thailand's* Ted, *Palau's* Jolanda, *Africa's* Jessie, who is Puerto Rican, and *Palau's* Janu, who is part Cuban. They also rated seven white contestants higher, and twenty-one

**Figure 8.1: Mean adjusted audience attitude index
for selected racial groups on *Survivor***

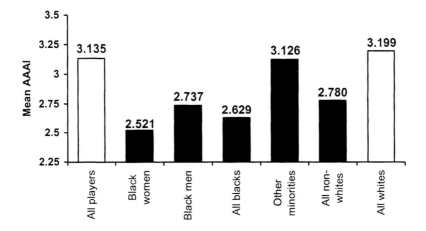

white contestants—many of whom suffered from their own negative stereotypes, depicted as "rednecks"—lower (see Table B.15, Appendix B).

African-American contestants also fare worse on *Survivor* game-wise, although because of the small sample size of sixteen, not to a statistically significant degree. A quarter of all white contestants have reached the final four,
but only one black person has—a success rate of 6.3 percent. To be fair, two
African-Americans were voted out at the final five; adding them to the mix
yields an 18.8 percent success rate vs. 31.5 percent for white contestants.

On the other hand, about the same percentage of white and African-
American contestants have wound up in a game-winning alliance. However,
two of the three to do so—*Marquesas'* Sean and *Thailand's* Ted—were the
first persons ousted once their alliance had eliminated all other players; the
third, *Marquesas'* Vecepia, was in danger until winning immunity at the
final four. These are the same three who reached the final five.

The AAAI ratings and adjective tallies are therefore consistent with the
beefs of the numerous critics referred to above: African-American contestants are depicted much more negatively on *Survivor* than white contestants.
The history of the show demonstrates that they also fare more poorly. But
why, and what can be done about it? Do the editors deliberately frame them
this way? Do producers purposely select African-American applicants who
are likely to create drama, just sit around camp all day, or not get along with
others? The problem is that casual viewers and children still undergoing political socialization may ignore these questions and merely assume that African-American people are as portrayed—this is, after all, a "reality" show.[4]

On *Survivor,* African-American contestants' often symbolically subordinate status dovetails with the enduring subordination of African-Americans in society at large. The exception: In *Survivor's* fourth season, *Marquesas,* the African-American contestants enjoyed extensive success; both became part of a successful alliance and one won the game. Race became a motif of the season, culminating in the penultimate episode, in which heroine Kathy was forced to decide whether to join up with two other white people—or the two African-Americans.

"Playing the Race Card" in the Marquesas

The first three seasons of *Survivor* had two African-American contestants each who, on occasion, made comments involving race. *Borneo's* Ramona said in Episode 4 that Jenna was her first "white friend" in a while (CBS, 24 June 2000). *Australian Outback's* Nick quipped to Alicia as their tribe ate chicken that "once you go dark meat, you don't ever go back" (CBS, 15 Feb. 2001). And *Africa's* Linda several times referred to the continent as the "mother land."

However, *Marquesas* was the first edition of *Survivor* where the African-American contestants—in this case Sean, a teacher from New York City, and Vecepia, an Air Force veteran and office manager—were shown *explicitly* discussing race on *multiple* occasions over the course of a season, resulting in a racial motif that climaxed in a somewhat awkward, black vs. white situation in the penultimate episode, one also rife with complicated instances of repetition and denial, and Vecepia's surprising victory in the season finale.

Sean refers to himself as a "Harlem brother" or some variation thereof numerous times in passing, but race first comes up at length in a scene in the Episode 2 (CBS, 7 March 2002). As it begins, Sean and Vecepia sit near the beach as the five other members of the Maraamu Tribe—all white—swim. We see the following exchange, intercut with solo confessionals:

> Sean (to camera): It's nice to bond with somebody [Vecepia] who understands. A lot of things are cultural. . . . [W]e don't even have to finish thoughts and we already know where we are. . . .
>
> Sean (to Vecepia): [T]he other five are different [from one another], but the commonality bond that bonds them is that . . . is *that.* . . .
>
> Sean: Even the fact that you and I are sitting here talking right now can be perceived as . . .
>
> Vecepia: We're strategizing. . . .

Sean (now speaking to camera): Sometimes the game isn't necessarily fair because me and [Vecepia], we're playing a whole other mental game that [the other Maraamu tribe members] don't even know. . . . Everybody [else] can just be themselves. We have to be ourselves, but then hold back a little bit. And on top of that [Vecepia and I are] bound by Christ. And that's a stronger bond, stronger than race. . . .

Vecepia: I can just tell what people are gonna say.

Sean: Yeah . . . "Those two ungrateful Negroes! You take them on an island and they're still complaining. Where's your Al Sharpton now?" (laughs)

In this way, the theme of race—and Vecepia and Sean's comfort in discussing it—is established early on in *Marquesas*. Sean asserts that the game of *Survivor* often isn't fair to African-Americans, and the show's history up to that point—African-American people on average finishing tenth in the first three seasons, and no higher than seventh—reinforces his belief. Indeed, the fact that these apparent difficulties are implied by him several times over the season forms a Jamesonian repetition of sorts, given that it is his friend Vecepia who wins in the end.

Note too, that the Sean and Vecepia themselves invoke race-based stereotypes in trying to guess how the white contestants will react to their being seen together, and in assuming that the others can all "be themselves." They also highlight perceived "cultural" differences between blacks and whites that previous seasons of *Survivor*—and most TV shows—largely ignored.

The following episode (CBS, 13 March 2002) contains a lighthearted scene that further cements *Marquesas'* racial undertones. Maraamu playfully has a "radio show" each morning at the campfire, with different members portraying the weather forecaster and so on. In this scene, Vecepia acts as the radio show's host, who has as her "guest" tribemate Hunter, who has been heavily bitten by tiny insects called "no-nos":

Vecepia: I heard a rumor that there's two types of no-nos, [black and white]. Which ones you think you bein' bit by?

Hunter: I think I've been bit by the black ones.

Sean: *Ring! Ring!*

(laughter)

Vecepia: . . .[T]he phones are lighting up! Brother, what do you say? . . .

Sean: This is Al Sharpton, and this is ludicrous! . . . The white ones are just as bad! [But] all the black ones get in trouble with the law . . .

The rest of the tribe applauds heartily at this—a far cry from later episodes, where Sean and Vecepia's discussion of race becomes a very serious

Table 8.3. Final five players on *Survivor: Marquesas*

Name	Age	Occupation	Notes
Vecepia	36	Office manager	Black, close friends with Sean; Air Force veteran
Sean	30	Teacher	Black, close friends with Vecepia; from New York
Kathy	47	Real est. agent	White, original tribemate with Neleh, Paschal; from Vermont
Neleh	21	Student	White, closely allied with Paschal; Mormon from Utah
Paschal	57	Judge	White, closely allied with Neleh; from Georgia

See Appendix B for more contestant details.

topic. Additionally, this foreshadows comments Sean makes during the "coconut challenge" discussed in Chapter 4, where after he and Vecepia are the first ousted from the challenge, he shouts that "it's a conspiracy" and that he's "calling Johnny Cochran."

As previously explained, following that immunity challenge, five contestants—Paschal, Neleh, Kathy, Sean, and Vecepia—unite to defeat an alliance of four others who were plotting their demise. They vote out this quartet of players at consecutive Tribal Councils, leaving only themselves by the time the race-saturated Episode 12 begins (see Table 8.3). This ignites another symbolic class struggle: Paschal and Neleh are close friends and admit to the others that they are allied and will not vote each other out. Sean and Vecepia are also close—but are they allied? And if so, does it have anything to do with their race? Much of the episode revolves around this question, and the conundrum Kathy faces in deciding who to side with for the end game.

This theme is clear from the episode's opening moments, as Vecepia and Sean sit by the fire with Kathy, who was the overwhelming choice to win *Marquesas* among respondents to the 2004 survey, and No. 4 among all 150 contestants, according to the AAAI in the 2005 survey. "I truly do not believe race is an issue on this beach," Vecepia says in a voice over while discussing Kathy's status as a swing vote, a statement of mock denial, given that she and Sean spend much of the episode implicitly accusing the others of assuming they are allied (CBS, 16 May 2002). Indeed, now speaking directly to Kathy, Vecepia explains how she perceives others as viewing her and Sean as a voting bloc: "There's two African-Americans, [so people are] going to think, 'Oh, those two are in together.' "

Kathy is clearly thrown by this. "It's gonna look big, playing the race card," she tells the camera. Thrusting race into the equation clearly perturbs Neleh and Paschal—who on an earlier episode had said "somebody like Sean" winning *Survivor* "would be an embarrassment" (CBS, 18 April 2002). Neleh opines that race has "never played a part in this game. Every once in a while, they'll just throw in [a comment about race]. It made me really irritated" (CBS, 16 May 2002). By denying race as an issue, Neleh furthers the episode's Jamesonian twist. She and Paschal have a brief conversation that dovetails with thoughts of African-Americans as victims vs. victimizers, with Neleh saying, "It's almost like a guilt thing," and Paschal replying, "It's like you owe 'em something."

These statements also tack closely with TV producer Norman Lear's belief about race: "I don't think there's any question that white America is uncomfortable with victimization, or however you want to term the black experience, that which makes you feel guilty, feel uncomfortable" (quoted in Jhally and Lewis, 106). Paschal and Neleh see Sean and Vecepia as trying to make the game about race by denying their alliance, and then accusing anyone who says otherwise as assuming it because they both are African-American. Neleh complains about Sean complaining too much, as Kathy semi-nods in confused agreement. Paschal says he's had "no reason from Day 1" to trust either Vecepia or Sean, with Neleh adding that she would become "absolutely pukey sick" if Kathy, Vecepia, and Sean were the final three.

It's likely that anyone would feel ill at the thought of three contestants other than themselves reaching the final three, yet because race has been injected into the episode by Sean and Vecepia (and by extension the series' editors), these statements take on racial overtones, combating Neleh's earlier denial. That evening, Vecepia arranges a campfire chat to try to clear the air, but it only makes matters worse. Note carefully these comments, which follow Paschal asserting that he and Neleh are in an alliance to the end:

Neleh: I feel that Sean and Vecepia . . . [are] gonna stick together. . . . [M]aybe that's just something that's not coming out.

Sean: You're assuming there's something underneath. . . . Vee and I never had a pact, although some people thought, OK, there's the black couple. They're definitely together.

Vecepia (a bit later): We haven't walked around saying "We're the two African-Americans, we're sticking together."

Only Sean and Vecepia mention race in this entire conversation, so far as viewers are shown. They bring it up, as Vecepia did at episode's beginning. Neleh does not. Does Neleh make racial implications with her comments, or is she honestly trying to keep race out of it? Is Sean's comment justified?

The next day, Paschal appears to link Sean and Vecepia's behavior with their "culture," as he fights to keep Kathy on his side:

Paschal: It's just sickening. . . . We've been duped by Vecepia and Sean, they duped everybody. . . .

Kathy: I just don't see it.

Paschal: It's cultural. It runs deep.

Kathy: I know it does. . . .

Paschal (to camera): I'm just kind of fed up about hearing that crap about them not being in an alliance. . . . Kathy's from Vermont. I'm from Georgia. Sean's from Harlem. This thing runs deeper than a game.

Note Paschal implying that their "culture" has led to Sean and Vecepia duping "everybody" else, i.e., the white players. Just what does he mean?

At Tribal Council, Sean offers Kathy a deal: If she gives him her immunity, he won't vote for her, and they'll be the final two. But that's only two votes. That means nothing, and so Kathy presses him for more details. The conversation continues (extraneous comments have been excised):

Sean: There's some things that are obvious. . . . You can read between the lines. . . . Because [Paschal and Neleh] had an alliance, I thought maybe that Kat could hook up with me . . . and Vee. [We] never had that kind of agreement where . . . it's two African-Americans, are they now gonna band together and oust me out. If [Paschal and Neleh] are gonna have a pact, then we need to have a pact. . . .

Vecepia: I would fall in line with that and have a threesome . . . .

Paschal: Sean's said . . . there's no association between him and Vecepia . . . [yet this comment] wasn't "Let me talk to Vee," it was "You can get with me and Vee and then we'll have the numbers." . . . It's disingenuous.

Sean: . . . We've been the underdog and it's not like we've had an agreement. None of this jives up, cuz if [Paschal and Neleh] had a pact, that means they're doing the same thing they're accusing me and Vee of doing!

Sean does not come off well here at all, first insinuating to Kathy that he and Vecepia *do* have an alliance, then spinning wildly once Paschal calls him on it. Paschal, on the other hand, is rather rude, at one point snapping at Sean to listen rather than "running your mouth" all the time. It's not a big surprise that moments later, Kathy sides with Paschal and Neleh and votes out Sean.[5]

Reflecting the racial divide in this episode, white survey respondents were significantly more likely to be pleased when Sean was voted out than nonwhite respondents. Similarly, nonwhite respondents were significantly more likely to be pleased when Vecepia persevered and won the game an episode later (see Figures 8.2 and 8.3; the former is from the 2005 survey, the latter from the 2004 survey).

Similarly, an OLS regression analysis found that nonwhite respondents rated Paschal and Kathy somewhat more negatively than whites on the raw

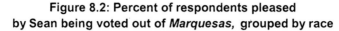

**Figure 8.2: Percent of respondents pleased
by Sean being voted out of *Marquesas,* grouped by race**

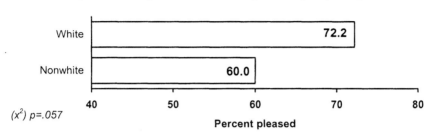

audience attitude question; there were no statistically significant differences for Neleh, Sean, and Vecepia. Paschal's questionable statements about Sean and Vecepia were the likely culprits for him, while for Kathy, perhaps nonwhite respondents remembered her as the reason Sean was sent packing, after she chose Paschal and Neleh alliance over Sean and Vecepia's "not an alliance but a bond" (see Table B.15, Appendix B).

The two contestants were so insistent on not having been allied that this talking point continued even with the post-show media tour. Million-dollar winner Vecepia said the following in a CBS.com chat with fans:

> One of the things I want to make clear is that people are confusing our relationship with an alliance. When we look at our relationship, there were so many things [Sean and I] had in common: our religion, we are African-Americans, we came over from Maraamu and stayed as long as we could and other relational things we had together and that's what the relationship was. Regarding the alliance, I see that as two people making an agreement to vote or not together and we never said that to one another . . . . We had a bond, there were times we had the opportunity to [vote] the same. We came to play our own game and have our own vote. (CBS.com, 2002)

Apparently, it depends on what the meaning of the word "alliance" is. However, almost no survey respondents believed Vecepia's argument. They were asked the following: ". . . Sean and Vecepia said that [Kathy, Neleh, and Paschal] should not assume they were in an alliance simply because they were both African-American. At episode's end, both voted for the same person, Neleh, at Tribal Council. When this occurred, what was your opinion of this set of events?" Less than 4 percent answered, "Vecepia and Sean were not in an alliance." Approximately 57 percent said that the pair was in an alliance that was at least "somewhat" based on their race. However, unlike the reactions to Sean's ouster and Vecepia's victory, there were no race-based differences to this question; whites and nonwhites held similar collective opinions.

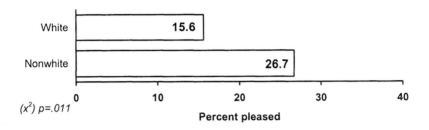

**Figure 8.3: Percent of respondents pleased
by Vecepia winning *Marquesas,* grouped by race**

Despite Paschal and Neleh's suspect statements (potentially only suspect thanks to the context the editors chose to place them in), it's difficult to
tag them as prejudiced. After all, they joined an alliance with Sean and Vecepia and maintained it to its natural conclusion. They could have voted out
two members of the erstwhile Rotu alliance (discussed at length in Chapter
4) and then joined with the remaining two members to form a four-person
majority and vote out both Sean and Vecepia. They did not. Additionally,
Paschal and Sean previously had bonded after winning a reward challenge
together—rolling around in the surf in celebration, then sipping tropical
drinks under an umbrella while discussing their differing backgrounds.

However, Paschal and Neleh's virulent reaction to Vecepia and Sean's
"don't assume that we're in an alliance just because we're both African-
Americans" line—along with Kathy's halting reluctance to discuss the
idea—reflects Jhally and Lewis' (1992) findings in their extensive qualitative study of *Cosby Show* audiences: White respondents were very uncomfortable with the idea of that program tackling racial issues. Granted, in the
case of *Survivor* we are talking about contestants on the show, rather than
viewers of the show, but the comparison holds since both respondent reactions and Paschal and Neleh's reactions reflect Lear's aforementioned comments.

"On the whole, [white] respondents want to be reminded neither that the
Huxtables are black nor, still less, of the existence of any form of racism,"
Jhally and Lewis write (105). These respondents thought well of the fact that
race was mentioned only very delicately on the *Cosby Show.* Some said
"they watched the show to enjoy it, not to be preached at; others stated that
the introduction of African-American issues would be 'alienating' and that
the show would 'lose a lot' if it dealt with racism, with the ominous consequence that they would 'probably lose the white audience they have'"(105).
The basic message, from these respondents and Paschal and Neleh as well:
"Don't talk about race!" Or as Donna Chrobot-Mason has argued, "Whites

in America tend to deny that racism exists. It's easier for them to believe that a society could exist where color doesn't matter at all" (Deggans 2004, 1E).

Yet all any of this proves is that much is open to interpretation. A person could reasonably conclude that Sean and Vecepia were trying to have it both ways, proclaiming an intention to "represent" Harlem, and noting the "cultural" differences between whites and blacks . . . then turning around and getting upset at their tribemates for assuming they are in an alliance—and that on top of that, that it's based on their race, or is "cultural." A person also could reasonably conclude that Neleh and Paschal were narrow-minded, holier-than-thou, and toeing a racist line with their comments and actions. Truth, as it often is, is in the eye of the beholder, as is the Jamesonian content of the episode: Is the repressed element a Sean/Vecepia alliance, "proved" by their voting together? Or is it race as an issue on the beach, "proved" by Kathy siding with her fellow Caucasians? According to Jameson, where there is collective repression, there is a hidden class context—and historically, it would appear race and class have been closely intertwined.

"I Almost Said White Values": The Class-Race Connection

As Jhally and Lewis describe in detail, in the industrial age African-Americans moved into segregated urban centers, particularly in the north. This segregation spurred a black middle class that served needs that the white service sector did not—doctors, lawyers, etc. "Discriminated against in housing and employment, the new black middle class lived in the same neighborhoods as their working class patrons and clients—the inner city," yielding social organization and a positive sense of community (1992, 65).

After 1960, industrial jobs began to leave inner cities, and shifts to a service-based economy created a need for more white-collar—and highly educated—workers, crippling inner-city economies (65) but avoiding the established black middle class:

> The expansion of the white-collar sector . . . along with affirmative action programs prompted by rising black political power, provided opportunities for higher-educated middle class blacks to get better-paying jobs and move out of the segregated inner city. . . . [Affirmative action's] impact on lower class blacks can be said to be entirely negative, for as the black middle class was able to leave its inner city homelands, it took with it the institutions that were needed to sustain community life. (1992, 66-67)

As a result, social order deteriorated. The poor and working-class blacks that are left in inner cities, Jhally and Lewis argue, have virtually no means to climb the social ladder and achieve the American Dream. They lack access to intergenerational transfers of wealth, the best education available, and cultural capital (1992, 68-69)—a fact that became tragically apparent following Hurricane Katrina in 2005. Therefore, this may be as much about class than race, or even more so. "The concepts of 'black person' and 'poverty' are so thoroughly intertwined in television news that the white public's perceptions of poverty appear difficult to disentangle from their thinking about African-Americans" (Entman 1994, 35, citing Peffley et al.).

Indeed, in the *Cosby* study, people of all racial stripes substituted "racial categories for class categories—hence the accusation sometimes leveled at middle-class blacks (like the Huxtables) that they have become 'too white'" (1992, 70).

The *Cosby* respondents—who found it difficult to discuss differences in class—"found themselves discussing the Huxtables as both black and white" (Jhally and Lewis 1992, 82). As one African-American respondent told them, "What's wrong with showing a black family that has those kinds of values? I almost said white values, but that's not the word I want" (83). The phrase this respondent wanted was "middle-class values," but instead "he reverts to the terms of the discourse that he knows and that make at least some sense: black equals poor, white equals affluent" (83).

In this way, *The Cosby Show* serves as a Jamesonian symbolic resolution to a real contradiction—thanks to what Jhally and Lewis call a "myth of classlessness" in America. We are all created equal in a world of capitalism, demonstrably the best economic system—albeit imperfect, hence attempts to intervene in the American economy to various degrees over time. *Cosby* helps maintain the illusion that we all have an equal shot at the American Dream—but for every John Edwards or Clarence Thomas, there are hundreds who, despite their best efforts, remain working class or poor.

Does class lurk beneath the surface of racial affairs on *Survivor*? At times it appears to. Take for instance *Marquesas*. As mentioned in Chapter 4, in the 2004 survey the greater one's income, the less likely one was to be pleased with Vecepia's win (and income strongly related to class in the survey sample). There was not a significant relationship between respondent income and reaction to Sean being voted out—but another demographic strongly linked to class, political party, did have a significant relationship. Recall that Republican respondents were significantly more likely to identify as upper class or upper middle class, politically independent respondents were significantly more likely to identify as working class, and Democratic respondents were no more likely to identify with one class or another. (There was not a significant relationship between race and party among those who took the survey.) The survey found that 77 percent of GOP respondents were "pleased" when Sean was voted out, versus 70 percent of Democrats and

Figure 8.4: Percent of respondents pleased by Sean's ouster from *Marquesas,* grouped by political party

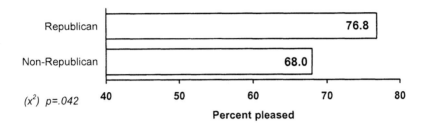

(x^2) *p=.042*

Percent pleased

65 percent of independents, or 68 percent of all non-Republican respondents (see Figure 8.4). An ordinary least squares regression analysis in fact found status as a Republican to be a bigger predictor than race regarding reaction to Sean's ouster—white female Republicans were the most likely to be pleased with this outcome, while nonwhite male non-Republicans were least likely to be pleased.[6]

Democrats, meanwhile, were the most likely to suspect Sean and Vecepia were in an alliance that was at least somewhat based on their race (62 percent), with Republicans in the middle (58 percent), and independents most likely to think they were not (47 percent).

The latter statistic is harder to pin down in terms of a class-based reading, but given the tendency of people to confuse class for race as found in the *Cosby* study, it makes sense that those with backgrounds associated with the upper class insofar as the survey sample was concerned—high income and Republican identification—would identify less with "lower class" players.[7] Some might argue that this is because people in those groups are more likely to be racially prejudiced, but based on Jhally and Lewis' evidence, class identification is at least partially at work here, not race, even if unconsciously.

Yet it is difficult indeed to ignore the Jamesonian protestations of *Marquesas'* Sean, who says that the game is harder for African-Americans to play—an argument bolstered by their lackluster performance the first three seasons—then repeatedly brings up racial separations, which in the backs of viewers' minds recalls his earlier comments.

Additionally, any time Sean says it is time to call Al Sharpton or Johnny Cochran, the somewhat subordinated role African-Americans play in society is conjured; he also refers to himself and Vecepia as the "underdogs" as late as the pivotal Tribal Council discussed earlier in this chapter. His own ouster from the program serves as a further denial. Meanwhile, we have Paschal,

Neleh, and Kathy repetitiously insisting that this is not about race, serving as a counterpoint to his comments.

The resolution to this Jamesonian equation comes twice: First, when Sean and Vecepia join with three others to overthrow the Rotu alliance, which was about to oust the two of them, resulting in significant audience pleasure; and second, when Vecepia outlasts everyone else to win the million despite being outnumbered 3-1, resulting in significant audience displeasure (that nonetheless seems more to do with her lack of character development and Kathy's immense popularity).

On the one hand, both incidents demonstrate that, at times, African-Americans in fact can do well at *Survivor*. But the fact that the pair's success has been a blip rather than a trend suggests this may be instead an exception that proves the rule. Sean's denials actually may be the repetition element of a larger Jamesonian framework spanning all eleven *Survivor* seasons thus far, with his, Vecepia's, and Ted's success serving only to deny the discomfiting truth: that African-Americans are indeed at a disadvantage on *Survivor*.

Notes

1. Note that these contestants were presented randomly with others from their respective seasons; respondents were given no other information, only a picture. Again, it is critical to understand that the stereotypes listed are based on how the contestants were portrayed on *Survivor* as recalled by respondents, not how they may be in real life.

2. The forty-nine white contestants chosen for this exercise wound up with a slightly higher mean AAAI than the entire pool of white contestants (3.262 vs. 3.199).

3. According to a T-test, the mean difference of 0.570 had a p value of .009. The raw AAI actually featured an even larger gap between white (3.268) and African-American (2.586) contestants, of 0.682, with a statistically significant T-test p value of .003. See methodology, Appendix C.

4. If the problem is an applicant pool full of people who really are drama queens and lazy bums, reality TV casting directors can certainly attempt to recruit minority contestants who would fit the mold of a "hero" or "America's Sweetheart" that a number of white contestants have fallen into. Wins by Vecepia and Sandra, a Latino, show minority contestants can indeed win. But they do appear to face a tougher road. Producers might also try casting more than three minority contestants at once. In fact, to be consistent with the diversity of the U.S. population, a season featuring sixteen contestants would need to include five members of racial minorities. But producers may fear that by casting four or more, those contestants might last long enough to form an alliance and wipe out everyone else. Do producers worry that the

key demographics for which advertisers hunger would be uninterested in a season-long plotline about that, or in a final four featuring, say, three African-Americans and a Hispanic? White audiences loved *The Cosby Show*, but they don't tune in as much for black-themed programs such as *RU The Girl* or *One on One*. *The Apprentice* has included as many as four minority members at once, several of whom advanced to the game's final stages, one of whom won the show's fourth Donald Trump-centric season. *The Amazing Race* has seen two African-American couples win in the first seven seasons, with another placing second. But in these cases, contestants aren't voted off by one another. There are no true alliances to be formed.

5. Note, too, that Vecepia and in particular Sean were perceived as greater immunity challenge threats than Paschal and Neleh.

6. Interestingly, according to a regression analysis, nonwhite respondents were also more likely to be displeased by the Koror tribe's dominance in *Palau* and pleased by Jabaru's win in Episode 1 of *Amazon*.

7. Note that, unlike most other class-based differences in survey results, these appear to be based on real-life attributes rather than in-game status. Obvious markers such as race and gender apparently override alliance-based factors.

Conclusion

"Always Historicize!"

Symbolic Resolutions and Contemporary Politics

THIS BOOK HAS USED a combination of textual analysis and survey research to demonstrate that *Survivor* both operates and resonates as a class discourse. Applying Fredric Jameson's concept of the political unconscious to the text has illuminated moments of repression, primarily related to alliances and power. Results from two surveys of 1,000 *Survivor* viewers, meanwhile, strongly suggest that social class impacts the show's consumption.

Executive producer Mark Burnett is the mastermind behind *Survivor*, so it is not surprising that he was the first to note his program's class structure. As noted earlier, writing about what he perceived as Tagi's strong work ethic and Pagong's laziness on *Survivor: Borneo*, he said that "if Tagi were the island's 'haves,' Pagong were definitely the 'have-nots.' Instead of empowering themselves by working harder, like Tagi, the Pagongs victimized themselves" (2000, 89). Eventually, this was borne out allegorically as the Pagong tribe (and Tagi outcast Sean), unable or unwilling to recognize their impending island doom and strategize on their own, fell prey to the Tagi alliance. As this study showed, survey respondents who identified as upper class or upper middle class—and/or were of demographic groups that strongly associated with those classes among the sample—generally were more likely to empathize with the Tagi alliance and later strategic players, such as *Survivor: The Amazon's* Rob.

The Life, and Wife, of Brian

No class-related survey results were more striking, however, that those regarding *Survivor: Thailand* victor Brian, a well-to-do used car salesman whose older Chuay Gahn tribe had "Pagonged" the generally younger members of the Sook Jai tribe following their merge.[1] Brian confided to the camera early on that he was in Thailand on a business trip, not to make friends,

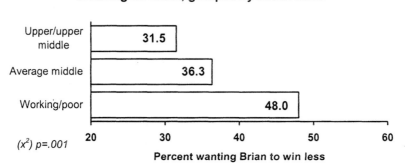

Figure 9.1: Percentage of respondents saying Brian's video made them want him to win less, as opposed to it having no effect, grouped by social class

and his eventual win utterly polarized survey respondents, with 50.9 percent pleased and 49.1 percent displeased.[2]

The survey also asked about a moment where Brian's suppression of his financial status came undone. In an episode midway through the show, the contestants viewed videotapes from home, and in Brian's, we watched as his wife wandered through their impressive abode, which housed a white grand piano, and then showed off the family's two new expensive automobiles. As this insertion of the "real" world into the manufactured world of *Survivor* reverberated, Brian frothed, fearing the revelation would undercut his plans—would his tribemates vote him out, feeling he didn't need the million-dollar prize? His alliance partner Helen (whom he eventually betrayed) raised this possibility in a confessional to the camera, and recounted in her e-mail interview:

> [The Brian video] was a *big* deal to me, but to me alone! I thought it was strange, because in a game where any little thing can get you voted off, I thought for *sure* this was an issue. . . . Rather than pick apart someone's personality, their wealth would be more of a deal breaker for me. But, like I said, that didn't seem to matter to the rest of them. . . . Much later on, Clay [who finished second] started to talk about how "well off Brian is" and how "Brian comes from a well-to-do family," but at that point it was too late to try and switch things up. (Glover 2004)

More than a third of survey respondents agreed with Helen's point of view. 1 percent wanted Brian to win the game more, 37.4 percent wanted him to win less, and 61.7 percent were unaffected in their opinion.

Broken down along class lines, however, we see a stark difference, one with a Chi Square p value of .001, the lowest among all cross-tabulations calculated between perceived social class and a non-demographic question.[3]

Figure 9.2: Percentage of respondents saying Brian's video made them want him to win less, as opposed to it having no effect, grouped by political party

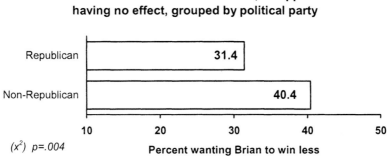

(x^2) *p=.004*   **Percent wanting Brian to win less**

We have nearly a 17 percentage point difference between upper/upper-middle-class and working-class respondents—the latter group far more likely to want Brian to win *Survivor: Thailand* less because of the car video (see Figure 9.1).

In addition to the question of class itself, the survey found statistically significant differences for related variables.[4] Non-Republicans were more likely to want Brian to win the game less after viewing his video than were Republicans; furthermore, as a respondent's household income increased, their likelihood of wanting Brian to win less decreased, showing a very large 20-point disparity between low and high income respondents. See Figures 9.2 and 9.3.

Furthermore, an OLS analysis shows several factors predicted reaction to Brian's video. A regression equation was created with reaction to the video as dependent variable. On a scale of 1 to 3, with 1 being "the video made me want Brian to win the game more" and 3 "the video made me want Brian to win the game less," a respondent who was male; upper class or upper middle class; made more than $100,000 in his household annually; and was neither Democrat nor Independent gave an average response of 2.1, the most positive for this equation. Conversely, a respondent who was female; working class, working poor or poor; made less than $35,000 annually in her household; and was a Democrat gave an average response of 2.6, the most negative for this equation.

These statistics suggest that when a contestant who is privileged in terms of the game is revealed to also be privileged in "real life," differences in viewer reaction can be magnified, indicating again that *Survivor* can indeed be associated with the culture that produced it. This reaffirms perhaps more than anything the class resonance of *Survivor*—something that, given these figures involve the show's fifth season, has not faded over time. Even

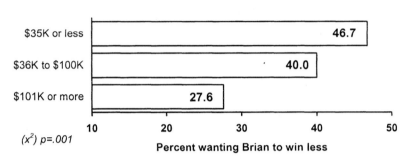

Figure 9.3: Percentage of respondents saying Brian's
video made them want him to win less, as opposed
to it having no effect, grouped by income

(x^2) p=.001

Percent wanting Brian to win less

the tenth season, *Palau*, had differing resonances among those of different class-related backgrounds, as will be discussed below.

"Concentric Frameworks" Revisited

As explained in Chapter 2, Jameson believes one can interpret a narrative within three concentric frameworks of generality that lead to the master code of the universal historical narrative. The first level examines the text as a symbolic or imaginary resolution of a real contradiction (such as apparent social inequalities in a society where all are purportedly equal). We saw this most precisely with Colleen and Gervase's wardrobe enhancements in *Borneo*, as well as John's nude diving in *Marquesas*. Elsewhere, soon after he formed his *Borneo* alliance, the editors chose to show "King Richard" strapping a hunting knife to his leg after his tribe won it in a reward. This symbolic display of political power helped highlight the fact that all were not equal on Tagi beach.

Symbolism is also built into the form of *Survivor* itself. Fire, as Jeff Probst announces to every new batch of contestants, represents life in the game. Contestants carry lit torches to and from every Tribal Council—except for the person who is voted out. That castaway's flame, of course, is dramatically extinguished. It would be just as easy to have contestants leave Tribal Council without the theatrics, but the torch-snuffing provides symbolic closure to that week's narrative, for both contestants and viewers. The immunity idol and necklace are also mere symbols, just as unnecessary—a contestant immune from the vote would be just as immune were the immunity necklace destroyed in a fire just before Tribal Council. One also could argue that they distract from the real contradictions at play—the alliances.[5]

Overall, these symbolic resolutions allow the real contradictions to carry on, unconfronted.

Moving to the second level of interpretation, which views a text as an ideologeme, a tiny part of an overall, "antagonistic collective [discourse] of social classes," (Jameson 1981, 76) one easily sees how *Survivor* is in many ways an "utterance of a class relationship" (Burnham 1995, 199). In some seasons of *Survivor*—particularly *Borneo* and *Thailand*—viewers watched the initial power players hold on to the very end. In others, an "overthrow" occurred. Along the way, we saw much repetition and denial regarding the existence of alliances, the symbolic bourgeoisie when its members play their cards right. But the existence of apparently dueling narratives shows both sides of the class relationship Jameson envisioned, where "the hegemonic relationship between dominant and dominated social classes or groups is most pronounced" (Hestetun 1993, 202).

Keeping in mind Jameson's opening mantra ("Always historicize!") and therefore pulling back to the third level, we find that the oppositional class discourses of the second horizon and the narrow textual readings of the first amalgamate into "the ultimate horizon of human history as a whole," (Jameson 1981, 76) where the master code of oppression and revolution is illuminated. This, in the end, is what the political unconscious represses, and we saw its manifestation on *Survivor* by the text's repetition and denial of the existence, or lack thereof, of alliances. Bringing such repression to the surface unearths *Survivor's* status as political allegory: It is a contrived sociopolitical contest where competing blocs of players seek to dominate one another, to symbolically play out the historical narrative and win a load of capital (i.e., $1 million). Moreover, the survey results demonstrate that, if subconsciously, *Survivor* viewers pick up on this. The fact that respondents of different social classes consume the same text differently—especially with respect to alliances—gives startling support to the Jamesonian method.

Additionally, looking at the specific moments in which *Survivor's* seasons were produced at times reveals odd parallels to American political culture. In most cases, these are certainly coincidental, yet nonetheless indicate how *Survivor* reflects the culture that produced it, even if entirely unintentionally.

For instance, the cultural context in which the first two seasons of *Survivor* took place is most appropriate. Consider the divisive 2000 presidential election, which occurred after the game of *Survivor* was staged yet still had its first tremors that summer as the series aired. In this election, a minority of voters gained power over a razor-thin plurality, thanks in part to a splintered base (Gore voters vs. Nader voters) and a controversial recount where the Republicans efficiently used the legal and political machinery available to them, while the hapless Democrats managed to create a ballot design that single-handedly may have swung the election.

Both sides accused the other of attempted electoral fraud, but such partisan squabbling is beside the point: If the election reflected the overall political climate at the time, then so did *Survivor*, with the minority (Tagi) using teamwork and hardball to outmaneuver the hapless majority (Pagong/Sean), a pattern that repeated to a degree in the following *Australian Outback*, with a five-person bloc of players using sleight of hand and political calculation to gain control over another five-person bloc (with three of the dominant five breaking away and maintaining control despite being in the minority).

All this is especially intriguing considering the survey results showing that upper class, high income, and GOP respondents—three groups highly interconnected in the sample—viewed more positively the Tagi alliance. In the 2000 election, despite the Democrats holding the White House at the time, the Republicans were the bourgeoisie.

A unique cultural moment drives home this connection: The White House Correspondents Dinner[6] in 2001 in fact featured a video parody linking *Survivor* with the Florida imbroglio. The video depicted Al Gore and George W. Bush seated at Tribal Council as host Jeff Probst "tallied the votes." He pulled from the Tribal Council urn one vote for Bush, one vote for Gore, another vote for Bush, and another for Gore. That left one unread ballot. "Here's the last vote," Probst said, and then turned it around, looking puzzled. It read "Bore." At that point, Florida Secretary of State Katherine Harris—whom Democrats had accused of lacking impartiality in the recount process and essentially controlled the election machinery in the ultimate swing state—stepped in and "re-interpreted" "Bore" as "Bush" (Oldenburg). In this way, she sent up portrayals of her as being a cheater, yet reinforced parallels between *Survivor* and political culture at large.

A year later, mere weeks after the Sept. 11 terrorist attacks, *Survivor: Marquesas* began filming; it aired in spring 2002. Just as the nation for some months united, without partisanship, in a patriotic fervor, so we saw Rotu declaring itself a "love tribe" full of unity, with contestant Paschal displaying on their beach the large U.S. flag he had brought as his "luxury item." Later, Paschal and four others united despite their diverse backgrounds and declared themselves above petty island politics, sticking to that promise for as long as the game's structure allowed them to. The season also had a strong religious theme, with four of the five finalists depicted as devout Christians. In this way, *Marquesas*—or at least most of its first eleven episodes, as Chapter 8 made clear—reflected the nation's mood at the time.

However, the show reverted to form soon after *Marquesas*. In another odd parallel, we had *All-Stars* air in the heat of the 2004 presidential campaign and *Palau* film and air in its immediate aftermath. In *All-Stars*, one

Table 9.1: Best-fitting overall structure of first eleven *Survivor* seasons

Category	Applicable seasons
Systematic elimination	*Borneo, Outback, Africa, Thailand, All-Stars, Palau, Guatemala*
Power shift	*Marquesas, Vanuatu*
Chaos	*Amazon, Pearl Islands*

bloc of contestants, despite having played the game before, did nothing to end the obvious two-person alliance of Rob M. and Amber, who went on to place first and second. Early in the 2004 race, Democrats saw the GOP strategy of painting Sen. John Kerry as a "flip-flopper" coming a mile away, yet were timid in their response. Timidity doesn't win races, hardball does. Perhaps Democrats could learn something if not from GOP strategists such as Karl Rove, than the success of *Survivor* winners: Despite having to earn the vote of his peers at the end, not often does the "nice guy" win the game; it's also most often manipulators like Rob C. and Jonny "Fairplay" who persevere to the final stages. Similarly, *Palau*—which coincidentally also had a war theme—filmed immediately after the Republicans swept nearly all the close races in 2004, consolidating their power base and control of the government. It's no surprise that Republican survey-takers identified more with *Palau's* Koror tribe, who defeated the hapless Ulong tribe (who had the advantage of being younger in a season filled with tough physical tasks) in every immunity challenge. Sixty percent of GOP respondents were pleased by Koror's dominance, while 52 percent of non-Republicans were (p=.081), with a regression analysis also finding this relationship. Unlikely as it seems that a relationship exists between political reality and a reality show springing from it (the *Marquesas* connection seems most plausible), it is intriguing indeed that in these cases, the apple did not fall far from the tree.

The form or structure of *Survivor's* seasons is also worth considering. Generally, they fall into one of three broad categories: *Systematic elimination*, in which one bloc takes control early and never lets go, riding to the end game by ousting everyone else (including, occasionally, one or more of their own, such as the bootings of Jerri and Amber on *Outback* and Jamie and Judd on *Guatemala*), known as "Pagonging" in fan parlance; *Power shift*, in which a group with power unexpectedly loses it; and *Chaos*, in which there are no successful long-lasting alliances at all, no one can be trusted, and many Tribal Council outcomes are highly unpredictable. Most seasons have featured elements of at least two of these structures (*Vanuatu* in particular is tough to pin down), but Table 9.1 shows which form has dominated: systematic elimination, where the proletariat nightmare is fulfilled. Indeed, it may be no accident that the show's first season fell along this format; with no one having played the game before, it seems likely that *Survivor's* virgin outing would most resemble the society from which it springs, one where Americans find themselves increasingly polarized, finding a political "alliance" and sticking to it virtually no matter what.

Indeed, related to the third level of Jameson's "concentric circles" is the ideology of form, as explained in Chapter 2. An argument Mark Andrejevic makes in *Reality TV: The Work of Being Watched* (2004) illuminates how reality TV's form relates to class. He notes that *An American Family*, "the first reality show based on the daily lives of real people," (67) arrived at the same time we saw a "demystification of authority" through Watergate—and the "return to an era of increasing economic inequality" (67). The average CEO's salary rose from 39 times the pay of an average worker in the early 1970s, to some 1,000 times more some thirty years later. (68) He continues:

> Reality TV . . . keeps alive the promise that "anyone" can make it in an era when the concentration of wealth and ownership in the hands of an increasingly rarefied group of elites is becoming increasingly obvious. . . . Reality TV is, in many of its incarnations, a lottery of celebrity; it invites viewers to submit tapes and apply to be on the shows with the promise that they might [be] transformed instantaneously into TV stars. Reality TV deploys the promise of greater equality based not just on the offer that anyone might become famous, but on the symbolic portrayal of celebrities who are "just like us"—if you overlook their fantastic wealth. (Andrejevic 2004, 68)

Andrejevic's thoughts, applied to Jamesonian theory, hammer home the point even more of the political nature of reality TV, not just in terms of its content, but in its basic structure and form.

Nature into History

Every week, as many as 20 million Americans receive messages from *Survivor* that appear to resonate differently for members of different social classes. This demonstrates that studying such "base" programming as reality television—and *Survivor*, along with *The Amazing Race*, is consistently the best-reviewed and of the highest quality in the genre—is indeed worthwhile, even if, to some, it seems too common to qualify. Indeed, programming that many cultural elites see as the most reprehensible form of television does contain messages about class, gender, race, and other factors. Perhaps elites who question the relevance of television suffer from their own political unconscious, refusing to examine (beyond basic questions such as "Is this bad for children?") a medium that affects virtually all Americans on a daily basis—far more, for better or worse, than any "classic" novel, painting, or poem.

This, again, is the danger, especially where reality television is concerned. It is not "real," as we have seen, but is presented as such, and the ideologies therein may more greatly impact viewers than obviously fictitious work. On fictional shows such as *Crime Scene Investigation*, those who lie, cheat, and steal are sent to jail—and if they are not caught, we can simply shrug our shoulders and say, "Well, it's fictional." On *Survivor*, however, real-life liars are not fined $1,000, but rather rewarded with $1,000,000. Real-life people are often presented in the worst possible light. Women become whiny, black men become lazy. These may be victims of selective editing, but they are presented as objective, *real* portraits. This "allows the audience to assume that the castaway interaction is a representation of contemporary morals, beliefs, and values" (Roth 2003, 35).

All this demonstrates the fears of Roland Barthes—he who urged us to interrogate the obvious—in that the purported reality of these texts makes the messages therein seem factual or *natural*, therefore imbedding them even more concretely in society and perpetuating them—or, as Barthes pronounced, transforming "history into nature" (1988, 129). Simply put, programs such as *Survivor* must be studied further to better understand their meaning and messages. In a world filled with ideologies that "support existing power structures and which purport to be natural," (McNeill 1996) we must continue to interrogate the obvious, and attempt to turn false nature back into history.

Notes

1. To clarify, technically once Chuay Gahn and Sook Jai merged, they were no longer members of those tribes, but rather members of the new Chuay Jai tribe. Voting, however, continued to generally split along original tribal lines.

2. Including those "neither pleased nor displeased" by Brian's victory, the numbers are 43.6 percent pleased, 42.0 percent displeased, and 14.4 percent neither.

3. By adding the negligible number of respondents who replied that the video made them want Brian to win more, the Chi Square value increases to .004.

4. Since doing so for the most critical variable, class, did not affect statistical significance, the handful of responses wanting Brian to win *more* based on the video have been removed from these results.

5. Only occasionally has immunity forced an alliance's hand, usually when only one non-allied member remains in the game and that person wins immunity.

6. This is an annual star-studded event in which politicians, celebrities, and the media come together for comic speeches by the president and others.

Appendix A
Synopses of First Eleven Survivor Seasons

1. *Borneo* (summer 2000)   Raw AAI: 5.16[1]; Rank: 2nd

Survivor's first season begins with sixteen castaways divided into the Tagi and Pagong tribes, with the former slightly older overall. The two tribes split their competitions, and each votes out three members before the remaining ten members merge. By now, four Tagis have formed a mostly secret alliance, and proceed to systematically vote out the other six players, who, despite their suspicions, fail to form an alliance of their own in time. The finals pit corporate trainer Rich against river guide Kelly, and Rich wins $1 million on a 4-3 jury vote following an excoriating speech by Kelly's pal-turned-enemy, Sue, who tells her she would leave her to die if she found her somewhere, dying of thirst.

2. *The Australian Outback* (spring 2001)   Raw AAI: 5.25; Rank: 1st

The Kucha and Ogakor tribes each arrive at the merge with five players—Kucha had threatened to come into the merge with a 6-4 majority until member Michael fell into their campfire, severely burned his hands, and had to be airlifted out of the game. At the merge, Ogakor takes control via a tie-breaking rule at Tribal Council and looks ready to do to Kucha what Tagi did to Pagong. However, players' dislike for Ogakor's Jerri and disrespect for member Amber lets two Kucha members, the very likable Elizabeth and Rodger, sneak into the final five—not long after a fierce rainstorm floods the players' camp. At the final three, Colby, who dominated the challenges, takes friendly Tina to the finals with him instead of the disliked Keith, and as a result loses the jury vote to her, 4-3.

3. *Africa* (fall 2001)   Raw AAI: 3.78; Rank: 7th

In Episode 5, when six members of both the Boran and the generationally split Samburu tribes remain, producers throw contestants the series' first major twist, swapping three members from each tribe into the other, resulting in splintered alliances and jumbled power structures. By the time the merge occurs, only four original Samburus remain, compared to six original Boran. Thanks to the Borans' dislike of their own member Clarence and unsubstantiated distrust of their own Kelly, soon the tribes are again even, 4-4. But the Samburu cannot overcome the distrust borne of their earlier generational divide, and Boran takes advantage of this to eliminate them one by one. In the end, the aging Kim shockingly wins the final two immunity challenges, and takes benevolent soccer pro Ethan with her to the finals rather than paranoid power player, and heavily tattooed, Lex. Ethan wins, 5-2.

4. *Marquesas* (spring 2002)   Raw AAI: 4.23; Rank: 5th

Even after a tribal swap similar to *Africa's*, the Maraamu Tribe is dominated by Rotu, which has seven members to Maraamu's three by the time the two tribes merge. Four Rotu members have by now formed an alliance much like Tagi's, and try to keep word of it from leaking to their other original tribemates (three of whom earlier had been switched into Maraamu). However, at the final nine immunity challenge, the pecking order becomes obvious—and as a result, the five non-allied contestants unite and eliminate the Rotu alliance one by one. This reversal of fortune constitutes *Survivor's* first major power swing. The season's end has other notable firsts: After a 2-2 tie at the final four Tribal Council, Paschal is eliminated by random chance. Then, after the favored Kathy flounders at the final immunity challenge, the quiet Vecepia beats ingénue Neleh before a bitter jury filled with former Rotu alliance members, 4-3, to become the game's first African-American champ.

5. *Thailand* (fall 2002)   Raw AAI: 2.66; Rank: 10th

Thailand begins with promise when for the first time, players choose their own tribes, with the two oldest contestants named team captains. One tribe, Sook Jai, winds up with youth on its side and dominates the early challenges—then loses one on purpose in order to evict one member, and begins to unravel. The older Chuay Gahn tribe faces controversy when one member accuses another of grinding her in the night. When ten players remain—five from each tribe—host Jeff Probst announces that the two tribes will live together on the same beach. Sook Jai outsider Shii Ann begins sidling up to the Chuay Gahn members, but then is stunned to learn the merge hasn't happened yet. Sook Jai thus ousts her, winding up in the minority, and as a result is systematically eliminated by the five-strong Chuay Gahn alliance once the tribes actually do merge, turning the season into monotony. Ultimately, used car salesman Brian defeats restaurateur Clay, 4-3, to win the million.

6. *The Amazon* (spring 2003)   Raw AAI: 3.99; Rank: 6th

Tribes are divided by gender for the first time here, with the women's tribe, Jabaru, more than holding its own against the men's, Tambuqui. *Amazon* also features the game's first deaf contestant, Christy, who overcomes initial social isolation to finish sixth. After both tribes have voted out two members, the youngest remaining man and woman are asked to pick new, mixed-gender tribes. At the merge, six men and four women remain, but instead of sticking with their gendered original tribes, several men side against bossy alpha-male Roger. The rest of the season is an unpredictable madhouse as contestant Rob hop-scotches from alliance to alliance—and a fire even torches the castaways' camp. At the final four, with the three remaining men aligned against her, swimsuit model Jenna beats the odds to win the last two immunity challenges, then wallops restaurant designer Matthew with a 6-1 jury vote.

7. *Pearl Islands* (fall 2003)   Raw AAI: 5.05; Rank: 3rd

Contestants are thrown for a loop when they must begin the game earlier than anticipated, jumping into the sea with only the clothes on their backs. They swim to a nearby village to barter for supplies. Drake wins the first three immunity challenges, but then Morgan returns the favor so that with ten players left, five remain from each tribe. Then comes *Survivor's* biggest-ever twist, as the six voted-out players return for a challenge and beat both Drake and Morgan, forcing each to vote out one more player—to be replaced by someone who had already been ousted once. Lillian and Burton are chosen to return to the game, and the former quickly aligns against those who had voted her out days earlier. Soon the fan favorite, jolly Rupert, is also ousted. When contestants' friends and relatives visit, Jon tricks the others into thinking his grandmother has died, earning their sympathy. In the end, Jon is dispatched at the final three by Lillian, who loses to Sandra in a 6-1 landslide for the million.

8. *All-Stars* (spring 2004)   Raw AAI: 3.20; Rank: 9th

Eighteen former castaways return in this much-hyped, long-anticipated edition that takes place, like its predecessor, in the Pearl Islands. For the first time, contestants initially are divided into three tribes of six players each. Early on, *Amazon* victor Jenna M. quits out of fear for her mother's health; *Borneo's* Sue also quits after one-time ally Rich appears to rub against her in a challenge while naked. *Marquesas'* Rob and *Outback's* Amber form an alliance early on and fall in love in the process; despite this obvious pairing, no one makes a serious move to vote them out, reviving memories of *Borneo* that are quite ironic considering the contestants' purported knowledge of the game. The predictability spurred by Rob and Amber's larger tribal alliance "Pagonging" the others leads many fans to be disappointed, though former Pagong member Jenna L. is on the "right" side of the alliance this time. Amber beats Rob 4-3 in the live finale moments after agreeing to be his bride.

9. *Vanuatu* (fall 2004)   Raw AAI: 3.69; Rank: 8th

This edition, like *Amazon*, divides the players by gender into two tribes. The men again fail on a balance beam obstacle in the opening immunity challenge, and the older men gang up on the younger ones at Tribal Council. After the women vote out a member the next episode, both tribes are forced to vote out one member each in Episode 3. Later, the tribes are jumbled somewhat, though the men remain a minority on one and a majority on the other. At the merge, the women snooker the men and unite in an all-female alliance, proceeding to vote out three men in a row, leaving just one, Chris. Chris, despite facing a 6-1 deficit, is able to take advantage of fissures in the women's alliance to worm his way into the endgame, where he prevails in the final immunity challenge and defeats fellow construction worker Twila, 5-2.

10. *Palau* (spring 2005)   Raw AAI: 4.95; Rank: 4th

As host Jeff Probst promises before the first episode aired, this is a "season of firsts." For the first time, twenty castaways enter the game, and are told to race to a nearby beach, with the first man and woman to arrive on shore immune from…something. Soon, a schoolyard pick 'em ensues (with the immune Ian and Jolanda "captains"), resulting in two tribes of nine, Ulong and Koror—and two contestants dumped off the bat. Koror wins every single immunity challenge, a *Survivor* first. Ulong is soon whittled to two, Stephenie and Bobby Jon, who face off in a Tribal Council challenge to see who will be their tribe's last member. Stephenie wins and in another first, spends a night alone at camp before joining Koror, where she lasts nine more days—three of those thanks to another contestant quitting—before being voted out. The core Koror alliance of five then shatters, and the remaining players become increasingly suspicious and outspoken regarding alliances. Ian sacrifices himself at the final three to preserve his friendship with firefighter Tom. Tom takes the generally unliked Katie to the final two, and wins, 6-1.

11. *Guatemala* (fall 2005)[2]

This season begins with intrigue as *Palau* players Bobby Jon and Stephenie return for a second try, then are, with the rest of the contestants, subjected to a grueling 11-mile hike through the sweltering jungle, by the end of which several of the men have collapsed in exhaustion. Some of the players also live amid Mayan ruins. In Episode 4, the tribes are rearranged, dooming several players who had looked to be in command. Stephenie, however, has bonded with several players and begins to take control of the game. She helps Bobby Jon reach the jury, but her allies vote him off after the intended target, Gary, finds a tiny immunity idol hidden in the woods. Danni is soon the last of her pre-merge tribe remaining. However, dissention and fear in the ranks of the dominant bloc, plus key challenge victories, enable her to reach the finals, where she clobbers Stephenie, who had simply betrayed too many people, 6-1.

Notes

1. The raw audience attitude index (AAI) based on results from 2005 survey. Respondents rated their recollected "overall attitude" toward each season at the time it aired on a scale from 0 (very negative) to 6 (very positive). The raw AAI is the mean of these responses. The results were not weighted (i.e., the AAAI) because doing so would not have changed the rankings. Only the first ten seasons are ranked.

2. *Guatemala* took place after the 2005 survey was conducted, with its finale airing just as this book went into production. It is therefore not rated with an AAI.

Appendix B
Contestant Profiles and Ratings

On the following pages are a series of tables; Tables B.2 through B.12 describe each contestant on *Survivor's* first eleven seasons. The following information is included in these eleven charts, with abbreviations also noted:

- **Name, age, occupation:** These are according to the official CBS Web site, at the time the season aired. Some occupation names are abbreviated.
- **AAAI:** The first number is the contestant's adjusted audience attitude index based on the 2005 survey. The highest value is 6.000, for a "very positive" audience attitude toward a contestant, while the lowest is 0.000, for "very negative." See Appendix C for details on how this was computed. The second number is the contestant's AAAI rank, with 1 being the most positively rated contestant and 150 being the most negatively rated. Table B.1 lists all 150 rated contestants in order of AAAI ranking.
- **Edgic:** Included as a supplemental measure of depictions, this is a player's season-long "Edgic" rating as computed by a group of viewers who conduct informal content analyses of episodes (the author is not among them). The ratings are included here with input from the group's founder, known online only as KernelQ, and four others: Chaperone, 9RedWing19, Pastordice, and Warrior. There are four ratings: *under the radar (UR), middle of the road (MR), complex personality (CP), and over the top (OT)*.

    UR applies to players who are generally "underutilized or deliberately hidden [and] kept out of focus.... [They] may be seen, but they aren't seen doing or saying" many significant things during their time on the show, although they may occasionally emerge as a main player. Even a contestant who lasts long or wins may be rated UR if his personality is quiet and/or his strategy kept hidden (Warrior 2005).

    MR players aren't "emphasized caricatures or developed personalities... These characters are more just kind of there." Neither ignored nor edited as in your face, they may have a few UR, CP, and even OT scenes, but not enough to receive such a rating overall (Warrior 2005).

    CP players' "editing has depth...their choices are presented to the audience so that we get an insight into their thinking. We generally see their strengths and flaws [and discussion of strategy]... These are the major players in the course of the game, and it is their choices that shape the story." In other words, this edit is multi-dimensional (Warrior 2005). The winner of each season often has fit best into this or the MR category, without many specifically OT or UR episodes.

OT players are often the "villains and heroes, the ones we love to love or hate. A consistently [OT] character is presented as a distraction." These may also include contestants edited one-dimensionally their entire time on the show, be it over the course of one episode or twelve, without progressive development of their personality (Warrior 2005).

These are only the most basic of Edgic analyses; many seasons also have per-episode ratings. The valence of a player's depiction is also measured; these were very similar to AAAI results. A player's "visibility" is also measured. The Edgic participants use the ratings to create statistical models in an attempt to predict each season's results, with some success. For more information, see historic Edgic ratings at http://p085.ezboard. com/fsurvivorsucksfrm9.showMessage?topicID=8141.topic.

- **Notes:** Significant events in the player's time on *Survivor*; in some cases, other contestant's reactions to them and information about their overall "edit" are included, in many case based on the author's own impressions. Finally, in cases where the player was a person for whom respondents to the 2005 survey could choose descriptions, the most common adjective cited is included in italics. See Appendix C, methodology, for details.

The remainder of Appendix B has tables with compiled survey results, including differences among respondent subgroups (such as income groups, political orientation and gender) regarding how they perceived certain contestants. Other tables list the most common adjectives used to cite various contestant subgroups. All of these tables are based on a survey conducted in May 2005, before *Guatemala* aired, so contestants from that season (except Stephenie and Bobby Jon, who also appeared on *Palau*) are not accounted for in them.

Abbreviations used in Appendix B

AAAI: Adjusted audience attitude index (see previous page)

UR: Under the radar (see previous page)

MR: Middle of the road (see previous page)

CP: Complex personality (see previous page)

OT: Over the top (see previous page)

TC: Tribal Council

IC: Immunity challenge

RC: Reward challenge

Bor.: *Borneo*, first season of *Survivor*

Out.: *Australian Outback*, second season

Afr.: *Africa*, third season

Marq.: *Marquesas*, fourth season

Thai.: *Thailand*, fifth season

Amaz.: *The Amazon*, sixth season

PIs.: *Pearl Islands*, seventh season

Van.: *Vanuatu*, ninth season

Pal.: *Palau*, tenth season

Table B.1: AAAI rankings of contestants from first ten *Survivor* seasons

Rank	Name, season	AAAI	Rank	Name, season	AAAI	Rank	Name, season	AAAI
1	Colleen, Born.	5.031	51	Tijuana, Pls.	3.511	101	Caryn, Pal.	2.684
2	Elizabeth, Out.	4.994	52	Butch, Amaz.	3.491	102	Jeanne, Amaz.	2.672
3	Ethan, Afr.	4.847	53	Jenna, Born.	3.431	103	Dirk, Born.	2.647
4	Kathy, Marq.	4.797	54	Sonja, Born.	3.428	104	Mitchell, Out.	2.615
5	Colby, Out.	4.790	55	Chris, Van.	3.412	105	Kel, Out.	2.611
6	Rodger, Out.	4.766	56	Jennifer, Pal.	3.399	106	Keith, Out.	2.600
7	Rudy, Born.	4.630	57	Darrah, Pls.	3.372	107	Jeff, Pal.	2.587
8	Stephenie, Pal.	4.613	58	Dolly, Van.	3.371	108	Ramona, Born.	2.579
9	Sandra, Pls.	4.552	59	Leann, Van.	3.347	109	Stephanie, Thai.	2.569
10	Gretchen, Born.	4.404	60	Brian, Thai.	3.338	110	Jolanda, Pal.	2.560
11	Rupert, Pls.	4.365	61	Alicia, Out.	3.326	111	James, Pal.	2.558
12	Rob, Amaz.	4.344	62	Gabriel, Marq.	3.293	112	Janet, Amaz.	2.551
13	Gina, Marq.	4.340	63	Rich, Born.	3.289	113	Jenna, Amaz.	2.541
14	Tom, Pal.	4.337	64	Twila, Van.	3.231	114	Nicole, Pls.	2.535
15	Bobby Jon, Pal.	4.336	65	Kim J., Afr.	3.186	115	Carl, Afr.	2.503
16	Tina, Out.	4.325	66	Eliza, Van.	3.156	116	Ryan, Amaz.	2.488
17	Teresa, Afr.	4.310	67	Ibrehem, Pal.	3.154	117	Susan, Born.	2.487
18	Paschal, Marq.	4.292	68	Jessie, Afr.	3.129	118	Willard, Pal.	2.473
19	Ian, Pal.	4.268	69	Ryan S., Pls.	3.119	119	Patricia, Marq.	2.453
20	Michael, Out.	4.235	70	Jan, Thai.	3.105	120	Roger, Amaz.	2.451
21	Christy, Amaz.	4.155	71	Frank, Afr.	3.074	121	Penny, Thai.	2.443
22	Jake, Thai.	4.109	72	Ami, Van.	3.055	122	Ashlee, Pal.	2.422
23	Chad, Van.	4.093	73	John K., Van.	3.051	123	Clarence, Afr.	2.402
24	Hunter, Marq.	4.055	74	Joel, Born.	3.047	124	Silas, Afr.	2.372
25	Tom, Afr.	4.048	75	Tammy, Marq.	3.042	125	Zoe, Marq.	2.326
26	Angie, Pal.	3.885	76	Amber, Out.	3.019	126	Jonathan, Pal.	2.296
27	Kelly, Born.	3.838	77	Burton, Pls.	3.013	127	Kimmi, Out.	2.295
28	Greg, Born.	3.832	78	Robert, Amaz.	2.999	128	Wanda, Pal.	2.274
29	Helen, Thai.	3.823	79	Sean, Born.	2.998	129	Daniel, Amaz.	2.269
30	Kim P., Afr.	3.779	80	Trish, Pls.	2.987	130	John, Thai.	2.260
31	Deena, Amaz.	3.772	81	Travis, Van.	2.980	131	Katie, Pal.	2.243
32	Lea, Van.	3.768	82	Erin, Thai.	2.972	132	Linda, Afr.	2.208
33	Jeff, Out.	3.753	83	Nick, Out.	2.971	133	Lindsey, Afr.	2.177
34	Matthew, Amaz.	3.735	84	Scout, Van.	2.934	134	Peter, Marq.	2.160
35	Coby, Pal.	3.734	85	Ted, Thai.	2.932	135	Heidi, Amaz.	2.159
36	Ken, Thai.	3.728	86	Rob M., Marq.	2.911	136	Diane, Afr.	2.124
37	Gregg, Pal.	3.710	87	Alex, Amaz.	2.879	137	Stacey, Born.	2.078
38	Julie, Van.	3.702	88	John P., Van.	2.874	138	B.B., Born.	2.040
39	Maralyn, Out.	3.700	89	Brandon, Afr.	2.863	139	Kimberly, Pal.	1.984
40	Ryan O., Pls.	3.694	90	Rory, Van.	2.856	140	Mia, Van.	1.938
41	Dave, Amaz.	3.685	91	Brook, Van.	2.853	141	Sarah, Marq.	1.918
42	Brady, Van.	3.677	92	Michelle, Pls.	2.847	142	Robb, Thai.	1.909
43	Tanya, Thai.	3.676	93	Jed, Thai.	2.813	143	Lillian, Pls.	1.906
44	Andrew, Pls.	3.664	94	Vecepia, Marq.	2.811	144	Debb, Out.	1.848
45	Christa, Pls.	3.656	94	Sean, Marq.	2.811	145	Jerri, Out.	1.842
46	Kelly, Afr.	3.638	96	John, Marq.	2.798	146	Joanna, Amaz.	1.821
47	Shii-Ann, Thai.	3.611	97	Janu, Pal.	2.775	147	Clay, Thai.	1.786
48	Lex, Afr.	3.609	98	Lisa, Van.	2.741	148	Jon, Pls.	1.745
49	Gervase, Born.	3.564	99	Shawna, Amaz.	2.706	149	Ghandia, Thai.	1.355
50	Neleh, Marq.	3.541	100	Shawn, Pls.	2.702	150	Osten, Pls.	1.203

Note: For explanation of AAAI, see first page of Appendix B and also Appendix C.

Table B.2. Contestants on *Survivor: Borneo* (CBS, summer 2000)

Placement and name	Age	Occupation	AAAI	Edgic	Comments on depiction
1 Richard Hatch	39	Corporate trainer	3.289-63	CP	*Shrewd* mastermind of "Tagi alliance"; known for walking on beach in the nude; during opening episode, confided to camera that he would win.
2 Kelly Wiglesworth	23	River guide	3.838-27	CP	Alliance's most guilt-ridden, wavering member; won four straight ICs to stay in game; voted out Sue to break TC tie, then incurred her wrath.
3 Rudy Boesch	72	Ret. Navy SEAL	4.630-7	UR	*Loyal*; known for hilarious, if prejudiced, comments; formed tight alliance with Richard despite the latter's sexuality. Nearly ousted early on.
4 Sue Hawk	38	Truck diver	2.487-117	OT	*Opinionated* "redneck"; gruff alliance member; befriended Kelly, then felt betrayed by her in finale; delivered famous "rats and snakes" speech.
5 Sean Kenniff	30	Neurologist	2.998-79	UR	Portrayed as dumb maker of useless fishing pole and beach bowling alley; alphabetical voting system helped doom Pagong; Tagi outsider.
6 Colleen Haskell	23	Student	5.031-1	OT	Cute as a button but often naïve, fit "America's Sweetheart" role to a T. Edited as having ill-fated affair with Greg; later denied this was true.
7 Gervase Peterson	30	Basketball coach	3.564-49	OT	*Lazy*; celebrated son's birth while on island; online glitch implied he won.
8 Jenna Lewis	22	Student	3.431-53	OT	Naïve mom of twin girls; cried when her video from home went missing.
9 Greg Buis	24	Journeyman	3.832-28	CP	Odd "coconut phone" inventor; won first solo IC; eschewed strategizing.
10 Gretchen Cordy	38	Teacher	4.404-10	OT	Hardy leader of oblivious Pagong; first player ousted by alliance at merge.
11 Joel Klug	28	Trav. salesman	3.047-74	MR	"Alpha male" booted by Pagong women after laughing at sexist joke.
12 Dirk Been	23	Farmer	2.647-103	MR	*Religious*, pensive; got too skinny, became first victim of Tagi alliance.
13 Ramona Gray	29	Chemist	2.579-108	OT	*Weak*; became ill in early going, failed to regain strength soon enough.
14 Stacey Stillman	27	Lawyer	2.078-137	MR	"Annoying"; wrongly trusted Sue; alleged producers engineered ouster.
15 B.B. Andersen	64	Retired contractor	2.040-138	OT	*Bossy*; failed to bond with younger players; all but asked to be ousted.
16 Sonya Christopher	63	Musician	3.428-54	OT	*Kind* cancer survivor; fell during first-ever IC, helping Pagong win.

Source for names, ages, professions: www.cbs.com/primetime/survivor/survivors

Table B.3. Contestants on *Survivor: The Australian Outback* (CBS, spring 2001)

Placement and name	Age	Occupation	AAAI	Edgic	Comments on depiction
1 Tina Wesson	40	Nurse	4.325-16	CP	Stealthy player; helped convince Colby to force tie at critical early TC; got Kimmi to spill critical Kucha secrets; gave up IC to Keith to aid tribe.
2 Colby Donaldson	26	Auto designer	4.790-5	CP	Proud Texan; refused to fall into Jerri's web; won string of ICs; loyalty in taking Tina to end cost him win; edited as alliance's decision-maker.
3 Keith Famie	40	Chef	2.600-106	MR	"Chef who couldn't cook"; Jerri's plan to oust him failed when Colby switched sides; rescued food from flood; carried to end by Tina, Colby.
4 Elisabeth Filarski	23	Shoe designer	4.994-2	OT	*Kind;* "America's Sweetheart" V.2.0; tight bond with Rodger; didn't kick butt in challenges, but benefited from others' dislike of Jerri. Religious.
5 Rodger Bingham	53	Teacher	4.766-6	OT	*Honest;* chummy "Kentucky Joe" so tight with Elisabeth he told Tina to vote him out first; rallied Kucha after Michael fell into fire. Religious.
6 Amber Brkich	22	Admin. assistant	3.019-76	UR	Buddy of Jerri's left dangling after Jerri was booted; Tina and company disrespected under-the-radar strategy; didn't appear to do much else.
7 Nick Brown	23	Student	2.971-83	UR	*Lazy,* quiet builder of camp "kitchen"; key IC win prompted Jerri ouster.
8 Jerri Manthey	30	Actress	1.842-145	OT	*Bossy,* "manipulative"; tactics spurred Kel boot; led early failed alliance.
9 Alicia Calaway	32	Pers. trainer	3.326-61	MR	*Strong* and confident; Jeff's pal; sparred with Kimmi over chickens' fate.
10 Jeff Varner	34	Internet manager	3.753-33	CP	Shrewd and gossipy; doomed by Kimmi discussing votes with Tina.
11 Michael Skupin	38	Company pres.	4.235-20	MR	Hunted pig; semi-arrogant leader airlifted from game after burning self.
12 Kimmi Kappenberg	28	Bartender	2.295-127	OT	*Opinionated,* "smelly" vegetarian; too attached to tribe's chicken reward?
13 Mitchell Olson	23	Songwriter	2.615-104	MR	Tall Jerri pal ousted in TC tie-breaker after Colby sided with Tina, Keith.
14 Maralyn Hershey	51	Ret. Police	3.700-39	OT	*Honest;* tough, jolly "Mad Dog"; fell in early IC, team sad to see her go.
15 Kel Gleason	32	Army officer	2.611-105	MR	*Strong;* didn't fit in; accused of smuggling beef jerky into camp by Jerri.
16 Debb Eaton	45	Prison officer	1.848-144	OT	Poor social skills trumped strength; embarrassed by her tribe's sex talk.

Source for names, ages, occupations: www.cbs.com/primetime/survivor2/

Table B.4. Contestants on *Survivor: Africa* (CBS, fall 2001)

Placement and name	Age	Occupation	AAAI	Edgic	Comments on depiction
1 Ethan Zohn	27	Soccer player	4.847-3	MR	Hard not to like but somewhat quiet; bonded with poor children at remote village after RC win; allied with Tom, Lex, Kim; edited as Jesus figure?
2 Kim Johnson	57	Ret. teacher	3.186-65	MR	*Weak*; blandly edited "mama"; failed at numerous challenges before winning final two to save self; chose "good" Ethan over "evil" Lex.
3 Lex van den Berghe	38	Marketing	3.609-48	CP	Paranoid central character; went on witch hunt after receiving mystery vote, wrongly blaming Kelly; liked by some despite (too?) negative edit.
4 Tom Buchanan	46	Farmer	4.048-25	CP	*Loyal*; marble-mouthed and jolly; closest to Lex and Ethan; evicted after Teresa sparked bout with Lex and Kim won IC, ending any male alliance.
5 Teresa Cooper	42	Flight attendant	4.310-17	MR	Charming, shrewd; cast mystery vote vs. Lex after making deal with Clarence, then watched as Lex's obsession almost destroyed his alliance.
6 Kim Powers	29	Marketing	3.779-30	MR	In younger bloc of generationally splintered Samburu; friendly; semi-betrayed by Brandon when he voted vs. Kelly without warning Kim.
7 Frank Garrison	43	Phone technician	3.074-71	CP	*Opinionated* "redneck" hard on the young; asked tribe "What is brunch?"
8 Brandon Quinton	25	Bartender	2.863-89	MR	*Complaining*; inexplicably ousted Kelly over Lex; had "date" with Frank.
9 Kelly Goldsmith	22	Behavior research	3.638-46	MR	Smart, snarky; unraveled Samburu plot; scapegoat for paranoid ally Lex.
10 Clarence Black	24	Basketball coach	2.402-123	MR	*Strong*; too big a threat at merge to last; Did he steal his tribe's beans?
11 Lindsey Richter	27	Advertising	2.177-133	OT	*Emotional*, competitive; booted when rejiggered tribe deadlocked at TC.
12 Silas Gaither	23	Bartender	2.372-124	CP	Cocky Samburu "mallrats" ringleader; doomed when swapped to Boran.
13 Linda Spencer	44	Career services	2.208-132	UR	*Religious*; "superstitious"; asks Lindsey if her mom had ever hugged her.
14 Carl Bilancione	46	Dentist	2.503-115	CP	Talked up his expensive cars; ousted after generational TC deadlock.
15 Jessie Camacho	27	Sheriff's deputy	3.129-68	UR	*Weak* but pretty; seemed to spend all her time under tribe's mosquito net.
16 Diane Ogden	42	Mail carrier	2.124-136	MR	Collapsed during first challenge; had dispute with Clarence over beans.

Source for names, ages, occupations: www.cbs.com/primetime/survivor3/

Table B.5. Contestants on *Survivor: Marquesas* (CBS, spring 2002)

Placement and name	Age	Occupation	AAAI	Edgic	Comments on depiction
1 Vecepia Towery	37	Office manager	2.811-94	UR	*Religious*; oft-underdeveloped surprise victor; cozied up to Rotu before coup; eschewed "drama"; struck deals to reach end; allied with Sean?
2 Neleh Dennis	21	Student	3.541-50	MR	*Naive*, religious; tight bond with Paschal, got "princess" edit late after offering half-eaten mint; scolded at end for starting to strategize so late.
3 Kathy Vavrick-O'Brien	47	Real estate	4.797-4	CP	*Intelligent* heroine; initial social outcast blossomed into contender; summit with Rob first stone in path to coup; felled by distraction in last IC.
4 Paschal English	57	Judge	4.292-18	MR	*Trustworthy*, pensive; sent with Kathy, pal Neleh to underdog tribe; wary of Sean, Vecepia's motives; ousted by random "purple rock" at tied TC.
5 Sean Rector	30	Teacher	2.811-94	CP	*Lazy*; religious; dialogue tinged with racial overtones; fearlessness of discussing alliances helped doom Rotu's; denied alliance with Vecepia.
6 Robert DeCanio	38	Limousine driver	2.999-78	MR	Longest-lasting, most sympathetic member of ill-fated Rotu alliance; tried in vain with Tammy to swing some of coup group their way.
7 Tammy Leitner	29	Crime reporter	3.042-75	MR	Shifted views on lying as game progressed; saved by IC win after coup.
8 Zoe Zanidakis	35	Fishing boat cptn	2.326-125	UR	Socially awkward; making tribemates jewelry post-coup didn't save her.
9 John Carroll	36	Registered nurse	2.798-96	CP	*Egotistical* alliance leader took support of Paschal, Neleh for granted.
10 Rob Mariano	26	Construction	2.911-86	CP	"Robfather" seized reins of his first tribe; spoke of alliances too loudly.
11 Gina Crews	28	Nature guide	4.340-13	OT	*Honest*; savored sole IC win then, outnumbered, bowed out gracefully.
12 Gabriel Cade	23	Bartender	3.293-62	MR	Overtly idealistic; refused to rule out voting vs. allies, ending his shot.
13 Sarah Jones	24	Account manager	1.918-141	MR	Seen as "lazy" and "vain"; done for once suitor Rob M. swapped tribes.
14 Hunter Ellis	33	FedEx Pilot	4.055-24	OT	*Strong*; leader undone early by Rob M.-led "knuckleheads." Liked Gina?
15 Patricia Jackson	49	Truck assembler	2.453-119	OT	Tribe's "mom" pushed image of hard worker, but still seen as weak link.
16 Peter Harkey	45	Bowl. alley owner	2.160-134	OT	"Fruit loop"; speech about bodily holes doomed him despite strength.

Source for names, ages, occupations: www.cbs.com/primetime/survivor4/

Table B.6. Contestants on *Survivor: Thailand* (CBS, fall 2002)

Placement and name	Age	Occupation	AAAI	Edgic	Comments on depiction
1 Brian Heidik	34	Used car salesman	3.338-60	CP	Oily manipulator followed in Rich's footsteps, saw game as "business trip"; won string of ICs; to fans, smart strategy mitigated a negative edit.
2 Clay Jordan	46	Restaurateur	1.786-147	MR	*Opinionated* "redneck" accused of racist remarks vs. Ted, whom he also secretly told rival Sook Jai members to vote against; "weasily, lazy."
3 Jan Gentry	53	Teacher	3.105-70	UR	*Weak*; selected dominant Chuay Gahn tribe's members; emotional, kind but "odd"; maintained cemetery for dead animals. Too trusting of Brian.
4 Helen Glover	47	Navy swim instr.	3.823-29	CP	Most morally aware alliance member? Recipe reciter; lost at sea with Jan, jokingly said thankful she didn't have a gun; deceived by Brian, Clay.
5 Ted Rogers Jr.	37	Software devel.	2.932-85	CP	*Strong*, drawn into blistering "he said, she said" sex harassment fight with Ghandia; somewhat "naïve", burned by alliance-mates in endgame.
6 Jake Billingsley	61	Land broker	4.109-22	CP	*Honest*; most sympathetic part of ill-fated Sook Jai tribe, whose members he had chosen; forced to choose between Ken and Erin as tribe crumbled.
7 Penny Ramsey	27	Pharma. sales	2.443-121	UR	Attempt at betraying Jake backfired when alliance ousted her instead.
8 Ken Stafford	30	NYPD officer	3.728-36	UR	*Strong*, a trait he downplayed; job meant respect, but seen as tough to beat.
9 Erin Collins	26	Real estate agent	2.972-82	UR	Season's female eye candy was first core Sook Jai member to be canned.
10 Shii Ann Huang	28	Executive recruiter	3.611-47	CP	*Intelligent*; cozying up to Chuay Gahn at fake merge felled snarky fan fave.
11 Robb Zbacnik	23	Bartender	1.909-142	OT	"Skater dude" hothead nearly choked Clay at intense RC; mellowed at end.
12 Stephanie Dill	29	Firefighter	2.569-109	MR	*Weak*; questioned others' work ethic; slept on wet beach, not in shelter.
13 Ghandia Johnson	33	Legal secretary	1.355-149	OT	*Quarrelsome*; lost tribe's lead in first IC; accused Ted of sex harassment.
14 Jed Hildebrand	25	Dental student	2.813-93	CP	Blamed for losing fishing net in ocean; Sook Jai threw IC to oust him.
15 Tanya Vance	27	Social worker	3.676-43	UR	Friendly, kind, but became ill in early going; classic "weak link" bootee.
16 John Raymond	40	Pastor	2.260-130	OT	Practical joke about tribe's water hole fell flat, helping to alienate him.

Source for names, ages, occupations: www.cbs.com/primetime/survivor5/

Table B.7. Contestants on *Survivor: The Amazon* (CBS, spring 2003)

Placement and name	Age	Occupation	AAAI	Edgic	Comments on depiction
1 Jenna Morasca	21	Swimsuit model	2.541-113	MR	*Lazy*; generally edited as spoiled beauty queen until final episode, when won last two ICs to save self; stripped with Heidi for food at merge IC.
2 Matthew Von Ertfelda	33	Restaurant design	3.735-34	CP	Seen as naïve tool to help Rob advance to endgame; targeted post-merge when others seemed to fear his sanity, but IC win led to Deena's ouster.
3 Rob Cesternino	24	IT projects coord.	4.344-12	CP	Played alliance hopscotch, depending on needs at the time; "horny" comic had negative edit but lauded as "best player not to win" thanks to strategy.
4 Butch Lockley	50	Principal	3.491-52	UR	*Loyal*; world-wise but quiet; motto: "believe in yourself"; apparent firewood obsession helped spur camp burning down; sole Matt voter at end.
5 Heidi Strobel	24	Phys. ed. teacher	2.159-135	OT	Jenna's pal and fellow stripper at IC; Rob's crush; depicted as somewhat dumb yet had season's high IQ; chided Joanna for doing too much work.
6 Christy Smith	24	Adventure guide	4.115-21	OT	*Emotional*; deafness led to social isolation early, but came into own after tribal switch; waffling before final-six TC left Rob to turn the tables on her.
7 Alex Bell	32	Triathlon trainer	2.879-87	UR	Final four slot foiled when told Rob he'd oust him then; liked Shawna.
8 Deena Bennett	35	Deputy D.A.	3.772-31	CP	*Opinionated*; leader of women's tribe sent away after growing too cocky.
9 Dave Johnson	24	Rocket scientist	3.685-41	MR	On wrong side of splintered men's tribe at merge; otherwise confident.
10 Roger Sexton	56	Corporate V.P.	2.451-120	OT	*Bossy*; sexist, homophobic; arrogant; tribe gleeful in ousting him at merge.
11 Shawna Mitchell	23	Clothing retail	2.706-99	UR	"Ill" until men showed up after swap, then fell for Alex, but didn't last.
12 Jeanne Hebert	41	Marketing director	2.672-102	MR	Joanna's friend booted when Heidi switched sides at first mixed-gender TC.
13 Joanna Ward	31	Guidance coun.	1.821-146	UR	*Religious*, bossy and quarrelsome; sang gospel at camp, feared IC idol.
14 Daniel Lue	27	Tax accountant	2.269-129	UR	*Weak* but muscular; lost first IC for his tribe, soon predictably ousted.
15 Janet Koth	47	Travel agent	2.551-112	MR	Accused of smuggling snackbar into game; generally weak from Day 1.
16 Ryan Aiken	23	Model	2.488-116	OT	*Lazy*; paired with Dan on fateful balance beam; talked smack about women.

Source for names, ages, occupations: www.cbs.com/primetime/survivor6/

Table B.8. Contestants on *Survivor: Pearl Islands* (CBS, fall 2003)

Placement and name	Age	Occupation	AAAI	Edgic	Comments on depiction
1 Sandra Diaz-Twine	29	Office assistant	4.552-9	CP	*Opinionated*, shrewd; survived failed alliance with Rupert by playing Jon and Burton; strategy included sneaking behind shrubbery to eavesdrop.
2* Lillian Morris	51	Scout troop leader	1.906-143	MR	*Emotional*; after pre-merge return to game, voted vs. tribe that earlier had ousted her; despondent; at first naïve to Jon and Burton's manipulations.
3 Jon Dalton	29	Art consultant	1.745-148	OT	*Shrewd*, egotistical "Jonny Fairplay" infamously had friend announce at RC that grandmother had died; dismissed women's chances of winning.
4 Darrah Johnson	22	Mortician	3.372-57	UR	*Kind/Weak*, classic long-term under the radar player; won late string of ICs to stave off execution; came up with plan to oust Burton at final five.
5* Burton Roberts	31	Marketing exec.	3.013-77	CP	Duped Rupert and other original tribemates after reentering game; bonded with Jon; a positive edit suddenly turned negative in last few episodes.
6 Christa Hastie	24	Computer progr.	3.656-45	CP	Friendly Sandra pal; suckered by Jon swearing on "grandmother's grave."
7 Tijuana Bradley	27	Pharma. sales	3.511-51	MR	*Kind*; overhearing alleged allies' plans with Sandra's help didn't save her.
8 Rupert Boneham	39	Teen mentor	4.365-11	OT	Overt hero edit; pirated rivals' shoes in premiere; betrayed by Burton, Jon.
9 Ryan Opray	31	Electrician	3.694-40	UR	Friendly and liked; simply on wrong side of then-dominant alliance.
10 Andrew Savage	40	Attorney	3.664-44	OT	*Self-confident*; led Morgan tribe, bond with Rupert; ousted thanks to Lil.
11* Shawn Cohen	29	Advertising sales	2.702-100	MR	Mocked Rupert sewing; poor work ethic outweighed tribe distrust of Jon.
11* Osten Taylor	27	Equity trade mgr.	1.203-150	OT	*Unreliable*; first player to quit game; scared of pelican; couldn't swim.
13* Trish Dunn	42	Sales executive	2.987-80	UR	Attempted conspiracy to oust Rupert backfired, leading to her defeat.
14* Michelle Tesauro	22	Student	2.847-92	UR	*Naïve*; offered to dupe rival tribe in gross-food IC, but failed miserably.
17* Ryan Shoulders	23	Produce clerk	3.119-69	MR	Close to Lillian; friendly and determined, but too weak to last long.
18* Nicole Delma	24	Massage therapist	2.535-114	OT	Too-early strategizing turned tribe's guns off weaker players and onto her.

* Lil was also the third to be voted out, and Burton the fourth; both were voted back in a twist. Shawn and Osten left at a double TC. Normally, Trish, Michelle, Ryan S., and Nicole would have placed 11th, 12th, 15th, and 16th, respectively. Source for names, ages, occupations: www.cbs.com/primetime/survivor7/

Table B.9. Contestants on *Survivor: All-Stars* (CBS, spring 2004)

Placement and name	Age	Prv season, finish	Edgic	Comments on depiction
1 Amber Brkich	25	*Outback*, 6th	MR	Latched onto Rob M. early in game, with some fans seeing her as riding his coattails; earlier, was only player to stay in initial tribe as all others switched, endangering her.
2 Rob Mariano	28	*Marquesas*, 10th	CP	Picked up where left off strategy-wise as "Robfather"; despite clear Amber pairing, others failed to mount serious challenge; duped Lex into saving Amber after swap.
3 Jenna Lewis	26	*Borneo*, 8th	MR	Sent into Rob and Amber's tribe when hers forced to disband; made up for *Borneo* naivete by joining winning alliance, yet did nothing to gain power over Rob, Amber.
4 Rupert Boneham	40	*Pearl Islands*, 8th	MR	Did "newcomer" status among all-stars (he appeared in two straight seasons) aid him? Lower-key this time, but overexposed; built below-ground shelter on beach.
5 Tom Buchanan	48	*Africa*, 4th	OT	Similar depiction to *Africa*; performed a jig after Sue quit; outsider in key alliance.
6 Shii Ann Huang	30	*Thailand*, 10th	MR	Won critical IC to stave off "Pagonging"; warned others Amber was good bet to win.
7 Alicia Calaway	35	*Outback*, 9th	MR	Somewhat calmer this time, but outsider in key alliance: ousted after Shii Ann won IC.
8 Kathy Vavrick-O'Brien	50	*Marquesas*, 3rd	CP	Devastated by Rob M.'s merge move, nearly handed Lex immunity but reconsidered.
9 Lex van den Berghe	40	*Africa*, 3rd	CP	Inexplicably evicted Colby, chum Ethan before ill-fated deal with Rob to save Amber.
10 Jerri Manthey	33	*Outback*, 8th	MR	More sympathetic this time, but got revenge on Colby. Ousted thanks to Lex's deal.
11 Ethan Zohn	30	*Africa*, 1st	MR	Longest-lasting former winner ironically put out at hands of former alliance-mate Lex.
12 Colby Donaldson	29	*Outback*, 2nd	MR	Stunned when tribe narrowly voted him out over the complaining, weaker Jerri.
13 Sue Hawk	42	*Borneo*, 4th	OT	Screamed at Probst, then quit after nude Richard had brushed against her at RC.
14 Richard Hatch	42	*Borneo*, 1st	CP	"Bamboozled" by tribe at its first TC; trademark nudity led to RC incident with Sue.
15 Rob Cesternino	25	*Amazon*, 3rd	UR	Tried to stay low-key following *Amazon* machinations, but tribe's mistrust cost him.
16 Jenna Morasca	22	*Amazon*, 1st	UR	Far more positive edit this time; in emotional move, quit, fearing for mother's health.
17 Rudy Boesch	76	*Borneo*, 3rd	MR	Injured early, but gruff as ever, drinking possibly tainted water; too weak to be kept.
18 Tina Wesson	42	*Outback*, 1st	UR	Weak link, combined with being a previous winner, sent this charmer packing first.

Note: AAAIs were not determined for this season. Source for names, ages, occupations: www.cbs.com/primetime/survivor8/

Table B.10. Contestants on *Survivor: Vanuatu* (CBS, fall 2004)

Placement and name	Age	Occupation	AAAI	Edgic	Comments on depiction
1 Chris Daugherty	33	Highway constr.	3.412-55	CP	*Cunning*; targeted in Ep. 1 after balance beam bobbling, but saved by older men's majority; splintered women's alliance despite facing 6-1 deficit.
2 Twila Tanner	41	Highway repair	3.231-64	CP	*Opinionated*; gruff but winning; early fight with Mia; assisted Chris in orchestrating overthrow of power-happy segment of female alliance.
3 Scout Cloud Lee	59	Rancher/entrepren.	2.934-84	MR	*Weak*, terrible at challenges; had to rest on way to camp on Day 1; one of two openly lesbian contestants on season; failed at earlier coup attempt.
4 Eliza Orlins	21	Pre-law student	3.156-66	OT	Edit flipped from negative to positive to negative again; failed at pig catching RC; too talkative; staved off ouster several times before getting ax.
5 Julie Berry	23	Youth mentor	3.702-38	UR	*Charming*, sunbathed nude after swap; fooled Twila into not trusting men.
6 Ami Cusack	31	Barista/model	3.055-72	CP	*Bossy*, openly gay women's alliance leader felled after Chris, Twila united.
7 Leann Slaby	35	Research assistant	3.347-59	UR	Earlier chopping-block status saved by Lisa's lips; first mini-coup victim.
8 Chad Crittenden	35	Teacher	4.093-23	UR	Impressed with abilities despite prosthetic leg; late strategic effort not enough.
9 Lea Masters	40	Drill sergeant	3.768-32	MR	Mildly bossy but positively edited; on wrong end of women's alliance.
10 Rory Freeman	35	Housing case man.	2.856-90	CP	*Opinionated*; semi-quarrelsome; evaded ouster while on women's team.
11 John Kenney	22	Mechanical bull op.	3.051-73	UR	Won Ep. 3 individual IC; strength, poor work ethic too much to overcome.
12 Lisa Keiffer	44	Real estate agent	2.741-98	MR	Offhand comment to power player Ami precipitated loss of trust, ouster.
13 Travis Sampson	33	Loss prevention	2.980-81	MR	*Loyal*; offed by women after whispered comment to ex-tribemates at RC.
14 Brady Finta	33	FBI agent	3.677-42	MR	*Strong*; climbed pole in "opening ceremony"; on wrong end of alliance.
15 John Palyok	31	Sales manager	2.874-88	MR	Seemed set to be strategy king, but upended early by "elder" male alliance.
15 Mia Galeotalanza	30	Finance manager	1.938-140	OT	Evicted with John P. at double TC; bitter feud with Twila sealed her fate.
17 Dolly Neely	25	Sheep farmer	3.371-58	OT	*Friendly*, but done in like *Amazon's* Christy by inability to choose sides.
18 Brook Geraghty	27	Project manager	2.853-91	MR	*Nice*; little explanation given for ouster; first victim of male elder alliance.

Source for names, ages, occupations: www.cbs.com/primetime/survivor9/

Table B.11. Contestants on *Survivor: Palau* (CBS, spring 2005)

Placement and name	Age	Occupation	AAAI	Edgic	Comments on depiction
1 Tom Westman	41	NYC firefighter	4.337-14	CP	*Strong*; won many ICs, RCs; Koror leader; speared shark early; fearing betrayal, offed Gregg with Caryn's aid; upset by Ian's view of their alliance.
2 Katie Gallagher	29	Advertising exec.	2.243-131	MR	Classic "riding coattails" edit; trusted Ian just enough to stick with him and oust Gregg; stunned when Ian chose Tom to join him for last reward.
3 Ian Rosenberger	23	Dolphin trainer	4.268-19	CP	Nice but had guilt complex; sacrificed self in final IC to salvage Tom bond.
4 Jennifer Lyon	32	Nanny	3.399-56	UR	Lost TC tiebreaker to Ian; all but doomed after love interest Gregg booted.
5 Caryn Groedel	46	Civil rights attor.	2.684-101	MR	Exposed rifts at TC, then ousted; blabbed to Tom about women's alliance.
6 Gregg Carey	28	Business consult.	3.710-37	MR	Nice; stunned by allies booting him when he thought he had upper hand.
7 Stephenie LaGrossa	25	Pharma. sales	4.613-8	CP	Survivor of hapless Ulong; hard-working, driven; the ultimate underdog?
8 Janu Tornell	39	Vegas showgirl	2.775-97	UR	Quiet; had to spend night alone on separate island; quit game, saving Steph.
9 Coby Archa	32	Hairstylist	3.734-35	CP	*Talkative*; in mold of Jeff V., Kelly G., Shii; grew as game progressed.
10 Bobby Jon Drinkard	27	Waiter	4.336-15	CP	Driven but frustrated; in Ulong "final 2" with Steph, lost TC tiebreaker.
11 Ibrehem Rahman	27	Waiter	3.154-67	UR	*Religious*; saved earlier by Koror giving him immunity; faltered at diving.
12 James Miller	33	Steelworker	2.558-111	OT	*Narrow-minded* "redneck" amazed by gay Coby's dominance in challenges.
13 Willard Smith	57	Lawyer	2.473-118	UR	*Weak*, nice, lazy, quiet; first Koror gone, ousted with Angie at dual TC.
13 Angie Jakusz	24	Bartender	3.885-26	MR	*Strong* challenge performer after initial lack of self-confidence; friendly.
15 Kim Mullen	25	Graduate student	1.984-139	OT	Seen as weak link and lazy; fourth straight Ulong to go; interested in Jeff?
16 Jeff Wilson	21	Personal trainer	2.587-107	CP	Strong but inured ankle early; asked to be voted out; shaken tribe complied.
17 Ashlee Ashby	22	Student	2.422-122	UR	Quickly exhausted, appeared to lose her will to continue playing game.
18 Jolanda Jones	39	Lawyer	2.560-110	OT	*Opinionated/Forceful*; bossiness, bad decisions doomed Ulong "leader."
19 Jonathan Libby	23	Sales/marketing	2.296-126	UR	Despite strength, not picked for a tribe after failing to bond with others.
19 Wanda Shirk	55	English teacher	2.274-128	OT	*Talkative*; odd singing, presumed weakness kept her from joining a tribe.

Source for names, ages, occupations: http://www.cbs.com/primetime/survivor10/

Table B.12. Contestants on *Survivor: Guatemala* (CBS, fall 2005)

Placement and name	Age	Occupation	Comments on depiction
1 Danni Boatwright	30	Sports radio host	May have benefited from Stephenie's bridges burned; strength at challenges clear from start; overcame 5-1 deficit in final stages; suspected Gary's secret, then befriended him.
2 Stephenie LaGrossa*	25	Pharma. sales	Clear focus of season; *Palau* heroine became near-villain—was it all in the editing or did circumstances change her? Often seen whining; multiple betrayals doomed her.
3 Rafe Judkins	22	Wilderness guide	Controlled, with Stephenie, most Tribal Council decisions; kind, seeming to struggle at times with need for betrayals; won several ICs; bond with Danni helped her get to end.
4 Lydia Morales	42	Fishmonger	Argued against an early eviction, then hung on as semi-outsider in winning alliance.
5 Cindy Hall	31	Zookeeper	Nice; may have hurt self by choosing to give self, rather than all others, car at final RC.
6 Judd Sergeant IV	34	Hotel doorman	Gruff, lied about hidden idol's locale; called supposed allies scumbags when ousted.
7 Gary Hogeboom	46	Ex-NFL Q'back	Strong; finding hidden idol delayed ouster; lied about identity, with only some success.
8 Jamie Newton	24	Water ski instruct.	Self-fulfilling prophecy: Paranoid of betrayal, then *was* betrayed. Loud at challenges.
9 Bobby Jon Drinkard*	27	Waiter	Questioned strength after draining hike, but recovered; similar depiction to *Palau*.
10 Brandon Bellinger	22	Rancher/farmer	First alliance victim at merge; only male on his tribe not sapped by opening hike.
11 Amy O'Hara	39	Police sergeant	Entertaining; injured ankle, bad luck in tribal swap kept her from going further.
12 Brian Corridan	22	Ivy League student	Shrewd student of game in Rob C. mold; engineered Blake ouster, but swap doomed him.
13 Margaret Bobonich	43	Nurse practitioner	Won respect at start for helping ailing men after hike; betrayed by Judd after swap.
14 Blake Towsley	24	Comm. real estate	Strong; poisoned when thorn stuck him on hike; attitude, Brian gambit led to ouster.
15 Brooke Struck	26	Law student	Judd defection after tribal swap spurred defeat; status in original tribe not too clear.
16 Brianna Varela	22	Makeup artist	Seen as not trying hard enough in basketball-like IC; tribe saw Lydia as more valuable.
17 Morgan McDevitt	21	Magician's asst.	Viewed as weak, not contributing; targeted Lydia survived after Brian intervened.
18 Jim Lynch	63	Ret. fire captain	Friendly, experienced, but an easy ouster choice after snapping his bicep in first IC.

*Also appeared on previous season, *Palau*. Note: This season aired after the 2005 survey was conducted, and therefore there are no AAAI rankings for it. Edgic ratings were incomplete at press time. Source for names, ages, occupations: www.cbs.com/primetime/survivor11

Table B.13: *Survivor* **contestants perceived significantly differently by male vs. female respondents**

Rated significantly higher by female respondents, and significantly lower by male respondents						Rated sig. higher by male resp., and sig. lower by female resp.		
Andrew	PIs.	*****	Alex	Amaz.	***	Eliza	Van.	*****
Brandon	Afr.	*****	B.B.	Born.	***	Heidi	Amaz.	*****
Carl	Afr.	*****	Christy	Amaz.	***	Jenna	Amaz.	*****
Chad	Van.	*****	Deena	Amaz.	***	Jerri	Out.	*****
Ethan	Afr.	*****	Ian	Pal.	***	Jon	PIs.	*****
Jed	Thai.	*****	Ibrehem	Pal.	***	Kelly	Afr.	*****
Roger	Amaz.	*****	Osten	PIs.	***	Kim P.	Afr.	*****
Rupert	PIs.	*****	Paschal	Marq.	***	Sarah	Marq.	*****
Scout	Van.	*****	Tom	Pal.	***	Ted	Thai.	*****
Shawn	PIs.	*****	Janet	Amaz.	**	Ashlee	Pal.	****
Twila	Van.	*****	Jonathan	Pal.	**	Gina	Marq.	****
Coby	Pal.	****	Maralyn	Out.	**	Julie	Van.	****
Colby	Out.	****	Ryan S.	PIs.	**	Brian	Thai.	***
Daniel	Amaz.	****	Sonja	Born.	**	Erin	Thai.	***
Hunter	Marq.	****	Angie	Pal.	*	Gervase	Born.	***
Joanna	Amaz.	****	Christa	PIs.	*	Jennifer	Pal.	***
John P.	Van.	****	Frank	Afr.	*	Jessie	Afr.	***
Lea	Van.	****	John K.	Van.	*	Katie	Pal.	***
Lex	Afr.	****	Ken	Thai.	*	Lindsey	Afr.	***
Lillian	PIs.	****	Kim J.	Afr.	*	Tanya	Thai.	***
Linda	Afr.	****	Michael	Out.	*	Clay	Thai.	**
Rodger	Out.	****	Mitchell	Out.	*	Darrah	PIs.	**
Ryan	Amaz.	****	Sean	Born.	*	Tammy	Marq.	**
Sandra	PIs.	****	Dolly	Van.	*			
Tom	Afr.	****	Tijuana	PIs.	*			

Key to Tables B.13 through B.19

(In layman's terms, as number of stars increases, so does gulf between the two groups of respondents listed, e.g., males and females, Republicans and non-Republicans. Results determined by ordinary least squares regression with raw AAI as dependent variable.)

*****   Statistically significant with p = .000, standardized coefficient .150 or up

****   Statistically significant with p between .01 and .001, standardized coefficient .150 or up

***   Statistically significant with p between .01 and .001, standardized coefficient between .125 and .149

**   Statistically significant with p generally between .02 and .05, standardized coefficient between .100 and .124

*   Approaches statistical significance, p between .06 and .15, standardized coefficient between .075 and .099

Table B.14: *Survivor* contestants perceived significantly differently by respondents age 50 and older vs. 30 and younger

Rated significantly higher by respondents age 50 and older, and significantly lower by respondents age 30 and younger						Sig. higher by resp. 50 & up, lower by 30 & young.		
Zoe	Marq.	*****	John	Marq.	***	Kim P.	Afr.	*****
Deena	Amaz.	****	Keith	Out.	***	Wanda	Pal.	*****
Lea	Van.	****	Kel	Out.	***	John K.	Van.	****
Richard	Born.	****	Kim J.	Afr.	***	Sonja	Born.	****
Robert	Marq.	****	Ted	Thai.	***	Brandon	Afr.	***
Roger	Amaz.	****	Butch	Amaz.	**	Elizabeth	Out.	***
Stacey	Born.	****	Chad	Van.	**	Greg	Born.	***
Tom	Pal.	****	Frank	Afr.	**	Silas	Afr.	***
			Ian	Pal.	**	Eliza	Van.	**
			Jeff	Out.	**	Gervase	Born.	**
			Lex	Afr.	**	Jennifer	Pal.	**
			Rupert	Pls.	**	John P.	Van.	**
			Sean	Born.	**	Jon	Pls.	**
			Susan	Born.	**	Neleh	Marq.	**
			Jerri	Out.	*	Tom	Afr.	**
			Maralyn	Out.	*	Ami	Van.	*
			Stephanie	Thai.	*	Coby	Pal.	*
						Paschal	Marq.	*

Table B.15: *Survivor* contestants perceived significantly differently by white respondents vs. nonwhite respondents

Rated significantly higher by white respondents, and significantly lower by nonwhite respondents						Sig. higher by nonwhite resp., lower by white resp.		
Mitchell	Out.	***	Chris	Van.	*	Janu	Pal.	****
Butch	Amaz.	**	Christa	Pls.	*	Ken	Thai.	**
Carl	Afr.	**	Clay	Thai.	*	Ted	Thai.	**
Chad	Van.	**	Hunter	Marq.	*	Ami	Van.	**
Frank	Afr.	**	Ian	Pal.	*	Jolanda	Pal.	**
John P.	Van.	**	James	Pal.	*	Angie	Pal.	*
Kathy	Marq.	**	Keith	Out.	*	Brian	Thai.	*
Lea	Van.	**	Lex	Afr.	*	Jessie	Afr.	*
Paschal	Marq.	**	Rob	Amaz.	*	Jonathan	Pal.	*
Tom	Afr.	**	Roger	Amaz.	*	Susan	Born.	*
			Rudy	Born.	*	Teresa	Afr.	*

Table B.16: *Survivor* contestants perceived significantly differently by politically independent respondents vs. non-independent respondents

Rated significantly higher by independent respondents, and significantly lower by non-independent respondents						Sig. higher by non-ind. resp., sig. lower by ind.		
Heidi	Amaz.	**	Ryan O.	Pls.	**	Shawna	Amaz.	**
Maralyn	Out.	**	Kel	Out.	*			

Table B.17: *Survivor* contestants perceived significantly differently by Republican respondents vs. non-Republican respondents

Rated significantly higher by GOP resp., and sig. lower by non-GOP respondents					Rated significantly higher by non-GOP respondents, sig. lower by GOP resp.			
Clay	Thai.	****	Ethan	Afr.	**	Ramo.	Born.	****	Ghand.	Thai.	**
Mich.	Out.	****	Hunter	Marq.	**	Angie	Pal.	***	Kathy	Marq.	**
Travis	Van.	****	Roger	Amaz.	**	Deena	Amaz.	***	Kimmi	Out.	**
B.B.	Born.	***	Shawn	PIs.	**	Jerri	Out.	***	Sonja	Born.	**
Chris	Van.	***	Darrah	PIs.	*	Leann	Van.	***	Jenna	Amaz.	*
Jake	Thai.	***	Eliz.	Out.	*				Sandra	PIs.	*
Rudy	Born.	***	Silas	Afr.	*						
Colby	Out.	**	Eliz.	Out.	*						
Dirk	Born.	**	Tom	Pal.	*						

Table B.18: *Survivor* contestants perceived significantly differently by Democratic respondents vs. non-Democratic respondents

Rated significantly higher by *non*-Democratic Respondents, and sig. lower by Dem. resp.					Rated significantly higher by non-Dem. respondents, sig. lower by Dem. resp.			
Frank	Afr.	*****	James	Pal.	**	Ami	Van.	*****	Scout	Van.	**
Lea	Van.	*****	Lisa	Van.	**	Stacey	Born.	***	Tijuana	PIs.	**
Tom	Afr.	****	Paschal	Marq.	**	Brandon	Afr.	**	Janu	Pal.	*
Carl	Afr.	***	Ashlee	Pal.	*	Christy	Amaz.	**	Jon	PIs.	*
Dolly	Van.	***	Jed	Thai.	*	Coby	Pal.	**	Jonathan	Pal.	*
Joel	Born.	***	Roger	Amaz.	*	Peter	Marq.	**			
Kim P.	Afr.	***									

Table B.19: *Survivor* contestants perceived significantly differently by respondents with household incomes of $100,000 or more vs. respondents with household incomes of $35,000 or less

Sig. higher by resp. in households earning $100,000 or more, and sig. lower by resp. in households earning $35,000 or less					Sig. higher by $35K; sig. lower by $100K		
Stephanie	Thai.	***	Ami	Van.	*	Katie	Pal.	**
Stephenie	Pal.	***	Carl	Afr.	*	Maralyn	Out.	**
Daniel	Amaz.	**	Chad	Van.	*	Christy	Amaz.	*
Leann	Van.	**	Gretchen	Born.	*	Ghandia	Thai.	*
Tammy	Marq.	**	Jennifer	Pal.	*	Jan	Thai.	*
Ted	Thai.	**	Lex	Afr.	*	Jolanda	Pal.	*
			Osten	PIs.	*	Kathy	Marq.	*
			Rob	Amaz.	*	Lillian	PIs.	*
			Tom	Afr.	*	Linda	Afr.	*
						Scout	Van.	*

Table B.20: Frequency of use of adjectives chosen by respondents to describe *Survivor* contestants, grouped by gender

	Percent of time adjective was chosen by respondents to describe...			
Adjective	Female contestants	Rank	Male contestants	Rank
Absent-minded	5.62%		5.18%	
Bossy	12.71%	10	9.41%	
Charming	10.54%		9.75%	
Complaining	11.89%		8.83%	
Cunning	6.29%		8.38%	
Egotistical	6.33%		13.29%	8
Emotional	17.92%	3	3.33%	
Forceful	10.19%		8.26%	
Honest	14.98%	6	18.75%	2
Intelligent	15.22%	5	14.17%	7
Kind	15.79%	4	9.05%	
Lazy	8.34%		14.23%	6
Loyal	7.90%		16.39%	4
Naïve	14.10%	7	8.77%	
Narrow-minded	5.36%		10.86%	
Opinionated	19.20%	2	15.79%	5
Productive	6.47%		9.71%	
Quarrelsome	12.47%		7.62%	
Religious	7.73%		6.78%	
Self-confident	12.82%	9	16.45%	3
Shrewd	9.70%		9.88%	
Strong/Vigorous	12.61%		19.95%	1
Stubborn	8.13%		9.96%	
Talkative	14.05%	8	10.07%	
Trustworthy	5.74%		10.69%	
Unreliable	7.13%		11.29%	10
Weak	20.79%	1	13.19%	9

Note: Percentages add up to more than 100 because respondents could select up to three adjectives per contestant. See Appendix C for definitions and other methodological information.

Table B.21: Frequency of use of adjectives chosen to describe
***Survivor* contestants 50 and older, overall and by gender**

Percent of time adjective was chosen by respondents to describe…

Adjective	All contestants 50 and up	Rank	Male cont. 50 and up	Rank	Female cont. 50 and up	Rank
Honest	31.7%	1	37.5%	1	24.2%	3
Weak	27.6%	2	13.8%	9	45.2%	1
Kind	27.0%	3	19.5%	4	36.4%	2
Loyal	24.2%	4	32.3%	2	13.8%	9
Trustworthy	20.8%	5	28.9%	3	10.6%	10
Intelligent	16.4%	6	18.2%	5	14.1%	8
Naïve	12.7%	7	3.7%		24.1%	4
Opinionated	12.7%	8	17.6%	6	6.4%	
Productive	11.1%	9	14.5%	8	6.8%	
Bossy	9.9%	10	15.4%	7	3.0%	
Emotional	9.3%		0.6%		20.4%	5
Self-confident	9.2%		9.6%		8.6%	
Absent-minded	9.0%		4.5%		14.8%	7
Talkative	8.8%		0.9%		18.9%	6
Charming	8.4%		8.2%		8.7%	
Narrow-minded	8.4%		12.7%	10	3.0%	
Stubborn	7.7%		10.8%		3.8%	
Unreliable	6.5%		4.4%		9.1%	
Forceful	5.7%		7.4%		3.6%	
Strong/Vigorous	5.5%		6.0%		4.7%	
Egotistical	4.9%		7.7%		1.5%	
Complaining	4.3%		4.2%		4.5%	
Religious	4.3%		5.5%		2.9%	
Lazy	4.2%		5.6%		2.4%	
Shrewd	4.2%		3.6%		4.9%	
Quarrelsome	3.2%		4.9%		1.1%	
Cunning	2.1%		1.8%		2.5%	

Note: Percentages add up to more than 100 because respondents could select up to three adjectives per contestant. See Appendix C for definitions and other methodological information.

Table B.22: Frequency of use of adjectives chosen to describe select *Survivor* contestants, by race and gender

Percent of time adjective was chosen by respondents to describe…

Adjective	All black cont.	Rank	White cont.	Rank	Black female cont.	Rank	Black male cont.	Rank
Lazy	23.6%	1	7.5%		8.0%		40.0%	1
Strong	21.9%	2	14.9%	6	20.0%	5	23.9%	3
Quarrelsome	19.7%	3	7.5%		26.4%	1	12.8%	9
Religious	19.7%	3	4.4%		24.8%	2	14.4%	6
Opinionated	19.1%	5	16.7%	2	24.3%	3	13.6%	7
Weak	16.6%	6	15.2%	4	15.0%	8	18.4%	5
Complaining	16.3%	7	8.6%		14.1%	9	18.6%	4
Unreliable	16.1%	8	6.5%		5.8%		26.9%	2
Self-confident	13.5%	9	15.0%	5	14.0%	10	13.1%	8
Forceful	12.0%	10	9.1%		19.6%	6	4.0%	
Bossy	12.0%		11.4%		20.7%	4	2.9%	
Emotional	10.4%		11.0%		16.6%	7	3.9%	
Stubborn	9.7%		8.6%		8.9%		10.5%	
Honest	9.6%		19.6%	1	7.5%		11.7%	10
Intelligent	9.3%		15.3%	3	12.5%		5.9%	
Talkative	8.5%		13.0%	9	10.2%		6.7%	
Naïve	7.9%		12.3%	10	5.4%		10.4%	
Egotistical	7.8%		10.8%		5.5%		10.2%	
Kind	7.6%		13.8%	8	7.0%		8.3%	
Charming	7.0%		11.4%		4.2%		9.9%	
Narrow-minded	5.9%		9.3%		7.9%		3.8%	
Loyal	5.2%		14.7%	7	2.4%		8.1%	
Productive	4.9%		9.2%		5.0%		4.9%	
Shrewd	4.9%		10.4%		7.0%		2.8%	
Trustworthy	4.1%		9.9%		2.7%		5.5%	
Absent-minded	4.0%		5.9%		2.4%		5.7%	
Cunning	2.7%		8.0%		2.6%		2.8%	

Note: Percentages add up to more than 100 because respondents could select up to three adjectives per contestant. White ratings are based on 49 contestants. See Appendix C for definitions and other methodological information.

Appendix C
Methodology

TO COMPLEMENT THE TEXTUAL ANALYSIS of this project, survey research was conducted, the intent being to measure audience expectations and desires in viewing *Survivor* and compute whether certain demographics, especially those relating to class, appeared to impact consumption of *Survivor*. Two surveys were conducted, each with 1,000 or more respondents, with the first occurring over three days in spring 2004 and the second, also over three days, in spring 2005. Additionally, a content analysis was conducted with a total of sixteen coders in two sessions in spring 2005, explained in further detail later.

Spring 2004 Survey

The primary hypotheses were as follows:

1. Overall, viewers of *Survivor* viewed negatively the program's Tagi and Rotu alliances on its *Borneo* and *Marquesas* editions, respectively, rooting for the powerless, "underdog" players to prevail instead.

2. Overall, viewers of *Survivor* experienced displeasure when the Tagi alliance prevailed in the *Borneo* edition, and pleasure when the Rotu alliance in the *Marquesas* edition was defeated.

3. Upper-class viewers viewed somewhat more favorably the Tagi and Rotu alliances than working-class viewers.

A 36-question survey was designed to test these hypotheses and related questions that were prompted by the accompanying textual analysis. It was hosted by Zoomerang, an online survey service then subscribed to by Georgetown University's Communication, Culture, and Technology graduate program. The survey was composed of four sets of questions, on *Survivor: Borneo*, *Survivor: Marquesas*, other seasons of *Survivor*, and demographics.[1]

The first set of questions measured audience expectations regarding the outcome of *Survivor: Borneo*; specifically, whether the Tagi alliance would dominate the game. It also determined audience desires and reactions regarding that alliance's ultimate dominance and contestant Rich's victory. Similarly, the second set of questions measured audience expectations regarding the outcome of *Survivor: Marque-*

sas; specifically, whether the Rotu alliance would dominate the game. It also determined audience desires and reactions to that alliance's ultimate demise and Vecepia's victory. The third set of questions regarded audience reaction to Brian, a well-to-do car salesman and winner of *Survivor: Thailand*, and the tactics of Rob C., an especially strategic player on *Survivor: The Amazon*. It sought to determine whether viewers were put off by Brian's wealth and Rob's deceptions. The fourth set of questions was demographic in nature, including level of *Survivor* fandom.

The survey was deployed by generating a unique URL and posting it to the *Survivor* fan message board SurvivorSucks (p085.ezboard.com/bsurvivorsucks), of which the author is a long-time member. The link was also sent to the Communication, Culture, and Technology program list-serv, consisting of hundreds of program students and alumni. The survey was set up so that it could not be completed more than once from the same computer.

The survey was completed anonymously by 1,509 respondents over a period of three and a half days, then was closed and the results aggregated. One response was deleted from the database because the subject had listed that she was over 76 years in age, lived with her parents, and belonged to the social class known as "Pooping." This left 1,508 responses for analysis. Eventually, the final 508 of those replies had to be dropped from the sample due to clear respondent priming problems. This situation is discussed later.

Analysis

Because nearly all variables were cateogorical in nature (such as respondents listing the player they most wanted to win *Survivor*), they were assigned numeric values. Responses such as "I didn't watch that season of *Survivor*" or "I don't remember how I felt" were treated as missing values.

Frequency tables were next run using SPSS 12.0 software, followed by cross-tabulation using the Pearson Chi Square Tests of statistical significance. For these, similar responses such as "very pleased" and "somewhat pleased" were grouped together, and waffling responses such as "I didn't care" were treated as missing since Chi Square Tests operate best with fewer choices, and "maybe"-type replies dilute "approve/disapprove" oppositional percentages.[2]

Ordinary least squares regression tests were run next to determine what independent variables, such as age, gender, and class, predicted a survey response. All responses to *Survivor*-related questions were included (other than disqualifiers mentioned two paragraphs prior) and not collapsed (e.g., "pleased" responses were divided into "very pleased" and "somewhat pleased"), as was the case for the cross-tabulations, in order to maximize their utility. As needed, the order of responses was rearranged to form a range. For example, Question 3 asked for respondents' desires regarding the fate of the Tagi alliance. After coding, "1" represented wanting the alliance to prevail, "2" represented wanting it to fail, and "3" represented not caring. For regression analysis, choices 2 and 3 were switched to create an accurate range.

Additionally, dummy variables were created to accommodate categorical variables. Some questions, such as gender and household union membership, were already dichotomous. But the political orientation question was used to create three dummy variables, "Republican or non-Republican," "Democrat or non-Democrat," and "Independent or non-Independent." This allowed party to be used as an independent variable in regression analysis.

Possible Error Sources

As with all survey research, certain caveats apply that may account for error. Among them:

The survey was a convenience sample, rather than a random sampling such as those conducted by the Gallup organization, something impossible to perform with the resources available. As a result, despite the large sample size, the data cannot be assumed to represent the opinions of all 20 million or so *Survivor* viewers. However, the statistically significant cross-tabulations and regression results still reveal patterns in key demographics that may well be embedded in the larger population. Additionally, many of those who took the survey were attentive *Survivor* fans with extensive knowledge of the program, giving the results additional merit.

It is possible that some respondents were misleading in their answers. However, this seems unlikely because of the minuscule level of risk involved with the survey (it was deployed online and was anonymous), the non-controversial nature of questions, and the fact that respondents could simply not answer a question if they so desired. The only two questions that required answers asked whether or not respondents had watched certain seasons of *Survivor*. Certainly downplaying the results of this survey because of the possibility of respondents being misleading would mean also disregarding virtually all survey research.

The disproportionate percentage of "online *Survivor* fans," females, Democrats, and younger viewers may have affected the results.

The survey asked respondents to "think back" to their opinions and thoughts while watching each season of *Survivor*, as far back as four years prior. They were asked to disregard any information that did not come from CBS, such as online "spoilers," that they were exposed to, as well as opinions they have formed since watching the show. This may have been difficult for some respondents to do. For instance, the author was displeased the night it was revealed Rich had won *Survivor: Borneo*, but later came to appreciate his strategy and respect his victory.

The Priming Problem

As noted earlier, the survey was posted to the Web site SurvivorSucks, a major online gathering place for *Survivor* fans, with more than 30,000 members. More than 75 percent of respondents reported belonging to an online *Survivor* community, and it is likely that the vast majority of these came from SurvivorSucks.

After the author (a long-time member of the community) posted the link to the survey in a new message thread, other community members began to reply, most saying "Good luck," "Nice survey," and so on. Approximately 32 hours after the survey was posted—by which point some 1,000 cases had accumulated—someone

Table C.1: First 1,000 vs. last 508 cases in 2004 survey

Variable cross-tabulated with class	First 1,000: Upper minus working (in percentage points)	Last 508: Upper minus working (in percentage points)	Change (in percentage points)
V2	12.6	-0.3	12.9
V3	11.4	3.1	8.3
V4	8.9	2.8	6.1
V5	-6.9	6.1	13.0
V6	13.4	-2.9	16.3
V7	16.2	8.1	8.1
V8	11.5	1.6	9.9
V10	-7.3	-14.5	7.2
V11	3.8	-8.0	11.8
V17	10.3	8.5	1.8
V18	-16.5	-12.3	4.2
V21	13.7	7.2	6.5

posted a "flaming" style message, questioning among other things the point of the study and highlighting the fact that *socioeconomic questions about class* were asked on the survey. The respondent alleged that the study was intended to discover socioeconomic data regarding *Survivor* viewers, not "Expectations and Desires in Viewing *Survivor*," as the survey was titled. The respondent claimed this to be a breach of research ethics.[3]

The author replied that the informed consent statement listed at the start of the survey specifically said the following: "The purpose of the study is to investigate the relationship between certain demographics and one's expectations and desires regarding the program." The author also noted that most public opinion surveys include demographic questions at the end.

The respondent continued to post flame-style messages, to other board members' consternation, and a back-and-forth developed between the "flaming" respondent and others. A second community member also posted several messages, claiming that because this was an Internet survey, any data gathered would be "bogus" due to potential lying by respondents. Others responded that this would be the case with any survey research, and that the anonymity of an online survey with little to no risk minimized any desire or need to lie (not to mention the option to leave any demographic question, and all but two *Survivor*-related questions, blank).

Indeed, if a great number of respondents had lied in answering survey questions, few Chi Square tests would have been significant due to the likely randomness of such replies, and no patterns would have emerged. Throughout this project, this has clearly been shown not to be the case.

However, data analysis clearly shows that the ranting/discussion that sprang up regarding socioeconomic questions[4] *dramatically affected later datasets involving the "perceived social class" question, v35.* Hence, while lying by survey respondents may be no more likely online than over the phone, outside a voting booth or in

Table C.2: Change in frequencies, first 1,000 vs. last 508 cases

Variable	Frequency (%) for most popular response, first 1,000 replies	Freq. (%) for same response, last 508 replies	Change (in percentage points)	Corresponding change, Table C.1
V2	51.5	51.8	0.3	*12.9*
V3	70.8	73.8	3.0	8.3
V4	78.1	81.4	3.4	6.1
V5	93.6	92.7	0.9	*13.0*
V6	63.6	63.3	0.3	*16.3*
V7	56.3	62.6	6.3	8.1
V8	25.2	27.6	2.4	9.9
V10	45.3	48.9	3.6	7.2
V11	89.2	85.9	3.3	11.8
V17	50.9	45.2	5.7	1.8
V18	62.3	60.5	1.8	4.2
V21	57.8	58.7	0.9	6.5

a shopping mall, the ability to comment on a live survey to other potential respondents jeopardizes the validity of later data.

This is borne out by the fact that cross-tabulations involving class swung markedly when one compares the first 1,000 responses and the last 508 (collected after the one respondent began complaining online). Table C.1 details this for cross-tabulations that involved the class question and had statistically significant, or approaching significant, differences. The table lists a survey question number; the difference between the percentage of upper class/upper-middle-class respondents and working-class respondents who gave that answer among the first 1,000 datasets; the difference between the percentage of upper class/upper-middle-class respondents and working-class respondents who gave that answer among the last 508 datasets; and the difference between those two figures. In a perfect world, the difference should be zero; realistically, one would expect the difference to be no more than five points or so when due to chance. This was, however, rarely the case.

Swings of at least six percentage points are seen in ten of the twelve relevant variables. Four have margins in the double digits. In ten of twelve cases, too, the margin decreased or even inverted from the first 1,000 to the last 508. This happened despite the fact that the proportions of respondents identifying under varied class groupings changed little from the first 1,000 to the last 508. For instance, the proportion of upper class/upper-middle-class respondents crept up from 29.0 percent to 29.3 percent, as did the proportion of working-class respondents, from 22.7 percent to 23.6 percent (the proportion of average middle-class respondents dropped 1.2 percentage points). Contrast these results with the differences between the first 1,000 replies and last 508 on three questions we will consider "control" variables, in that priming should not influence replies: Whether one watched *Survivor: Borneo*; whether one watched *Survivor: Marquesas*; and gender. For *Borneo* and *Marquesas*, the proportion saying they had watched each of those seasons dropped 2.1 percentage points, and the proportion of female respondents climbed three points. There was greater change, then, for these "control" variables than the one brought into the open by the "priming incident." There was little overall change, too, in the variables for which there was great change in cross-tabulated differences (see Table C.2).

Only two out of 12 variables had more than a five-point change. Furthermore, even though variables 2, 5, and 6 had the greatest shift in Table C.1 (difference in class reaction between first 1,000 and last 508), they shifted little in overall frequencies. This, coupled with the fact that overall class frequencies barely changed, suggests that upper-class respondents and working-class respondents began consciously or subconsciously "switching" their replies in the final 508, in a way that overall narrowed the margin between their cross-tabulated replies. This resulted in fewer statistically significant differences for cross-tabulations involving the class question when all 1,508 cases are compiled. Using all 1,508 cases, five questions had statistically significant differences when cross-tabulated with class; that number jumped to eight when only the first 1,000 cases were counted. This is in spite of the fact that, because of the smaller sample, statistical significance *should* be harder to achieve, all things being equal.

However, further suggesting that the priming problem *only* affected the class question, *every other demographic variable*, when cross-tabulated against *Survivor*-related questions, had as many or *fewer* statistically significant results (according to Chi Square) when only the first 1,000 cases were counted:

All these factors strongly suggest that the online comments criticizing the inclusion of socioeconomic questions significantly affected later responses involving that question, and that question alone. As a result, following the recommendation of the author's statistics adviser, the final 508 cases were dropped from this analysis.

Spring 2005 Survey

In April 2005, the author decided to deploy a second online survey to ask additional questions on reactions to certain events and, most importantly, develop a ranking system of all 150 contestants in an attempt to seek patterns in audience reactions to depictions.

As a result, the survey became quite long. The key questions asked were these three (with photographs of contestants provided to help refresh memories):

1. Considering a contestant's OVERALL DEPICTION on *Survivor*, what was your OVERALL ATTITUDE toward each of these contestants AT THE TIME THEIR SEASON AIRED? (You may wish to consider their personality; behavior at camp; physical abilities and challenge performances; mental and emotional makeup; game-play and strategy; treatment of other players; etc. For contestants who also appeared on *Survivor: All-Stars*, please primarily consider their first season on the show.)

2. For each contestant, please briefly describe (i.e., in five words or less) the first thing you remember about him or her. It may be a specific incident that occurred on the show, a personality trait, or something in their biography. However, please don't simply write what place they came in (e.g., "finished third" or "was first person voted out.") Anything else, however, is fine. If you

don't know what to put or did not watch this season, please leave the space blank and move on.

3. Next to each contestant's name are three drop-down menus. Each has on it a short list of adjectives. Please pick one adjective from each menu that best describes that particular contestant. If none do, select "none of these." Since there are three menus, you should pick up to three adjectives for each contestant. Definitions of each adjective appear here [link to separate Web site was provided]. If you don't know what to put or did not watch this season, please leave the space blank and move on.

As this was only the first part of the survey, it would have been unreasonable to ask respondents to answer the above questions for all 150 contestants, and could lead to priming if more than one of the above questions were answered for the same contestants. Therefore, several steps were taken:

Although the entire pool of 150 contestants was used for Question 1, a smaller pool of seventy-two—eight from each season—was used for Questions 2 and 3. The author selected all racial minority members, all contestants age 50 and older, and a number of others either important to their season's "plot" or members of another group (i.e., homosexuals, overtly religious, "rural").

The author arranged the survey so that a single respondent would only answer one of the three questions for each season—never, for instance, rating a depiction (No. 1) and then also choosing adjectives (No. 3) for the same set of contestants. Since No. 1 was deemed most important, and No. 2 least, the survey was set up so that a respondent was asked No. 1 for at most six seasons of contestants, No. 2 for one season, and No. 3 for two seasons.

After answering questions for four seasons (question No. 1 twice and Nos. 2 and 3 once each), respondents could either continue to rate contestants or move on to the rest of the survey (just under 60 percent elected to rate more contestants).

The author devised nine separate paths through the first part of the survey, each with a different order of seasons. Respondents were asked to select which day of the month their birthday fell on, and this determined their path through the survey. For instance, respondents who said their birthday fell on the 28th, 29th, 30th, or 31st received questions in this order: *Borneo* and *Outback*, question No. 1; *Vanuatu*, No. 2; *Pearl Islands*, No. 3; respondents who chose to rate more contestants then were given *Amazon* contestants, question No. 2; and then *Africa, Marquesas, Thailand,* and *Palau*, No. 1. The author purposely arranged the survey so that the most popular birthday groupings (i.e., those with a four-day range rather than a three-day range) started out with the least-watched seasons, and vice versa, in order to maximize likelihood of getting about equal response sets for all contestants. The order of the birthday list was also randomized partway into deployment to mitigate the effects of respondents simply choosing the first range of dates listed.

Following is further information about questions 1, 2, and 3:

- **Question 1, Overall Depiction:** This question was devised to gain a rating for each contestant regarding their overall depiction on *Survivor* (see question text above). Respondents rated each contestant on a seven-point scale from "very negative" to "very positive," with "don't recall/didn't watch" also an option. The ratings given had a normal, bell-curve distribution and

Table C.3: Adjectives used in 2005 survey, question No. 2

Adjective (list[*])	Valence[**]	Gender[***]	Definition
Absent-minded (3)	213	464	Unaware of one's surroundings or actions
Bossy (1)	112	498	Inclined to domineer
Charming (1)	430	373	Extremely pleasing or delightful
Complaining (1)	127	401	To express dissatisfaction; lament, gripe
Cunning (2)	430	n/a	Crafty in attaining an end; sly, wily
Egotistical (2)	116	575	Having too high an opinion of oneself; overly concerned with one's desires, needs, interests
Emotional (2)	283	254	Markedly aroused or agitated in feeling or sensibilities; having or expressing great depth of feeling
Forceful (3)	263	723	Marked by or uttered with forcefulness; possessing or filled with force
Honest (3)	555	527	Free from fraud or deception; marked by integrity and sincere expression
Intelligent (3)	537	501	Having or indicating a high or satisfactory degree of mental capacity; smart
Kind (2)	520	374	Of a sympathetic or helpful nature
Lazy (3)	126	601	Disinclined to activity or exertion
Loyal (2)	547	464	Unswerving in allegiance
Naïve (3)	270	n/a	Deficient in worldly wisdom, informed judgment
Narrow-minded (3)	80	n/a	Lacking in tolerance or breadth of vision
Opinionated (2)	257	602	Prone to vocalizing one's beliefs; unduly adhering to one's own opinion or to preconceived notions
Productive (1)	468	n/a	Having the quality or power of producing especially in abundance; yielding results or benefits
Quarrelsome (3)	101	475	Apt or disposed to quarrel or argue in an often petty manner; belligerent
Religious (2)	387	n/a	Faithful devotion to an acknowledged ultimate reality or deity
Self-confident (2)	421	614	Confidence in oneself and in one's abilities
Shrewd (3)	328	522	Clever discerning awareness
Strong/vigorous (1)	443	707	Having or marked by physical power
Stubborn (1)	196	599	Unreasonably unyielding
Talkative (1)	352	307	Given to talking
Trustworthy (1)	539	n/a	Worthy of confidence
Unreliable (2)	104	n/a	Unsuitable to be relied on; undependable
Weak (1)	159	384	Lacking physical strength, energy, or vigor

* Numerals refer to drop-down menus, see p. 179.
** 0 = most negative, 600 = most positive; Source: Anderson 1968, 272-279;
*** 0 = most feminine, 1000 = most masculine; Source: Williams and Best 1981.
Note: The ten "female" adjectives had a mean valence of 284.4, but one, "bossy," was barely feminine at all. Discounting this gives the nine remaining words a mean valence of 303.5. The ten masculine adjectives had a mean valience of 324.2, but discounting the barely masculine "intelligent" leaves us with a mean valence of 300.6. The twenty gendered words had a mean "gendered" value of 498.3. The twenty-seven words had a mean valence of 309.8, slightly on the positive side, although more of the words had a negative valence.

were compiled to form an audience attitude index for each contestant on a scale from 0 to 6. Later, based on respondent feedback and to minimize biases, an alternative index called the adjusted audience attitude index was formed and used in selected cases in this text. This process is detailed later in this section.

- **Question 2, Open-ended:** This question was asked to measure what respondents most recalled about a contestant off the top of their heads, and what patterns would emerge.

- **Question 3, Adjective Selection:** The purpose of this question was to see whether respondents recalled contestants as being depicted stereotypically. Twenty-seven adjectives were selected from Anderson's "Likeableness Ratings of 555 Personality-Trait Words" (1968), based on notable adjectives from the Princeton Trilogy studies of African-American stereotypes and a later study (Madon et al. 2001), Williams and Best's U.S. sex-stereotype index list, and from the author's impressions of common depictions of contestants. The words (and their definitions, which respondents could view) are listed in Table C.3.

    The twenty-seven words were divided into three groups of nine and presented in drop-down menus. Respondents could indicate if no word on a list described a particular contestant. Words that were degrees of each other or antonyms (weak vs. strong/vigorous, self-confident vs. egotistical) were grouped together whenever possible. The drawback of this method is that at times, more than one word on a list may have applied to a specific contestant. However, presenting one long list may have confused or frustrated takers of an already complicated survey, thereby increasing attrition. Results from this question were compiled in a number of ways—both by specific contestants and by grouping results from contestants who shared a specific trait, such as gender, race, or age group.

The rest of the survey involved varied questions, some important to this study, such as reaction to Sean's ouster from *Marquesas*, and others included for "entertainment purposes only," such as favorite episode. A limited number of demographic questions were included at the end; most socioeconomic questions, including social class, were eschewed out of fear that many participants would have either completed the 2004 survey or read its results, and therefore expect such a question, causing priming. Instead, the author stressed that this survey had a very different purpose than the last. These worries may have been unfounded, as less than 15 percent said they had taken the prior survey.

The survey was tested by six *Survivor* viewers and reviewed by the author's thesis statistics adviser, then deployed using SurveyMonkey.com by generating a unique URL and posting it to SurvivorSucks. This time the author requested that a site administrator lock the thread to mitigate possible priming, and asked that anyone sending the survey link to others not discuss its contents with them. The link was also sent to the Communication, Culture, and Technology program list-serv and posted on two other Web sites with the same instructions. The survey was set up so that it could not be completed more than once from the same computer. After 1,001 anonymous response sets were compiled over three days (305 other people started the survey but did not advance past the first set of contestant ratings), the survey was closed and the results aggregated.

Analysis, Possible Error Sources, and the Adjusted AAI

Analysis was similar in method to the 2004 survey, with cateogrical variables assigned numerical values. Responses such as "I didn't watch that season of *Survivor*" or "I don't remember how I felt" were treated as missing values.

Frequency tables were next run using SPSS 12.0 software, followed by cross-tabulation using the Pearson Chi Square Test of statistical significance. Ordinary least squares (OLS) regression models again were performed following the method described earlier.

Possible sources of error were also similar to the earlier survey as described above—with the nonrandom sampling, though the sample size is quite large and consists largely of a highly informed population, the main issue, although unavoidable with the resources available. Pains were taken to minimize the potential for priming. Additionally, in this case the survey was so extensive (taking as long as 45 minutes to complete) that it is highly unlikely anyone would have wanted to take it multiple times even if they determined a way to do so.

The most significant potential error source, however, was that out of necessity, the survey was deployed in the week following the conclusion of *Survivor: Palau*. Respondents were reminded before certain questions that "if you choose a more recent contestant, please be careful that you are not doing so simply because it is fresher in your mind." Nonetheless, this occasionally appeared to affect results, such as that season's winner, Tom, being named the most deserving of *Survivor's* then ten victors. Certain contestants from *Palau* and the preceding season, *Vanuatu*, also appeared to be rated "too high" or "too low" in the audience attitude index, the theory being that respondents reacted more emotionally to recent *Survivor* events, thereby rating up contestants they liked more than normal—and rating down those they did not. Additionally, contestants from some of the less-liked seasons (particularly *Vanuatu* and *Thailand*) were inexplicably high in the rankings. The author surmised this was because, when presented with a list of sixteen contestants from the same season, many respondents felt compelled to rate at least one or two of them very highly, since all sixteen were being compared at once.

To mitigate the above two bias sources, as well as demographic imbalances in the sample (particularly the necessarily high percentage of respondents belonging to an online *Survivor* community), the raw audience attitude index was weighted in various ways and recomputed to form an adjusted audience attitude index. This "corrected" index makes more sense in terms of viewer reaction to various contestants, although the method used to obtain it may appear arbitrary. Because of this, the AAAI is used only for individual contestant ratings throughout this text; furthermore, when the mean AAAI of multiple contestants is mentioned, their mean raw AAI is also noted.

The AAAI was computed as follows:
- 70 percent came directly from the original AAI, with the scores of *Palau* contestants either reduced or enlarged by 25 percent of the portion of their

AAI that fell above or below an overall neutral rating (3.0); *Vanuatu* contestants' AAIs were similarly adjusted by 20 percent. For instance, a *Palau* contestant with an original AAI of 4.500 would wind up with a score of 4.125 after 25 percent of the score above 3.0—in this case, .375 is 25 percent of 1.5—was subtracted. This 4.125 would then comprise 70 percent of the AAAI.

- 15 percent of the AAAI came from a second "survey about the survey" that 85 respondents, 75 percent of whom had taken the first 2005 survey, completed after certain results were posted online at SurvivorSucks. Respondents were asked to say whether each of the 150 contestants had wound up rated way too high, somewhat too high, about right, somewhat too low, or way too low in the posted results. These terms were defined for the respondents, and given those five choices, they chose "about right" 55 percent of the time. The results were converted into a value used for 15 percent of the AAAI.
- 7.5 percent of the AAAI was based on the percentage of offline fans who rated each contestant slightly, somewhat, or very positively on the survey.
- 7.5 percent of the AAAI was computed by taking the percentage of respondents who rated each contestant slightly, somewhat, or very positively on the survey and weighting it based on demographic information from the U.S. Census (CensusScope 2001). For instance, since younger people made up a disproportionately large percentage of the respondent pool, those datasets were given less weight, and older respondents given more weight, and so on.

The four values for each contestant were added together and then, using proportions, converted into a value on a scale from 0 to 6.

Content Analysis

To further supplement this project, two brief content analysis sessions were conducted with eight coders each in spring 2005. Coders viewed Episode 1 of *Borneo* in the first session and Episode 1 of *The Amazon* in the second. The point was to measure whether certain contestants' and tribes' depictions in those episodes were positive or negative.

For the *Borneo* episode, the ten most prominently featured contestants were selected for coding and assigned to three coders each; for *Amazon*, eight contestants, four from each gender-divided tribe, were selected and also assigned to three respondents each, as was one of the two tribes. Two coders of each gender were assigned each tribe. Coding instruments were prepared that divided the two episodes into sixteen and twenty-two scenes, respectively, with spaces for coders to indicate whether each contestant was depicted very positively, somewhat positively, neutrally, somewhat negatively, or very negatively (or not applicable) in that specific scene.

After signing informed consent statements, respondents received a training session that included sample scenes to code. Their instructions read, in part:

Be careful to not confuse liking or feeling sympathy for a contestant with thinking they have been portrayed positively. For instance, if an otherwise likable contestant becomes seasick and vomits off the side of a boat, this would likely be regarded as a negative portrayal of that person for that particular scene, even if you felt sympathy for them. Likewise, if an unlikable contestant won a physical challenge, this would likely be regarded as a positive portrayal for that particular scene. Also, consider the context of comments made by one contestant about another. If Bob says, "I don't like Ron because he's a jerk," that would likely be regarded as a negative portrayal of Ron for that particular scene. However, if Bob says, "I don't like Ron because he's gay," that might be a negative portrayal of Bob, rather than Ron.

After the "practice coding" and a question-and-answer period in which participants discussed why the practice scenes viewed might be coded a certain way, the episode tape was played. For the *Amazon* episode, the coders were also asked to rate their assigned tribe's depiction in each scene according to two categories. The first category was "depiction of survival/outdoors skills and physical abilities"; the second was "depiction of social/emotional behavior and attitude." For the *Borneo* coders, a Scott's pi of 83.3 was reached, an acceptable figure; for the *Amazon* group, one of 83.4 was reached.

Additionally, at three points during the *Amazon* episode, the tape was paused and the coders given sheets of adjectives; they were instructed to circle any they felt applied to their assigned tribe. These were similar to those listed in Table C.6. For this exercise, coders were not given definitions of the words being used.

Notes

1. The 2004 survey was approved by Georgetown University's Institutional Review Board.

2. However, to test this proposition, "maybe"-type replies were left in, and all *Survivor*-related questions were cross-tabulated again against perceived social class. Of eight results that had previously been statistically significant ($p=.05$ or less), six remained so, with the other two approaching significance. However, these results were discounted in the analysis since cross-tabs are easier to interpret when fewer "cells" are involved.

3. The respondent also claimed to have taken the survey twice from the same computer, using different Internet browsers. As noted earlier, the survey was specifically designed to be taken no more than once from the same machine.

4. Over the course of the surveying period, several respondents also posted comments regarding the survey's *Survivor*-related questions, which the author, new to survey research, considered more important to be kept secret to avoid priming—figuring, again, that demographic queries would pose no surprise to respondents since they are omnipresent in survey research. The author enlisted the help of SurvivorSucks moderators, who deleted three or so such comments from the message board. The author also then posted a note asking respondents to refrain from making comments that detailed survey questions, asking them instead to send the author a private message if they had questions or concerns.

Bibliography

Anderson, Norman H. "Likeableness Ratings of 555 Personality-Trait Words." *Journal of Personality and Social Psychology* 9, No. 3 (1968): 272-279.

Andrejevic, Mark. *Reality TV: The Work of Being Watched.* Critical Media Studies. Lanham, Md.: Rowman & Littlefield Publishers, 2003.

Atchley, Robert C. *Social Forces and Aging: An Introduction to Social Gerontology.* 7th ed. Belmont, CA: Wadsworth Publishing Co., 1994.

Baker, Sean. "From *Dragnet* to *Survivor:* Historical and Cultural Perspectives on Reality Television." In *Survivor Lessons: Essays on Communication and Reality Television*, ed. Matthew J. Smith and Andrew F. Wood, 57-69. Jefferson, N.C.: McFarland and Company, 2003.

Barthes, Roland. *Mythologies.* Translated by Annette Lavers. New York: Noonday Press, 1988.

Bellin, Roger. "On Jameson's *The Political Unconscious*—the Horizons of Theory: Jameson, Marxism, and Poststructuralism." 1998. Accessed 14 Sept. 2005. Available from http://alum.hampshire.edu/~rb97/jameson.html.

Benjamin, Walter. *Illuminations: Essays and Reflections.* Translated by Harry Zohn, ed. Hannah Arendt. New York: Schocken Books, 1968.

Biunculli, David. "*Survivor* a Winner." *New York Daily News*, 1 June 2000, 100.

Bogle, Donald. *Toms, Coons, Mulattoes, Mammies, and Bucks: An Interpretive History of Blacks in American Films.* New expanded edition. New York: Continuum, 1989.

Boone, R. Thomas. "The Nonverbal Communication of Trustworthiness: A Necessary *Survivor* Skill." In *Survivor Lessons: Essays on Communication and Reality Television*, ed. Matthew J. Smith and Andrew F. Wood, 97-110. Jefferson, MI: McFarland Press, 2003.

Burnett, Mark with Martin Dugard. *Survivor: The Ultimate Game.* New York: TV Books, 2000.

Burnham, Clint. *The Jamesonian Unconscious: The Aesthetics of Marxist Theory.* Durham: Duke University Press, 1995.

CBS. "The Marooning (Ep. 1)." In *Survivor*, 2000, 31 May.

———. "The Generation Gap (Ep. 2)." In *Survivor*, 2000, 7 June.

———. "Pulling Your Own Weight (Ep. 5)." In *Survivor*, 2000, 28 June.

———. "Udder Revenge (Ep. 6)." In *Survivor*, 2000, 7 July.

———. "The Merger (Ep. 7)." In *Survivor*, 2000, 12 July.

———. "Thy Name Is Duplicity (Ep. 8)." In *Survivor*, 2000, 19 July.

———. "Old and New Bonds (Ep. 9)." In *Survivor*, 2000, 26 July.

———. "A Crack in the Alliance (Ep. 10)." In *Survivor*, 2000, 2 Aug.

———. "Long Hard Days (Ep. 11)." In *Survivor*, 2000, 9 Aug.

———. "Trust No One (Ep. 3)." In *Survivor: The Australian Outback*, 2001, Feb. 8.

———. "The Killing Fields (Ep. 4)." In *Survivor: The Australian Outback*, 2001, 15 Feb.

———. "The Gloves Come Off (Ep. 5)." In *Survivor: The Australian Outback*, 2001, 22 Feb.

———. "The Gods Are Angry (Ep. 3)." In *Survivor: Africa*, 2001, 25 Oct.

———. "The Young and the Untrusted (Ep. 4)." In *Survivor: Africa*, 2001, 1 Nov.

———. "The Twist (Ep. 5)." In *Survivor: Africa*, 2001, 8 Nov.

———. "Dinner, Movie and a Betrayal (Ep. 9)." In *Survivor: Africa*, 2001, 13 Dec.

———. "The Final Four: No Regrets (Ep. 13)." In *Survivor: Africa*, 2002, 10 Jan.

———. "Nacho Mamma (Ep. 2)." In *Survivor: Marquesas*, 2002, 7 March.

———. "No Pain, No Gain (Ep. 3)." In *Survivor: Marquesas*, 2002, 13 March.

———. "The Winds Twist (Ep. 4)." In *Survivor: Marquesas*, 2002, 20 March.

———. "The End of Innocence (Ep. 5)." In *Survivor: Marquesas*, 2002, 28 March.

———. "The Underdogs (Ep. 6)." In *Survivor: Marquesas*, 2002, 4 April.

———. "True Lies (Ep. 7)." In *Survivor: Marquesas*, 2002, 11 April.

———. "Jury's Out (Ep. 8)." In *Survivor: Marquesas*, 2002, 18 April.

———. "A Tale of Two Cities (Ep. 12)." In *Survivor: Marquesas*, 2002, 16 May.

———. "Desperate Measures (Ep. 9)." In *Survivor: Thailand*, 2002, 14 Nov.

———. "Boys vs. Girls (Ep. 1)." In *Survivor: The Amazon*, 2003, 13 Feb.

———. "Storms (Ep. 2)." In *Survivor: The Amazon*, 2003, 20 Feb.

———. "Trapped (Ep. 4)." In *Survivor: The Amazon*, 2003, 6 March.

———. "Girls Gone Wilder (Ep. 7)." In *Survivor: The Amazon*, 2003, 26 March.

———. "The Chain (Ep. 9)." In *Survivor: The Amazon*, 2003, 10 April.

———. "Q and A (Ep. 10)." In *Survivor: The Amazon*, 2003, 24 April.

———. "Sour Grapes (Ep. 11)." In *Survivor: The Amazon*, 2003, 1 May.

———. "Reunion." In *Survivor: The Amazon*, 2003, 11 May.

———. "Mutiny (Ep. 13)." In *Survivor: Pearl Islands Panama*, 2003, 11 Dec.

———. "Double Tribal, Double Trouble (Ep. 3)." In *Survivor: Vanuatu*, 2004, 30 Sept.

———. "Reunion." In *Survivor: Guatemala*, 2005, 11 Dec.

CBS.com. "Vecepia's Final Chat." 2002. Accessed 16 Sept. 2005. Available from www.cbs.com/primetime/survivor4/survivors/chat_archive/vecepia/chat1.shtml.

Census.gov. "Historical Income Tables: People." Accessed 16 Sept. 2005. Available from www.census.gov/hhes/www/income/histinc/p04.html.

CensusScope.org. *CensusScope: Census 2000 Data, Charts, Maps and Rankings*. 2001. Accessed 15 Sept. 2005. Available from www.censusscope.org/.

Chandler, Daniel. *Semiotics for Beginners*. University of Wales, 2002. Accessed 14 Sept. 2005. Available from www.aber.ac.uk/media/Documents/S4B/semotic.html.

CNN.com. *National Exit Polls Results*. 2000. Accessed 15 Sept. 2005. Available from www.cnn.com/ELECTION/2000/results/index.epolls.html.

Cohn, Angel. "*Survivor's* Casting Chaos." TVGuide.com, 2005, 7 March. Accessed 16 Sept. 2005. Available from tvguide.com/News/Insider/default.htm?rmDate= 03072005&cmsGuid={0C043A6F-4F9F-4413-B6AC-FA9BDED7F0D0}.

Couldry, Nick. "Teaching Us to Fake It: The Ritualized Norms of Television's 'Reality' Games." In *Reality TV: Remaking Television Culture*, ed. Susan Murray and Laurie Ouellette, 57-74. New York: New York University Press, 2004.

Coupland, Nikolas. "Age in Social and Sociolinguistic Theory." In *Handbook of Communication and Aging Research*, ed. Jon F. Nussbaum and Justine Coupland, 69-90. Mahwah, N.J.: Lawrence Erlbaum Associates, 2004.

Craig. Commentary on *Survivor* fan survey. 2005, 10 June. Accessed 16 Sept. 2005. Available from p085.ezboard.com/fsurvivorsucksfrm17.showMessageRange? topicID=5756.topic&start=886&stop=890.

Curnutt, Hugh Phillips. "The Real World." *Georgetown University*, 2002.

D'Acci, Julie. "Gender, Representation and Television." In *Television Studies*, ed. Toby Miller, 91-94. London: BFI Publishing, 2002.

Dawidziak, Mark. "Front-Runner; CBS Is Still Taking Risks." *Cleveland Plain Dealer*, 15 Jan. 2003, E1.

De Moraes, Lisa. "For 2000-01, CBS Wins by a Hair—a Gray One, Alas." *The Washington Post*, 25 May 2001, C05.

Deggans, Eric. "TV Reality Not Often Spoken Of: Race." *St. Petersburg Times*, 22 Oct. 2004, 1E.

Delisle, Jennifer Bowering. "Surviving American Cultural Imperialism: *Survivor* and Traditions of Nineteenth-Century Colonial Fiction." *The Journal of American Culture* 26, no. 1 (2003): 42-55.

Dixon, Travis, and Daniel Linz. "Race and the Misrepresentation of Victimization on Local Television News." *Communication Research* 27, no. 5 (2000): 547-573.

Donlon, Margie M., Ori Ashman, and Becca R. Levy. "Re-Vision of Older Television Characters: A Stereotype-Awareness Intervention." *Journal of Social Issues* 61, No. 2 (2005): 307-319.

Dowling, William C. *Jameson, Althusser, Marx: An Introduction to the Political Unconscious*. Ithaca: Cornell University Press, 1984.

Dyer, Richard. "Male Sexuality in the Media." In *The Sexuality of Men*, ed. Andy Metcalf and Martin Humphries. London: Pluto Press, 1985.

Elasmar, Michael, Kazumi Hasegawa, and Mary Brain. "The Portrayal of Women in U.S. Prime Time Television." *Journal of Broadcasting & Electronic Media* 43, No. 1 (1999): 20-34.

Entman, Robert M. "African Americans According to TV News." In *Race: America's Rawest Nerve*, ed. Everette E. Dennis, 8, 29-37. New York: Columbia University, 1994.

Eschholz, Sarah, Jana Bufkin, and Jenny Long. "Symbolic Reality Bites: Women and Racial/Ethnic Minorities in Modern Film." *Sociological Spectrum* 22, No. 3 (2002): 299-334.

Farhi, Paul, and Lisa de Moraes. "Television's *Survivor* Instinct; Novelty and Marketing Pay Off for CBS' Unlikely Hit." *The Washington Post*, 15 June 2000, A01.

Farhi, Paul. "Reality TV Broadcasts 'Bad Black Guy' Stereotype." *The Washington Post*, 20 Feb. 2001, C01.

Fetveit, Arild. "Reality TV in the Digital Era: A Paradox in Visual Culture?" In *Reality Squared: Television Discourses on the Real*, ed. James Friedman, 119-137. New Brunswick, N.J.: Rutgers University Press, 2002.

Feuer, Jane. "The Concept of Live Television: Ontology as Ideology." In *Regarding Television: Critical Approaches—an Anthology*, ed. E. Ann Kaplan. Los Angeles: American Film Institute, 1983.

Fiske, John, and John Hartley. *Reading Television*. London: Methuen, 1978.

Foster, Derek. "'Jump in the Pool': The Competitive Culture of *Survivor* Fan Networks." In *Understanding Reality Television*, ed. Su Holmes and Deborah Jermyn, 270-289. London: Routledge, 2004.

Garbotalk. *"Survivor* Fans Rank the Seasons.*"* SurvivorFever.net, 2005. Accessed 15 Sept. 2005. Available from www.survivorfever.net/gt_rank_the_seasons. html.

Gillespie, Tarleton. "Narrative Control and Visual Polysemy: Fox Surveillance Specials and the Limits of Legitimation." *The Velvet Light Trap*, no. 45 (2000, Spring): 36-49.

Glover, Helen. "E-Mail Interview with *Survivor: Thailand* Contestant Helen Glover." ed. Christopher J. Wright, 2004.

Gray, Herman. *Watching Race: Television and the Struggle for "Blackness."* Minneapolis: University of Minnesota Press, 1995.

Greenberg, B.S., F. Korzenny, and C.K. Atkin. "Trends in the Portrayal of the Elderly." In *Life on Television: Content Analysis of U.S. TV Drama*, ed. B.S. Greenberg, 23-33. Norwood, N.J.: Ablex Press, 1980.

Haralovich, Mary Beth, and Michael Trosset. "Expect the Unexpected: Narrative Pleasure and Uncertainty Due to Chance in *Survivor*." In *Reality TV: Remaking Television Culture*, ed. Susan Murray and Laurie Ouellette, 75-96. New York: New York University Press, 2004.

Healey, Tim, and Karen Ross. "Growing Old Invisibly: Older Viewers Talk Television." *Media, Culture & Society* 24, No. 1 (2002): 105-121.

Hestetun, Oyunn. "A Prison-House of Myth?: Symptomal Readings in *Virgin Land*, the *Madwoman in the Attic*, and the *Political Unconscious*." Thesis doctoral— Uppsala University, 1993.

Hummert, Mary Lee, and Teri A. Garstka. "Stereotypes of the Elderly Held by Young, Middle-Aged, and Elderly Adults." *Journal of Gerontology* 49, no. 5 (1994): 240-249.

Hummert, Mary Lee, Teri A. Garstka, Ellen Bouchard Ryan, and Jaye L. Bonnesen. "The Role of Age Stereotypes in Interpersonal Communication." In *Handbook of Communication and Aging Research, 2nd Ed.*, ed. Jon F. Nussbaum and Justine Coupland, 91-109. Mahwah, N.J.: Lawrence Erlbaum Associates, 2004.

Hurt, Alyson. "Psychoanalyzing *Buffy*, Redux." 2002. Accessed 12 Sept. 2005. Available from www.morethanthis.net/blog/archives/2003/01/11/000031.html.

Jameson, Fredric. *Marxism and Form; Twentieth-Century Dialectical Theories of Literature*. Princeton, N.J.: Princeton University Press, 1972.

————. *The Prison-House of Language; a Critical Account of Structuralism and Russian Formalism*. Princeton, N.J.: Princeton University Press, 1972.

————. *The Political Unconscious: Narrative as a Socially Symbolic Act*. Ithaca, N.Y.: Cornell University Press, 1981.

————. *Postmodernism, or the Cultural Logic of Late Capitalism*. Durham: Duke University Press, 1991.

————. *Brecht and Method*. London; New York: Verso, 1998.

Jenkins, Henry. *Convergence Culture*. Manuscript in progress.

Jewell, K. Sue. *From Mammy to Miss America and Beyond: Cultural Images and the Shaping of Us Social Policy*. London: Routledge, 1993.

Jhally, Sut, and Justin Lewis. *Enlightened Racism:* The Cosby Show, *Audiences and the Myth of the American Dream*. Cultural Studies. Boulder: Westview Press, 1992.

Kellner, Douglas. *Media Culture: Cultural Studies, Identity, and Politics between the Modern and the Postmodern*. London: Routledge, 1995.

————. "The Lord of the Rings as Allegory: A Multiperspectivist Reading" In *From Hobbits to Hollywood: Essays on Peter Jackson's Lord of the Rings*, ed. Ernest Mathijs; Murray Pomerance. Amsterdam: Rodopi. Forthcoming.

Lance, Peter. *The Stingray: Lethal Tactics of the Sole Survivor*. Berryville, Va.: Cinema 21 Books, 2000.

Larson, Stephanie Greco. *Media & Minorities: The Politics of Race in News and Entertainment*. Spectrum Series, Race and Ethnicity in National and Global Politics. Lanham: Rowman & Littlefield, 2005.

Levin, Gary. "Men vs. Women on CBS' *Survivor*." *USA Today*, 14 Jan. 2003, 1D.

Levi-Strauss, Claude. *Tristes Tropiques*. 1st American ed. New York,: Criterion Books, 1961.

Lorber, Judith. *Paradoxes of Gender*. New Haven: Yale University Press, 1994.

Macherey, Pierre. *A Theory of Literary Production*. London: Routledge & Kegan Paul, 1978.

Madger, Ted. "The End of TV 101: Reality Programs, Formats, and the New Business of Television." In *Reality TV: Remaking Television Culture*, ed. Susan Murray and Laurie Ouellette, 137-156. New York: New York University Press, 2004.

Madon, Stephanie, Max Guyll, Kathy Aboufadel, Eulices Montiel, Alison Smith, Polly Palumbo, and Lee Jussim. "Ethnic and National Stereotypes: The Princeton Trilogy Revisited and Revised." *Personality and Social Psychology Bulletin* 27, no. 8 (2001): 996-1010.

Marable, Manning. "Reconciling Race and Reality." In *Race: America's Rawest Nerve*, ed. Everette E. Dennis, 8, 11-18. New York: Columbia University, 1994.

McCarthy, Anna. *Ambient Television: Visual Culture and Public Space*. Consoling Passions. Durham: Duke University Press, 2001.

McDaniel, Mike. "*Survivor* Contestants Go for Thrills." *Houston Chronicle*, 31 May 2000, 1.

McNeill, Tony. 1996. "Roland Barthes: Mythologies (1957)." Accessed 15 Sept. 2005; Available from http://orac.sund.ac.uk/~os0tmc/myth.htm.

McWhorter, John H. *Authentically Black: Essays for the Black Silent Majority*. New York: Gotham, 2003.

―――. "Still Losing the Race?" *Commentary* (2004, Feb.): 37-42.

Mifflin, Lawrie. "A Dissertation on Mr. Ed? New Scholarly Center to Study Pop Television Culture." *The New York Times*, 15 Oct. 1997, E01.

Oldenburg, Meg. "Bush Survives Night of Jokes." *USA Today*. 30 April 2001, 2D.

Ouellette, Laurie, and Susan Murray. "Introduction." In *Reality TV: Remaking Television Culture*, ed. Susan Murray and Laurie Ouellette, 1-15. New York: New York University Press, 2004.

Petrozzello, Donna. "*Survivor* River Rumble Will Be Guys vs. Gals." *New York Daily News*, 14 Jan. 2003, 75.

Pittsburgh Post-Gazette. "*Survivor* Holds Its Own Opposite *Millionaire*." 3 June 2000, D11.

PollingReport.com. *Race and Ethnicity*. 2005. Accessed 16 Sept. 2005. Available from www.pollingreport.com/race.htm.

Powell, Kimberly A., and Lori Abels. "Sex-Role Stereotypes in TV Programs Aimed at the Preschool Audience: An Analysis of *Teletubbies* and *Barney & Friends*." *Women & Language* 25, no. 2 (2002): 14-22.

Roberts, Adam. *Fredric Jameson*. Routledge Critical Thinkers. London; New York: Routledge, 2000.

Robinson, James D., and Thomas Skill. "The Invisible Generation: Portrayals of the Elderly on Prime-Time Television." *Communication Reports* 8, no. 2 (1995): 111-119.

Roth, April L. "Contrived Television Reality: *Survivor* as a Pseudo-Event." In *Survivor Lessons: Essays on Communication and Reality Television*, ed. Matthew J. Smith and Andrew F. Wood, 27-36. Jefferson, N.C.: McFarland and Co., 2003.

Schaefer, Richard T. *Racial and Ethnic Groups*. 6th ed. New York: HarperCollins College Publishers, 1996.

Shales, Tom. "*Survivor*: An Island Not Remote Enough; Contestants May Outlast Viewers on CBS Show." *Washington Post*, 1 June 2000, C01.

Sheppard, Fergus. "*Apprentice* Is Praised for Helping Racial Harmony." *The Scotsman*, 29 June 2005, 9.

Signorielli, Nancy, and Aaron Bacue. "Recognition and Respect: A Content Analysis of Prime-Time Television Characters Across Three Decades." *Sex Roles* 40, no. 7/8 (1999): 527-545.

Signorielli, Nancy. "Aging on Television: Messages Relating to Gender, Race, and Occupation in Prime Time." *Journal of Broadcasting & Electronic Media* 48, no. 2 (2004): 279-301.

Siri on *Survivor*. "Lesson 2: Men Are Pigs: The Women's Tribe Has the Upper Hand." *The Ottawa Citizen*, 20 Feb. 2003, E1.

Spigel, Lynn. *Make Room for TV: Television and the Family Ideal in Postwar America*. Chicago: University of Chicago Press, 1992.

SurvivorFever.net. *Survivor Host Jeff Probst Talks About Survivor: Palau—Media Teleconference Transcript*. 2005, Feb. 10. Accessed 12 July 2005. Available from www.survivorfever.net/s10_jp_media_teleconference.html.

Thackaberry, Jennifer. "Manual Metaphors of *Survivor* and Office Politics: Images of Work in Popular *Survivor* Criticism." In *Survivor Lessons: Essays on Com-*

Thackaberry, Jennifer. "Manual Metaphors of *Survivor* and Office Politics: Images of Work in Popular *Survivor* Criticism." In *Survivor Lessons: Essays on Communication and Reality Television*, ed. Matthew J. Smith and Andrew F. Wood, 153-181. Jefferson, N.C.: McFarland and Company Inc., 2003.

Thorson, James A. *Aging in a Changing Society*. 2nd ed. Philadelphia: Brunner/Mazel, 2000.

Tinkcom, Matthew. "Lecture and Discussion on Walter Benjamin." Georgetown University, 2002.

Van Evra, Judith Page. *Television and Child Development*. 3rd ed. Lea's Communication Series. Mahwah, N.J.: Lawrence Erlbaum Associates, Publishers, 2004.

Vander Zanden, James Wilfrid. *Sociology: The Core*. 4th ed. New York: McGraw-Hill, 1996.

Vrooman, Steven. "Self Help for Savages: The 'Other' *Survivor*, Primitivism, and the Construction of American Identity." In *Survivor Lessons: Essays in Communication and Reality Television*, ed. Matthew J. Smith and Andrew F. Wood, 182-198. Jefferson, N.C.: McFarland and Company, 2003.

Warrior. *Edgic Guidelines*. 11 Aug. 2005. Accessed 30 Nov. 2005. Available from p085.ezboard.com/fsurvivorsucksfrm9.showMessage?topicID=8949.topic.

White, Mimi. "Ideological Analysis and Television." In *Channels of Discourse, Reassembled*, ed. Robert C. Allen, 161-202. Chapel Hill, N.C.: University of North Carolina Press, 1987.

Williams, Frederick, Robert La Rose, and Frederica Frost. *Children, Television, and Sex-Role Stereotyping*. New York, N.Y.: Praeger, 1981.

Williams, John E., and Deborah L. Best. *Measuring Sex Stereotypes: A Thirty-Nation Study*. Cross-Cultural Research and Methodology Series. Beverly Hills: Sage Publications, 1982.

Wiltz, Teresa. "The Evil Sista of Reality Television; Shows Trot out Old Stereotypes to Spice up Stagnant Story Lines." *The Washington Post*, 25 Feb. 2004, C01.

Wright, Chris. *Borans Don't Cry*. PopPolitics.com, 22 Oct. 2001. Accessed 29 Nov. 2003. Available from www.poppolitics.com/articles/2001-10-22-borans.shtml.

———. *Harold and Maude?* PopPolitics.com, 18 Dec. 2001. Accessed 30 Dec. 2003. Available from www.poppolitics.com/articles/2001-12-18-outofsight.shtml.

———. *Whitewash*. PopPolitics.com, 26 Nov. 2001. Accessed 21 Dec. 2003. Available from www.poppolitics.com/articles/2001-11-26-whitewash.shtml.

———. *Bet on Black*. PopPolitics.com, 9 May 2002. Accessed 20 Dec. 2003. Available from www.poppolitics.com/articles/2002-05-09-betonblack.shtml.

———. *Spoiler Sports*. PopPolitics.com, 10 Jan. 2002. Accessed 9 Dec. 2003. Available from www.poppolitics.com/articles/2002-01-10-spoilers.

———. *The Invisible Woman*. PopPolitics.com, 29 May 2002. Accessed 12 Dec. 2003. Available from www.poppolitics.com/articles/2002-05-29-vecepia.shtml.

Wyman, Bill. "Reality TV Stereotypes Harshest on Blacks." *The Atlanta Journal-Constitution*, 20 May 2002, 8D.

Index

Note: Contestants listed by first name.

227, 111, 112, 113

A Streetcar Named Desire, 19
AAAI (adjusted audience attitude
    index), 5; *Borneo* blocs, 31, 43n6,
    by contestant gender, 91; by
    contestant race, 120, 121, 132n2;
    Marquesas blocs, 52, 61n7, *see
    also* Appendix B
acculturation, 98–99
Adorno, Theodor, 18
age, xix, 73, *96*, *97*; alliances and, 102–
    104, *102*, *103*, 107n4, 107nn6–7;
    cultural representations of, 95–97;
    invisibility and, 96–98; repression
    and, 102, 104, 106; on television,
    95–97; *see also* content analysis
    results; and survey results, age
Alex, *Amazon*, 56, 58, 70; ouster, 56,
    57
Alicia, *Outback*, 91, 116, 122; survey,
    91
allegory, 4, 13, 19, 32, 33, 38, 48–49,
    51, 55, 60, 73, 95, 98, 99, 100,
    131–132, 135, 139; *Survivor* as
    society model and, 30, 32, 33, 37,
    38, 42–43, 46–47, 48, 51–52, 55,
    57, 60, 72, 142. *See also*

bourgeoisie; class; Jameson,
    Fredric; political unconscious;
    politics; and repression
alliances, 13, 22, 105, 107n4, 107n6,
    107n10, 118, 121, 138, 141; age
    and, 101–104, 106; on *Africa*, 45;
    on *All-Stars*, 61n10; on *Amazon*,
    55–57; on *Borneo*, 27–45, 63, 91,
    95, 104, 105; class, repression,
    and, 22, 24, 95, 135, 139; on
    Marquesas, 47–53, 60, 61n2, 91,
    104, 105, 124, 125, 126, 127, 128,
    129, 131, 134; on *Outback*, 45; on
    Pearl Islands, 86–88; race and,
    121, 122; on *Vanuatu*, 86
Althusser, Louis, xviii, 16
The Amazing Race, 133n4, 142
Amber, *All-Stars*: romance with Rob
    M., 66, 141
An American Family, 142
American Idol, 11, 12
Ami, *Vanuatu,* 91; survey, 105
Andrejevic, Mark, 10, 142
Andrew, *Pearl Islands*, 91
Angel, 19
The Apprentice, 12, 13, 114, 133n4
The Bachelor, 12
Bacue, Aaron, 74

Barthes, Roland, xix–xx, 3, 11, 143
Beavis and Butthead, 19
B.B., *Borneo*, 8, 96, 97, 106, 119; and age stereotypes, 99–100, 101; survey, 100
Bellin, Roger, 17
Benjamin, Walter, 8
Bianculli, David, 2
Big Brother, 10, 11, 14n6
Bobby Jon, *Guatemala*, 6n3; *Palau*, 114
Bogle, Donald, 111, 115
Boran alliance, 45, 67, 68, 107nn4–5
bourgeoisie and proletariat, xviii, 3, 23, 32, 33, 34, 35, 40, 47, 52, 64–66, 72, 75, 84, 86, 92, 98, 115, 118, 122, 124, 130–131; bourgeoisie nightmare, 32, 34, 35, 50, 51, 60, 76, 84, 87, 89–90, 141; proletariat nightmare, 30, 33, 35, 36, 38, 60–61, 141–142; *see also* allegory; class; repression; political unconscious; politics; and Jameson, Fredric
Brandon, *Africa*, 10 23, 67; survey, 91, 105
Brian, *Thailand*, 55, 65, 86, 135–137, *136, 137, 138*; survey, 91, 136–137, 143nn2–4
Buffy the Vampire Slayer, 17, 80
Burnett, Mark, 1, 7, 12, 13, 28, 45, 76, 98, 114, 135; editing and, 34, 53, 63, 65, 66, 68, 69, 72n3, 81, 83
Burnham, Clint, 18
Burton, *Pearl Islands*, 86–89, *89*, 81, 93; second ouster, 90; survey, 90
Bush, President George W., 140, 141
Butch, Amazon, 56, 57, 58, 96, 104; ouster, 57

Caryn, *Palau*, 91
causality, 16–17
Cheers, 19–20
Chris, *Vanuatu*, 86
Christy, *Amazon*, 56, 58, 119; ouster, 57
Chuay Gahn, *Thailand*, 25, 55, 107nn4–5, 107n9, 135, 143
Clarence, *Africa*, 116

class, xvii, xix, 3, 13, 16, 18, 72, 124; age and, 95; form of reality television and, 142; gender and, 92–93; Jamesonian analysis and, 18, 19, 21, 73; race and, 129–132; *Survivor* and, 21, 23, 137, 139; *see also* allegory; bourgeoisie; Jameson, Fredric; political unconscious; politics; and repression
Clay, *Thailand*, 24, 86, 136
Coby, *Palau*, survey, 91, 105
Colby, *Outback*, 45, 91; alliance, 45, 66, 69; obscured relationship with Tina, 66, 68
Colleen, *Borneo*, 8, 10, 14n3, 18, 29, 31, 33, 34, 50, 58, 118; faux romance, 63–66, 69, 72nn1–2; as heroine, 33–36; ouster, 36; strategy, 31, 32, 33, 35; survey, 33, 39, 41; symbolic resolution and, 35–36, 138
Content analysis results, 82–83, 98, 99, 101
Cops, 7, 10
The Cosby Show, 111, 112, 128, 130, 133n4
Couldry, Nick, xx
Curnutt, Hugh Phillips, 7

Daniel, *Amazon*, 76, 79, 81
Darrah, *Pearl Islands*, 86, 87, 88; denial of women's alliance, 88–89
Dave, *Amazon*, 58, 70; ouster, 56, 57; stereotypes and, 79, 81, 84
The DaVinci Code, 80
de Saussure, Ferdinand, xix
Deena, *Amazon*, 56, 70, 119; ouster, 56, 57; stereotypes and, 76, 77, 80, 91; survey, 91, 105; as symbolic male, 77, 81, 84
Delisle, Jennifer Bowering, 9
denial. *See* repression
Diane, *Africa*, 116
Dirk, *Borneo*, 8, 28; ouster, 28, 29, 30, 34
Dirty Harry, 80
Dowling, William C., 16

Eagleton, Terry, 21
editing, 7–8, 11; on *Africa*, 67–69; on
    Amazon, 69–72, 76–85; apparent
    manipulation through, 10, 14n3,
    34, 64–65; on *Borneo*, 32, 34, 35,
    63–66, 101; on *Outback*, 66, 69;
    on *Pearl Islands*, 85–90;
    suppression and, 22, 24, 28, 29,
    66–69; *see also* stereotypes
Edwards, Sen. John, 130
Elizabeth, *Outback*, 8, 114; survey, 105
Ethan, *Africa*, 91; Kim J. and, 66–69;
    survey, 72n3

Fables of Aggression, 20
"fake final four," 10, 14n3
fandom, 10–11, 14n3, 34, 43n8, 44n12,
    45, 61nn12–13, 90; "invisible
    pair," 66–67; in regression
    equations, 42, 54; *see also*
    "pagonging"
Farhi, Paul, 113, 114
Fetveit, Arild, 10
Feuer, Jane, 11
Finding Nemo, 20
Fiske, John, 11
Flieger, Jerry Aline, 21
form. See ideology, of form; and
    Survivor, structure of
Foster, Derek, 14n5
Frank, *Africa*, 8, 67, 91, 106
Freud, Sigmund, xviii, xix, xx, 15–16,
    23, 79

Gabe, *Marquesas*, 46, 47, 49
gender, xix, 17, 73, 83; repression and,
    84–85; stereotypes and hierarchies
    on *Survivor*, 73–94; television
    and, 74–75; *see also* content
    analysis results; stereo-types; and
    survey results, gender
Gervase, *Borneo*, 9, 10, 14n3, 30, 31,
    32, 33, 34, 44n11, 58, 63–64, 85–
    86, 99, 115, 116, 120; denial of
    alliance, 30, 33; ouster, 35–36;
    racial stereotypes and, 118;
    symbolic resolution and, 35–36,
    138; Web site glitch, 14n3, 34
Ghandia, *Thailand*, 24–25, 117; survey,
    94n9

Gillespie, Tarleton, 11
*Global Aesthetic: Cinema and Space in
    the World System*, 20
Gore, Vice President Al, 139–140
Gosford Park, 19
Gray, Herman, 111, 112
Greg, *Borneo*, 28, 29, 30–31, 32, 43n3,
    50; faux romance, 63–66; ouster,
    32, 33, 65; survey, 41
Gretchen, *Borneo*, 28, 29, 99; ouster,
    30, 33, 64; survey, 41, 43n7

Haralovich, Mary Beth, 3, 11, 23
Harris, Katherine, 140
Harry Potter series, 20
Hartley, John, 11
Heidi, *Amazon*, 56, 57, 58, 70, 76;
    gender stereotypes and, 76, 77, 79,
    80, 81, 82, 85; ouster, 57
Helen, *Thailand*, interview with, 8, 24–
    25, 136; ouster, 86
Hestetun, Oyunn, 17, 18, 20, 21
homosexuality, 21, 73; gay contestants,
    47, 61n9, 79, 91, 105; survey,
    61n9, 91, 105
Hunter, *Marquesas*, 46, 123
Hurricane Katrina, 110, 115, 130
Hyperrealism, 11

ideologeme, 18, 55, 139
ideology, 1, 3, 11, 15, 18, 19, 113, 121,
    142–143; defined, xviii
Iffland, James, 20–21

Jabaru, *Amazon*, 75–85, 92, content
    analysis, 82-83; survey, 94n8,
    132n6; *see also* stereotypes,
    gender and
Jake, *Thailand*, 25, 96, 97
Jameson, Fredric, 3, 13, 15–25, 32, 35,
    40, 72, 73, 129, 135; allegory and,
    19, 32, 43, 138, 139, 142;
    criticism of, 20; Marx, Freud, and,
    15; *see also* allegory; bourgeoisie;
    class; political unconscious;
    politics; and repression
Jan, *Thailand*, 96, 102; ouster, 86
Janu, *Palau*, 120
Jeanne, *Amazon*, 120
Jeff, *Outback*, 116

Jenkins, Henry III, 14n5
Jenna M., *Amazon*, 56, 57, 70, 90;
    editing of, 61n13; gender
    stereotypes and, 77, 78, 79, 80, 81,
    85; recognition of Rob's power,
    58; spoiler on, 61nn12–13; survey,
    59, 61
Jenna L., *All-Stars*, 61n10; *Borneo*, 28–
    29, 31, 33, 34, 58, 63–64, 65, 116,
    118, 122; suspicions and denial,
    28, 30, 31, 32; ouster, 34–35,
    44n11;
Jerri, *Outback*, 21, 23, 114; survey, 105
Jessie, *Africa*, 120
Jewell, K. Sue, 111, 115
Jhally, Sut, 111, 128, 129, 131
Jim, *Guatemala*, 96, 97, 106
Joanna, *Amazon*, 8, 117; gender
    stereotypes and, 80; ouster, 120;
    racial stereotypes and, 119–120
Joe Millionaire, 12
Joel, *Borneo*, 99, 118; ouster, 85–86
John, *Marquesas*, 46, 47, 48, 49;
    forming alliance, 46–47; ouster,
    51–52; similarity to Rich, 47;
    symbolic resolution and, 47, 138
John, *Thailand*, 24
Jolanda, *Palau*, 117; survey, 91, 120
Jon, *Pearl Islands*, 86–89, 90, 93, 114,
    141; recruitment of, 106n2

Kathy, *Marquesas*, 22, 23, 46, 47, 48,
    49, 50, 61n3, 122; as heroine, race
    and, 112, 124–129, 132; 48;
    strategy of, 22, 23, 47, 49, 51, 52,
    125–128; survey, 48–49, 50, 53,
    54, 60, 132; suspicions, 47–48
Keith, *Outback*, 45, 66, 69
Kel, *Outback*, 23
Kellner, Douglas, 19, 73
Kelly, *Africa*, 90
Kelly, *Borneo*, 27, 28, 29, 31, 36,
    44n11; apparent wavering of, 29,
    32, 33, 34, 35, 36; argument with
    Sue, 34, 43n8; denial of alliance,
    31, 33; survey, 39
Kerry, Sen. John, 141
Kim J., Africa, 96, 106, 107n9; Ethan
    and, 66–69; survey, 72n3
Kim P., *Africa*, 67

Kimmi, *Outback*, 116
Koror, *Palau*, 107n5, 107n7; survey,
    132n6, 141

Lance, Peter, 7, 34, 43n2, 65
Lear, Norman, 125, 128
Levi-Strauss, Claude, 17, 35
Lewis, Justin M., 111, 128, 129, 131
Lex, *Africa*, 9, 25, 45, 67,–68, 91;
    survey, 72n3, 105
Lillian, *Pearl Islands*, 86, 87, 88, 89,
    96, 107n8; denial and women's
    alliance, 87, 88, 89
Linda, *Africa*, 9, 106, 116, 122
Lindsey, *Africa*, 8
The Lord of the Rings, 19

Macherey, Pierre, 15
male gaze, 79
Maraamu, *Marquesas*, 46, 47, 122–123
Maralyn, *Outback*, 96
Marugault-Stallworth, Omarosa, 114
Marx, Karl, xviii, xx, 13; and Jameson,
    20, 33
Marxist analysis, xviii, 15, 16; parallels
    with Freudian analysis, 15
Marxism and Form, 20
Matthew, *Amazon*, 56, 57, 58, 77;
    spoiler and, 61n12; as tool of Rob,
    56;
McWhorter, John H., 111, 113
Miller, Mark Crispin, xvii
The Mole, 12
myth, xx, 9, 95, 130, 143

Nader, Ralph, 139
narrative, 16, 19
Neleh, *Marquesas*, 22, 46, 47, 48, 49,
    105, 132n5; denial and acceptance
    of alliance, 22, 48, 49, 50, 51;
    Paschal and, 47, 50; survey, 61;
    race and, 124–129, 132
Nick, *Outback*, 9, 116, 122

Osten, *Pearl Islands*, 44n12; survey,
    117

Pagong, *Borneo*, 28, 61n10, 85–86, 99–
    100, 101, 105, 118, 135, 140; faux
    romance, 63–66; mean AAAI, 31,

43n6; merge with Tagi, 28–29; suspicion and denial of alliance, 28, 30, 32, 33, 34

"pagonging," 44n12, 45, 55, 135, 141

Paschal, *Marquesas*, 22, 46, 49, 96, 132n5, 140; denial and acceptance of alliance, 22, 48, 50–51, 52; Neleh and, 47, 50; race and, 124–134, 131; survey, 61n2, 105

phallic symbolism, 17, 79–82

Phillips, Trevor, 109

political parties in U.S., 139–141; *see also* survey results, political orientation

The Political Unconscious. See political unconscious

political unconscious, 3, 4, 13, 15–25, 138–140; oppositional cultures and, 21, 73, 84. *See also* allegory; bourgeoisie; class; Jameson, Fredric; politics; and repression

politics, 13; *Survivor* and, 13; American, 139–141, 142; *see also* allegory; bourgeoisie; class; Jameson, Fredric; political unconscious; and repression

Poltergeist, 19

Postmodernism, or the Cultural Logic of Late Capitalism, 20

presidential election of 2000, 139–140

presidential election of 2004, 140–141

Princeton Trilogy, 110, 120

Probst, Jeff, 2, 11, 13, 29, 32, 34, 35, 36, 56, 57, 76, 79, 103, 119, 138, 140

proletariat. *See* bourgeoisie

Queer Eye for the Straight Guy, 7

race, 17, 73; cultural history of, 112, 129–130; makeup of *Survivor* contestant base and, 110, *116–117*; polling on, 115; repression and, 122, 125, 129; stereotypes and hierarchies on *Survivor*, 109–133, *121*, *127*, *128*; on television, 109–115, *111*; see also stereotypes; and survey results, race

Ramona, *Borneo*, 99, 116, 122

reality television, 1–3, 7–12, 109–110, 113–122, 123, 132n4, 142–143; defined, 1;

The Real World, 1, 7, 12

repetition. *See* repression

repression, xix, 3, 4, 15–16, 19, 23, 25, 139; on *Africa*, 67–69; African-American contestants and, 132; alliances and, 22, 24; on *Amazon*, 56–57, 58, 70, 84–85; on *Borneo*, 29, 31, 34–35, 36, 64–66; defined regarding *Survivor*, 23; editing and, 4, 24; on *Marquesas*, 48, 49, 122, 125, 129; older contestants, 102, 104, 106; on *Pearl Islands*, 87–90; suppression and, 22; *see also* allegory; bourgeoisie; class; Jameson, Fredric; political unconscious; and politics

Richard, *Borneo*, 2, 7, 18, 29, 32, 33, 37, 47, 43n3, 61n9, 63, 64, 65, 91, 102, 118; forming alliance, 27–28; Rudy and, 98, 102; survey, 38, 39, 40, *40*, 41, 43, 105; symbolic resolution and, 138; worries of, 32, 34

Rob, *Amazon*, 24, 55–61, 69, 70, 84, 104, 135, 141; ouster, 58, 59; stereotypes and, 77, 79, 90; strategy of, 55–58; survey, 58, *59*, 59–60, 61n14, 56, 91

Rob M., *All-Stars* romance with Amber, 66, 141; *Marquesas*, 25n3, 46, 47, 48, 49, 91; ouster, 49; strategy, 47, 48; survey, 53, 61n2;

Robert, *Marquesas*, 46, 47, 50–51; ouster, 52; survey, 61n2

Roberts, Adam, 15, 20

Rodger, *Outback*, 96

Roger, *Amazon*, 56, 58, 91, 96, 104; gender stereotypes and, 76, 77, 79, 81; ouster, 56, 57, 69–72; survey, 70–71, *70*, *71*, 72nn4–5, 90; suspicions and denial, 70, 84

Rory, *Vanuatu*, 117

Rotu, *Marquesas*, 21–22, 46–55, 91; alliance, 21–22, 46, *50*, *51*, *105*, 128; downfall of alliance, 50–51

Rove, Karl, 141

Rudy, *Borneo*, 10, 27, 28, 29, 33, 34,
    43n3, 96, 97, 98, 99, 101, 102,
    118; age stereotypes and, 98–99,
    100, 101; Rich and, 98, 102;
    survey, 32, 39, 41, 43n7, 100
Rupert, *Pearl Islands*, 86, 91
Ryan, *Amazon*, 24, 84; ouster, 81; as
    symbolic female, 77, 80–81, 84

Samburu, *Africa*, 45, 67
Sandra, *Pearl Islands*, 86, 87, 88,
    132n4; denial of alliance, 88, 89
Sarge, *Vanuatu*, 8, 91
Scout, *Vanuatu*, 96, 102
Sean, *Borneo*, 10, 27, 28, 29, 30, 33,
    34, 36, 37, 43nn4–5, 44n11, 135,
    140; alphabetical voting strategy,
    34, 35, 36; ouster, 36; survey, 31,
    105; suspicions and denial of
    alliance, 28, 29, 30, 31, 33, 35
Sean, *Marquesas*, 22, 46, 47, 49, 101,
    116, 121, *127*, *131*, 132n5;
    alliance and, 50–51; race and,
    122–129, 132; survey, 61n2, 127,
    131
semiotics, xix–xx
Sept. 11, 2001, 140
Shales, Tom, 2
Shawna, *Amazon*, 8, 79
Shii-Ann, *All-Stars*, 10, 44n12
Signorielli, Nancy, 74
socialization. *See* television
Sonja, *Borneo*, 96, 97, 101, 106;
    survey, 100, 105
Sook Jai, *Thailand*, 25, 55, 107n7, 135,
    143n1
Spigel, Lynn, 11, 74
spoilers. *See* fandom
Stephenie, *Guatemala*, 6n3; *Palau*, 8
stereotypes, 8, 9, 75, 143; age and, 95–
    102, *96*, 105, 106; defined, 74;
    gender and, 74–83, 87, 88, 89, 91,
    143; on news programs, 112–113;
    race and, 110–120; *111*, *116–117*;
    see also Appendix B
*The Stingray: Lethal Tactics of the Sole
    Survivor*, 7, 33, 65
Sue, *Borneo*, 27, 29, 32, 33, 35, 36,
    118; argument with Kelly, 34,

43n8; denial of alliance, 31, 32;
    survey, 105; worries, 32, 34
survey results, 4–5, 6n6, 132nn1–2,
    139; cross tabulations, 38–42,
    44nn14–15, 53–54, 59, 60, 70–71,
    72n4, 85, 89, 104–105, 126, 130,
    131, 136–138; regression analysis,
    42m 44n16, 50, 54, 59–60, 72n5,
    126,127, 131, 133n6, 137;
    respondents' age and, 54, 60, 104,
    105, *105*, 107n8, 107n10;
    respondents' class and, *38*, 39–40,
    39, *40*, 42, *58*, 60, 72n4, 92, 136–
    137, *136*; respondents' education
    level and, 40, 59, *59*, 60, 71, *71*;
    respondents' employment status
    and, 54; respondents' fandom
    level, 42, 54; respondents' gender
    and, 54, 55, 85, *85*, 89–93, *89*,
    131, 135; respondents' housing
    status and, 53, *53*; respondents'
    income and, 41, *42*, 54, *54*, 93,
    130, 131, 137, 138, *138*;
    respondents' occupation and, 53,
    59, 60, 71; respondents' political
    orientation and, 41, *41*, 42, 54, 60,
    70, *70*, 72n5, 92, *92*, 93, 130, 131,
    131, 137, *137*; respondents' race
    and, 54, 55, 92, 120, 126–127,
    127, 128, *128*, 130, 131, 133n6;
    respondents' union status and, 42,
    59, 60, 71; *see also* individual
    contestants, seasons; *see also*
    Appendix B
Survivor, 2–3; contestant demographics
    on, 96–98,*97*, 110, 132n4;
    marketing of, 97, 98, 110; *The
    Mole* and, 12; parallels to U.S.
    politics of, 139–141; racial
    discussions on, 122–129; ratings,
    2, 12, 65; society and, 12, 13, 30,
    32, 33, 37, 38, 42–43, 46–47, 48,
    51–52, 55, 57, 60, 72, 101, 121,
    139, 142–143; stereo-types in
    general on, 75; structure of, 12,
    23, 37, 55, 69, 138, 141–142, *141*;
    see also individual seasons and
    contestants
Survivor: Africa, 9, 23, 25n4, 45, 55,
    67, 90, 91, 96, 104, 105, 106, 116,

120, 122; "invisible pair" and, 66–69; repression and, 67–69; structure of, 141; survey, 72n3; *see also* individual tribes and contestants

Survivor: All-Stars, 4, 6n3, 6n7, 10, 25n4, 44n12, 55, 66, 91, 106n1, 107n4, 140; parallels to U.S. politics, 140; structure of, 141; *see also* individual contestants

Survivor: The Amazon, 4, 24, *56*, 57, *57*, *77*, *82*, *83*, *85*, *92*, 96, 104, 105, 117, 118, 119–120; gender and, 75–85, 87, 90, 91, 133; repression on, 56–57, 58, 70, 84–85; Roger's ouster on, 69–72; strategy of Rob on, 55–61; structure of, 141; survey, 56, 59, 60, 62n14, 70–71, 84–85, 133n6; *see also* individual tribes and contestants

Survivor: The Australian Outback, 6n7, 23, 45, 55, 66, 91, 96, 105, 116, 119, 122, 141; alliance on, 107n4; "invisible pair" on, 66; ratings of, 2; parallels in U.S. politics, 139–140; structure of, 140, 141; *see also* individual contestants

Survivor: Borneo, 4, 13, 6n7, 7, 25, 27–44, *28*, *31*, *37*, 50, 55, 61n5, 85–86, 91–96, 105, 115, 116, 120; lawsuit regarding, 14n1; older contestants on, 97–101, *100*; parallels in U.S. politics, 139–140; race on, 118, 122; ratings of, 2; repression on, 29, 31, 34–35, 36, 64–66; structure of, 139, 141; survey, 14n1, 31, 34, 37–42, 43n5, 44nn9–10, 61n5, 98–101, 104; Tagi alliance on, 27–44; *see also* individual tribes and contestants

Survivor: Guatemala, 6n3, 96, 97, 106, 106n1, 110; structure of, 141; *see also* Stephenie; Bobby Jon; and Jim

Survivor: Marquesas, 4, 9, 21–22, 25n3, 43, 45–55, *46*, *50*, *51*, *52*, 67, 91, 96, 104, 105, 107, *124*, *127*, *128*, *131*, 138; alliance and "coup" in, 45–55; parallels in U.S.

politics, 140, 141; race and, 109, 116–117, 121, 122–129, 131; repression and, 48, 49, 122, 125, 129; structure of, 141; survey, 48, 49–50, 52,53, 61n2, 61nn4–8; 52–54, 126, 127, 130, 131; *see also* individual tribes and contestants

Survivor: Palau, 6n3, 91, 96, 103, 105, 106, 107n4, 107n7, 138; parallels to U.S. politics, 140, 141; structure of, 141; survey, 91, 120, 133n6, 141; *see also* individual tribes and contestants

Survivor: Pearl Islands, 44n12, 75, *87*, *89*, 93, 96, 102, 106n2, 117, 141; gender and, 85–90; repression on, 87–90; structure of, 141; survey, 89–90; *see also* individual contestants

Survivor: Thailand, 8, 24–25, 86, 94n9, 96, 97, 102, 107, 117, 121, 135–138; similarities to *Borneo*, 55; structure of, 139, 141; survey, 91, 136–137, 143nn2–4; *see also* individual tribes and contestants

Survivor: The Ultimate Game (book), 28, 65

Survivor: Vanuatu, 86, 93, 96, 102, 104, 107n10, 117; structure of, 141; *see also* individual contestants

SurvivorSucks, 10, 38, 90, 10–11; *see also* fandom

symbolic resolutions of real contradictions, 17, 35–36, 47, 82, 86, 130, 138–139

Tagi, *Borneo*, 13, 27–28, 65, 91, 98–99, 119, 135, 138, 140; alliance, 13, 27–45, *31*, *38*, *39*, *41*, *42*, 60, 63, 104, 105, *105*, 106n4; denial of alliance in, 28, 31, 32; mean AAAI, 31n 43n6

Tambuqui, *Amazon*, 72, 75–85, 93; content analysis, 82–83; men's alliance in, 70; survey, 85, 92, 94n8; *see also* stereotypes, gender and

Tammy, *Marquesas*, 46, 47, 49, 50–51; ouster, 52

Ted, *Thailand*, 117, 121, 132; survey, 94n9, 120
television and socialization, xvii–xviii, 11, 142–143; age and, 95–97; authenticity and, 11; digitalization and, 10; gender and, 74–75; natural-inaction and, xviii, 1, 3, 11, 101, 113, 121, 142–143; race and, 109–115, 123; *see also* reality television
Teresa, *Africa*, 67, 68
Thackaberry, Jennifer, 13
Thompson, Robert, xvii
Thomas, Justice Clarence, 130
Tijuana, *Pearl Islands*, 117
time compression, 7, 11, 14n1
Tina, *Outback*, 45, 66, 69; obscured relationship with Colby, 66, 68
Tinkcom, Matthew, 25n2
Titanic, 19
Tom, *Africa* 67, 68
Tom, *Palau*, 91; survey, 91, 105
Tribal Council, 2, 3, 8, 13, 25, 36, 37, 141; age and voting patterns at,

95, 101–102; editing and, 36, 63, 69, 138; "fake Final Four" videoclip at, 10, 14n3; parody of, 140; race and voting patterns at, 121, 123
Trosset, Michael, 3, 11, 23
"twists" in *Survivor's* structure, 10, 45, 46, 55, 67

Ulong, *Palau*, 141

Vecepia, *Marquesas*, 22, 46, 49, 50, 52, *52*, *53*, *54*, 116, 121, *128*, 132n4, 133n5; alliance and, 51; race and, 122–129, 132; survey, 52–55, 127, 128, 130
Vrooman, Steven, 9

Wanda, *Palau*, 96
Willard, *Palau*, 96, 106
Wiltz, Teresa, 113, 114

Zoe, *Marquesas*, 47, 48, 50, 51; ouster, 52

About the Author

CHRISTOPHER J. WRIGHT BEGAN WRITING about political and cultural implications of *Survivor* in 2001 for *PopPolitics.com*. *Tribal Warfare* springs from his work toward his master's degree in Communication, Culture, and Technology at Georgetown University, where he focused on the intersection of media, culture, and politics and completed multiple projects on reality TV, in particular *Survivor*. The *Journal of American Culture* published his article "Welcome to the Jungle of the Real: Simulation, Commoditization, and *Survivor*" in summer 2006; another piece, "Parking Lott: The Role of Weblogs in the Fall of Sen. Trent Lott," was included in the anthology *Blogs: Emerging Communication Media* from ICFAI University Press (2006). He works in the political media in Washington, D.C.